Finding Queensland in
  Australian Cinema

Anthem Studies in Australian Literature and Culture

Anthem Studies in Australian Literature and Culture specialises in quality, innovative research in Australian literary studies. The series publishes work that advances contemporary scholarship on Australian literature conceived historically, thematically and/or conceptually. We welcome well-researched and incisive analyses on a broad range of topics: from individual authors or texts to considerations of the field as a whole, including in comparative or transnational frames.

Series Editors

Katherine Bode – Australian National University, Australia
Nicole Moore – University of New South Wales, Australia

Editorial Board

Tanya Dalziell – University of Western Australia, Australia
Delia Falconer – University of Technology, Sydney, Australia
John Frow – University of Sydney, Australia
Wang Guanglin – Shanghai University of International Business and Economics, China
Ian Henderson – King's College London, United Kingdom
Tony Hughes-D'Aeth – University of Western Australia, Australia
Ivor Indyk – University of Western Sydney, Australia
Nicholas Jose – University of Adelaide, Australia
James Ley – *Sydney Review of Books*, Australia
Susan Martin – La Trobe University, Australia
Andrew McCann – Dartmouth College, United States
Elizabeth McMahon – University of New South Wales, Australia
Susan Martin – La Trobe University, Australia
Brigitta Olubus – University of New South Wales, Australia
Anne Pender – University of New England, Australia
Fiona Polack – Memorial University of Newfoundland, Canada
Sue Sheridan – University of Adelaide, Australia
Ann Vickery – Deakin University, Australia
Russell West-Pavlov – Eberhard-Karls-Universität Tübingen, Germany
Lydia Wevers – Victoria University of Wellington, New Zealand
Gillian Whitlock – University of Queensland, Australia

Finding Queensland in Australian Cinema

Poetics and Screen Geographies

Allison Craven

ANTHEM PRESS

Anthem Press
An imprint of Wimbledon Publishing Company
www.anthempress.com

This edition first published in UK and USA 2019
by ANTHEM PRESS
75–76 Blackfriars Road, London SE1 8HA, UK
or PO Box 9779, London SW19 7ZG, UK
and
244 Madison Ave #116, New York, NY 10016, USA

First published in the UK and USA by Anthem Press 2016

© Allison Craven 2019

The moral right of the authors has been asserted.

All rights reserved. Without limiting the rights under copyright reserved above,
no part of this publication may be reproduced, stored or introduced into
a retrieval system, or transmitted, in any form or by any means
(electronic, mechanical, photocopying, recording or otherwise),
without the prior written permission of both the copyright
owner and the above publisher of this book.

British Library Cataloguing-in-Publication Data
A catalogue record for this book is available from the British Library.

ISBN-13: 978-1-78527-188-5 (Pbk)
ISBN-10: 1-78527-188-1 (Pbk)

This title is also available as an e-book.

In loving memory of Ruth and Vince Craven

CONTENTS

List of Figures   ix

Acknowledgements   xi

Introduction: Regional Features   1

Part 1   **Backtracks: Landscape and Identity**

Chaper 1.   Period Features, Heritage Cinema: Region, Gender and Race in *The Irishman*   17

Chaper 2.   Heritage Enigmatic: The Silence of the Dubbed in *Jedda* and *The Irishman*   31

Part 2   **Silences in Paradise**

Chaper 3.   Tropical Gothic and the Music of the Cane Fields in *Radiance*   45

Chaper 4.   Island Girls Friday: Women, Adventure and the Tropics   57

Part 3   **Masculine Dramas of the Coast**

Chaper 5.   The Sunshine Boys: Peter Pan and the Iron Man in the Coastal Cinema of Queensland   71

Chaper 6.   A Pacific Parable: Cave and Coastal Masculinities in *Sanctum*   85

Part 4   **Regional Backtracks**

Chaper 7.   Unknown Queensland in Torres Strait Television: *RAN* and *The Straits*   97

Chaper 8.   Back to the Back: Genre Queensland and Westerns in Winton   113

Conclusion: On Location in Queensland   127

Notes	133
Filmography	137
Works Cited	141
Index	149

FIGURES

5.1	The day of the race: Surfers Paradise and the cast of thousands in *The Coolangatta Gold* (1984)	74
5.2	Steve (Joss McWilliam) takes counsel with his mother (Robyn Nevin) outside the family home in *The Coolangatta Gold* (1984)	75
7.1	Helen (Susie Porter, foreground) attends church on the Island with Paul Gaibui (Luke Carroll, with child in arms) in *RAN: Remote Area Nurse* (2006)	98
7.2	The bikie goes into the swimming pool with the stingers as Noel (Aaron Fa'aoso, centre) and Harry Montebello (Brian Cox, right) look on in *The Straits* (2012)	108

ACKNOWLEDGEMENTS

Several earlier sole or co-authored publications, or parts thereof, are reproduced within the chapters of this book. Permission to republish this material is gratefully acknowledged as follows.

'Period Features, Heritage Cinema: Region, Gender and Race in *The Irishman*' was first published in *Studies in Australasian Cinema*, 5, no. 1 (2011): 31–42; 'Heritage Enigmatic: The Silence of the Dubbed in *Jedda* and *The Irishman*' was first published in *Studies in Australasian Cinema*, 7, no. 1 (2013): 23–34. *Studies in Australasian Cinema* is fully acknowledged as the original source of publication of these works, and I am grateful to the editor-in-chief, Dr Anthony Lambert, and the journal's publishers, Taylor & Francis, for kind permission to republish these essays.

'Paradise Post-national: Landscape, Location and Senses of Place in Films Set in Queensland' was first published in *Metro*, no. 166 (2010): 108–13, www.metromagazine.com.au/magazine. The publishers, the editorial board and the Australian Teachers of Media (ATOM) are gratefully acknowledged for permission to republish this essay. I warmly thank Associate Professor Jane Stadler, the guest editor of the landscape feature in *Metro*, in which the essay appeared.

'Tropical Gothic: *Radiance* Revisited' was first published in *etropic: electronic journal of studies in the tropics* 7 (2008); 'The Girl with the Bush Knife: Women, Adventure and the Tropics in *Age of Consent* and *Nim's Island*' was co-authored by Allison Craven and Chris Mann and first published in *etropic: electronic journal of studies in the tropics*, 9 (2010); 'Parables of Pacific Shores: Caves and Coastal Masculinities in *Cast Away* and *Sanctum*' was first published in *etropic: electronic journal of studies in the tropics*, 10 (2011): 158–65, www.jcu.edu.au/etropic. *etropic: electronic journal of studies in the tropics* is fully acknowledged and I am grateful to the editor, Professor Stephen Torre, and to James Cook University for kind permission to republish these essays.

'Fence Lines and Horizon Lines: Queensland in the Imaginary Geographies of Cinema' was first published in *Lectures in Queensland History 2009–2012*, edited by Annette Burns, 61–73. Townsville, Queensland, Australia: Townsville City Council. 2013. Permission from CityLibraries, Townsville City Council, to republish parts of this essay is gratefully acknowledged.

With warm thanks, the following permissions for use of film and television stills are fully acknowledged. Images from *The Coolangatta Gold* (Auzin 1984) in Chapter 5 are reproduced courtesy of kind permission from John Weiley and Heliograph Pty Ltd. Image from *RAN: Remote Area Nurse* in Chapter 7 is reproduced courtesy of kind permission from Penny Chapman and Matchbox Pictures Pty Ltd (www.matchboxpictures.com). Image from *The Straits* in Chapter 7 is reproduced courtesy of kind permission from *The Straits*, Matchbox Pictures Pty Ltd (www.matchboxpictures.com), and Andrew Watson Photography.

I acknowledge the traditional owners of the land on which the work in this book was developed and written, the Bindal Wulgurukaba people, and pay respects to their elders, past, present and future. Warm thanks are also extended to the following people for their support: Cheryl Taylor, Stephen Torre, Michael Ackland and, especially, Chris Mann. Chris co-authored 'The Girl with the Bush Knife: Women, Adventure and the Tropics in *Age of Consent* and *Nim's Island*', which forms the basis of Chapter 4 in this book, and his support to republish material from the earlier essay is much appreciated. Thanks to the staff of CityLibraries Townsville, Judith Jensen and Trish Fielding for convening the Queensland Cinema film series in 2007, and again to Judith and Trish, and Annette Burns at CityLibraries Townsville, for the Lectures in Queensland History Series. Sebastian Hernage at Matchbox Pictures went to much trouble to assist with obtaining images and permissions. In addition to the acknowledgements that appear in the book, thanks to Sebastian for his generous assistance. Thanks and acknowledgements, too, to my colleagues at Eddie Koiki Mabo Library of James Cook University, Townsville, for their support and assistance; to the many students who have engaged in lively conversations about Australian cinema in my subjects 'Studies in Film and Place' and 'Regional Features'; to Don and Mary Gallagher for their support and friendship; to Aaron Clarke and Vicky Seal for help with editing and proofreading; and to Emma Cooper for the happy thought about the crocodile and Queensland in *Peter Pan*. A nod is due, too, to Miss Holly and Mr Milton, who retain reserved seats in the study during working hours.

INTRODUCTION

REGIONAL FEATURES

Region, like gender, is a form of difference. (Whitlock 1994, 71)

The many spectacles of places shown in Australian cinema are typically assimilated to all of Australia in terms of its difference from non-Australian places. The regional histories and participation in production and poetics of narrative are submerged, typified by a view of the region as the space of the 'nation writ small' (Moran 2001, 2). This book brings a magnifying glass to a selection of films either wholly or partly made in Queensland in a period, from the 1970s to the present, during which Queensland has come to the fore in Australia as a place of film production. The four sections of this book suggest its emergence from passive participant in an era when the hegemony of national cinema was unquestioned, to a competitive presence in the present transnational environment of film production.

The expansion of film production infrastructure in Queensland and elsewhere in Australia corresponds to the increasing transnationalism of the international industry. Cross-border film production is now regarded as normal (Goldsmith and O'Regan 2008), and this reflects trends in the de-nationalising of film and television as the effects of globalisation (O'Regan and Potter 2013).

Within this era of change, debate about Australian national cinema has persisted, and questions are asked as much about what is 'subsume[d]' by the 'national cinema' (Khoo, Smaill and Yue 2015, 8), as much as what is revealed of or about the place of Australia. Various approaches have highlighted the inherently 'international' character of Australian cinema (O'Regan 1996; Danks and Verevis 2010; Goldsmith 2010) or its 'transnational' scope (Goldsmith, Ward and O'Regan 2010; Khoo et al. 2015). Some investigate the inner cultural diversity of films that represent Australia (Simpson, Murawska and Lambert 2009), and speculate on the post-national connotations (Craven 2010; Khoo 2011a). The aim in this book is to pose the idea of region as a source of cinematic identity, and to examine how location affects a film's meaning.

Region, however, is not posed in the sense of regionalism, or distinct cultural practices or traditions, or the specific cultural geographies of diasporic identities. It is treated as a geographic construct, as the spaces and places 'outside the dominant metropolitan centres' (Khoo 2011b, 462). In Queensland, that includes coastal and inland regions within its land borders, and offshore islands of the Great Barrier Reef and the Torres Strait. In the transnationalised environment of film production, regional landscapes and film locations signify place as something of a trade commodity. Australia, including Queensland, has been promoted more actively as a film production destination for some time now, especially its rich offerings of places and spaces for location shooting. The 'Locations Gallery' on the Screen Queensland website currently lists nearly 1,500 places, landscapes, landforms and properties, private and public, available for use.[1] The attractions of locations are often supplemented through hosting by state and national agencies, Screen Queensland and Screen Australia, and the benefits of co-production networks and regimes of financial and taxation-based incentives. These regimes are modelled on comparable schemes in other nations that participate in the transnational production industry. In film production, as in the arts of the information age, the digitisation of the real is endlessly subversive of the constraints and contingencies of geographic place, and hence of that which it most commodifies: cultural desires for a sense of place.

A Cinematic Sense of Place

The setting of a film may be read as a symbolic representation of the work the text does 'to find a place in which to speak and an audience on which to act' (Freadman 1988, 84). A sense of place in a film does not only result from setting. Film and moving image media have, arguably, uniquely mobile potential to evoke persuasive fictions of place. The conventions of realist cinema suggest place in a range of disparate and fluid sensory markers, visual, aural, verbal and non-verbal cues, through vision of settings, allusions to known or unknown places, or persons or events, and with supplementary devices such as voice-overs and inter titles, all orchestrated through establishing and action images, and mise-en-scène. Cultural and political discourses are filtered in these processes, and in the performances of race and gender. Location of production does not always anchor any of these elements, and its effects are variable in the utterance of regional differences, as much as differences of race and gender.

If this is the effect of the medium, it is inculcated more deeply through the institutional and cultural processes of cinema that apply provenance to a production. Production discourses, including the facts and contingencies of locations, hold the potential to reinforce or disrupt the experience of the sense of place in the poetry of the film. Queensland on screen does not always mesh with local geography and knowledge, as in *Radiance* (Perkins 1998) when the church and pub are unrecognisable because the film's locations in Central Queensland are not the same as the diegetic place of North Queensland, or in *Mystery Road* (Sen 2013) when a recognisable site is renamed in keeping with the horror of racial violence. A sense of place, therefore, is more than a process of recognition; it is an 'experience' arising from 'regimes of affect' that induce 'a sense of intimacy, of being at home' and 'mingles with a sense of immensity or disproportion' (Routt 2001, 4).

The approach to place as a cinematic construct is therefore informed by ideas from the poetics of space (Bachelard 1994) insofar as these can be applied in film and television (Routt 2001). Anthropological notions of space and place underpin the connection to location, as elliptically framed by Michele de Certeau's idea of a place 'of whatever sort' as 'containing the order "in whose terms elements are distributed in relations of coexistence" and in a specific "location"' (Augé 1995, 53–54). Marc Augé says of this definition that it does not stop us thinking about how the elements are singular or distinctive, or about the 'shared identity conferred on them by their common occupancy of a place' (54). In these conventions, images or other signs suggest only a diegetic place, or, to use a term coined by William Routt, a 'narrative place' that is relational to how 'story space should appear on the screen, not upon the field of vision one is liable to employ in everyday life' (Routt 2001, 2). Narrative Queensland, or the people and places performed in its locations, suggests not only, to adapt Augé, what is singular or distinctive as evidence of Queensland, but what is contingent and even arbitrary in the signification of shared identity in the common occupancy of narrative Queensland, its regions and micro-sites.

Locating Queensland in Australian Cinema

Film technologies came to Queensland in the 1890s, like many other places in the world. The earliest films were government productions by official artists and photographers showing civic events and various regional spectacles of agriculture and engineering, including wheat harvesting on the Darling Downs, the sugar industry on the Sunshine Coast and the building of railways in North Queensland (Laughren 1996). A.C. Haddon's Cambridge expedition films of Torres Strait Islanders are among the first films created in Queensland in 1898 (Laughren 1996). The Salvation Army, through its Limelight Department, was also an early film-maker, who incorporated footage into its touring lecture presentations (Laughren 1996). While most of the Salvation Army's films are lost, the organisation holds the quirky distinction of shooting Australia's first bush-ranging film – *Bushranging in North Queensland* – in Winton, Western Queensland, in 1904 (Gaunson 2010, 89; and see Chapter 8).[2] The Limelight Department also filmed sheep shearing for the first time in Australia, in Hughendon, Western Queensland (Laughren 1996).

This early history forms a distant part of the much later corpus that Albert Moran (1989) characterises as 'institutional documentary', in which Queensland figures prominently but in that pattern of emergence from passive to focal presence in the spectacle of nation. In *The Cane Cutters* (McInnes 1948), the regional difference of North Queensland is submerged in the evocation of the place of 'Australia', and in a narrative steeped in sexual difference. A rhythmic (male) voice-over intones the identity of 'we' the 'cane cutters' of 'almost half a million acres of sugar land in tropical Australia'. 'Stoop, chop, straighten, top; stoop, chop, straighten, top' – the rhyming refrain is repeated to the 'simple music of the swinging knife' in unambiguous identification of the 'men' who work the land. Their wives at home are said to work harder than the men. Unannounced in the voice-over, but visible in the swinging pan across the cane-growing region are landmarks of Far North Queensland. Road signs point to the regional towns of 'Cairns', 'Innisfail', 'Ingham'. But there is no explicit mention of Queensland in 'this 1300 mile Australian sugar belt', identified as 'tropical Australia', that is always ready with a 'tall crop' for the 'men with the knives', whose 'families come from all four corners of the earth'. The nationalist and nation-building rhetoric (Moran 1989) is unmistakable in this era of documentary.

A dramatic change is suggested in *From the Tropics to the Snow* (Mason and Lee 1964), the parodic documentary that satirises the making of a film about Australia. It figures Queensland as, not the hard-working place of nation building, but the holiday tropics, in featuring various locations that predict some of the images in the Location Gallery of today's Screen Queensland: the Gold Coast, 'sun and sand' and a 'tropical island complete with palms', an isolated Barrier Reef island; a mangrove-lined stalking ground for a crocodile hunter. The aesthetic is modernist, and the narrative world of the film is 'elaborated inside the classical Hollywood narrative' (Moran 1985, 107). Moran observes that *From the Tropics to the Snow* 'points forward' (107), referring to the direction of documentary style. This film also predicts the future of Queensland as a destination for production of film fictions of the tropics.

An erotic variation emerges in *Will the Great Barrier Reef Cure Claude Clough?* (Milson 1968). Queensland is imagined as a region of the unconscious, of repressed desires. Claude finds himself in therapy for anxiety, counselled by a red-headed woman psychiatrist who advises him to take a 'holiday'. 'Think of it', she says, 'the tropical north, blue seas, white sands, coconut palms'.

Claude descends into a reverie and fantasises the vision shown to the cinema audience: a splendid aerial view of the Great Barrier Reef, the coastline and islands of Queensland. But the place is not named. Deep in his reverie, Claude's fantasy of the holiday tropics is diagnosed by the psychiatrist as an 'ideal girl fixation' stimulated by 'old television movies'. The girl appears as the psychiatrist in dusky-maiden drag, with a long black wig and – an unlikely accessory – large, horn-rimmed spectacles. 'She's beautiful but mysterious,' says Claude. The fantasy merges images of Queensland with a fantasy of female sexuality derived from the Hollywood South Seas films of the middle twentieth century. As the 'local girl' draws him into the interior of a Barrier Reef island, he experiences it as 'jungle', and sexual threat, and then boredom. 'Island beauties went out with the *Mutiny on the Bounty*,' the psychiatrist observes. Claude conjures a mermaid, the same swinging psychiatrist with a long, blonde wig who takes him underwater snorkelling among the coloured fishes and coral beds, her hair waving around like marine vegetation. The fantasy concludes, after Claude's James Bond–style adventures in nightclubs and a pirate fantasy, with Claude and the psychiatrist swapping places on the couch.

The inspiration from Hollywood is spotted in the allusion to the *Mutiny on the Bounty*.[3] Perhaps the slip reflects that the period of this documentary was one in which Australian domestic film production had subsided. But it was soon to re-emerge, and an influence was an international production set on an island in Queensland, *Age of Consent* (Powell 1969). Queensland is not a mystery destination in *Age of Consent*, but it is still a place of escape for an artist seeking refuge from the art world, in the fiction, at least. The tropical setting represented a break from the productions of the intervening period, which typically featured outback landscapes in figuring Australia. The contrasting scenic identity of Australia, emerging in the tropics of Queensland, underpins the chapters in this book, the regional semiotics of the productions and the passages of change in the film industry in Queensland.

The approach is framed, moreover, by the profound cultural influences of the Mabo Native Title legislation in 1993, and the longer-term outcome of the successful challenge in the High Court of Australia in 1992 that overturned the historical concept of *terra nullius* in upholding Torres Strait Islanders' territorial claims. Among the cultural implications, Felicity Collins and Therese Davis (2004) argue, is the paradigm shift in historical consciousness and structures of spectatorship on Australian films. While there is debate about the long-term impact of Native Title for Indigenous people (Collins and Davis 2004, 4; Keon-Cohen 2013), Collins and Davis's framework of 'backtracking' and 'aftershock' of the Mabo decision remains an insightful framework of interpretation of Australian cinema. 'Backtracking' is a lens whereby they revisit Australian films in the years since the Mabo decision. Their book, like this one, is not about Mabo, nor do they perceive that Mabo resolved issues to do with land rights for Indigenous people. Backtracking, with its dual connotations of traversing land already travelled, and a changing of perspective, is an interpretive strategy, which they contextualise within wider domestic and international debates in the intervening era about history and culture. The time of cinema 'after Mabo' suggested for them an 'afterwardness' of colonialism 'during a moment of intense globalisation' (8). It is adopted in a more limited way here with attention to films made in Queensland since the re-emergence of Australian cinema in the 1970s to the more prominent role of Queensland within the industry in the present.

Backtracks through Landscape and Identity in Part 1

In the first section, 'Backtracks', the films presented are seen as artefacts of a national cinema in which the notion of Australian identity was more monolithic, and these films were made in the era before the Mabo Native Title claims. *The Irishman* (Crombie 1978) is highlighted first, in Chapter 1 'Period Features', as an example of a New Wave, or revival, film. This period of the 1970s was a decade of cascading film production that followed what is now generally accepted to have been a lengthy period of relative inactivity in Australian film production during the years following the Second World War. The revival bore the signs of a quest for a national identity, and it arose with a significant level of government support and hence public interest in its oeuvre, and is now seen as a threshold period in the national film industry. The analysis of *The Irishman* in Chapter 1 suggests how these revival films might be seen as a collection of regional voices and images that were shaped in production and distribution by a national, and occasionally, an international lens. In spite of its authorisation as a 'national' film through the provenance of the Australian Film Commission (AFC), *The Irishman* exhibits regional semiotics arising from its almost exclusive production relationship to Queensland, and its basis on a novel set in the region. Its production converges with the gentrified aesthetic of the AFC-genre films, and it becomes a heritage film, as I argue. It poses the construction of Australian identity as gendered, racial and bound, predominantly, to an outback setting, defined as man's country versus the homesteads and houses defined as the domain of the white woman.

The Irishman is also exemplary of the landscape aesthetic of Australian cinema. Australian films have tended to exhibit landscapes somewhat in excess of the conventions of classic Hollywood realism, and due to the historic tendency in both literature and film to bring meaning to Australia through various mythologised, often ironised, topographies, such as the bush, the beach, the outback, the suburbs (Collins and Davis 2004). The 'landscape-cinema' of Australia 'assert[s]' its 'difference from the rest of the world' (Gibson 1994, 49). If place, as Edward Casey writes, is generally 'unlike the unconscious' in that it is 'not so controversial or so intrusive as to require repression' (Casey 1998, x), then the landscape aesthetic contributes to a particularly unrepressed sense of place in Australian cinema. But this is not to say that it is not without potential for some repressions.

Chapter 2, 'Heritage Enigmatic', extends the discussion of *The Irishman* through comparison with another earlier landmark film associated with the landscape aesthetic, *Jedda* (Chauvel 1955).[4] *Jedda* remains a distinctive and yet contentious film (see Jane Mills 2012), in spite of its 2015 anniversary screening at the Cannes Film Festival, subtitled in French (Bodey 2015). It is contentious for its representational discourse and its production history, to both of which Mills alludes. In Chapter 2, *Jedda* is compared with *The Irishman* as films that include two of only a handful of principal roles for Indigenous women in feature films and were made decades apart. In each film the visual image supersedes the voice in terms of identity construction. This is apparent in the use of vocal dubbing whereby the heritage aura of the revival film is aligned with foregoing values. The dramatic spectacle of landscape in *Jedda*, of which the Aboriginal subjects were, in fact, dispossessed, is magnified as a national and cinematic asset.

Backtracking over landscape and identity in the opening section suggests how the landscape tradition operates not only as an aesthetic, but as a device that deflects other silences in identity formations of Australian cinema. Yet the landscape tradition is not monolithic, and the subtleties are visible even in these two films. *Jedda* exhibits landscape in an exotic way, more typical of the Western-style films the international Ealing studios made in the 1940s and 1950s, including *The Overlanders* (Watt 1946) and *Bitter Springs* (Smart 1951). In the case of Charles Chauvel in the making of Jedda, it was accompanied by a particular machismo of production adventure, termed 'locationism' by Stuart Cunningham (1991) (see Chapter 2). *The Irishman*, as a period film, on the other hand, adopts the more romantic and painterly convention associated with the period revival films in the 1970s. It descends from visual art of the nineteenth century, including the Heidelberg School of painters, who, among other characteristics, chose to paint '"on location"' and under the influence of outdoor light and its effects on the landscape (Elliott 2010, 148). This is echoed in twentieth-century film-makers who practise their art on location.

The 'landscape-tradition' in Australian cinema, as Gibson terms it, signifies more than 'an environmental setting for local narratives' (1994, 45). The role of landscape in Australian cinema suggests how the act of illustrating landscape involves a grafting of ideas that supplant foregoing ones, and how this process also signifies a sense in which the 'society is also to some contentious extent a "natural" outgrowth of the habitat' (49). The landscape tradition promotes the 'significance of European society in "the Antipodes"', he argues (45). The construal of the Australian landscape as 'empty space' suggests not only overlooking of inhabitants and signs of precolonial culture but how the Australian landscape was unassimilated into the European symbolic order, 'except as a motif of the "extra-cultural", as a sublime, structuring void' (45). The concept of *terra nullius* came to name this phenomenon, and continues to haunt visions of landscape even long after Mabo. A number of the films discussed in this book use the landscape convention more consciously to contest, disrupt and redress the earlier connotations.

In making visible narrative places, landscape is also implicated in making culture seem natural, and this is often the ideological effect in Australian cinema. As a sign, it has 'customarily been construed as a sign of nature', or of something preternatural (Gibson 1994, 49–54). This is in spite of the reality of Nicholas Rothwell's observation that 'landscape', in its historical distinction from both 'wilderness' and 'town', is a construct that is intrinsically 'closer to culture than nature' yet is invoked as an 'emblem' of the 'natural order', alluding to the derivation of 'landscape' from old German and Dutch words, 'landschip', which refers to the distinction between wilderness and town (Rothwell 2007b). This tendency becomes more conscious and pronounced in the films discussed in the subsequent sections. While Collins and Davis suggest that coastal landscapes 'have yet to take on the iconic status of the desert and the bush' (2004, 115), I suggest how this occurs when Queensland is the figured place in the region of the coastal tropics and islands, and how a mythic cultural discourse of Queensland as paradise pervades these regional settings.

Tracks Forward: Silences in Paradise in Part 2

The notion of the tropics as paradise derives from classical sources and is transmuted to the classical notion of the 'antipodes' (Jericho 2005). Paradise myths are ancient, but most recently have been reinvented in white settler societies (Moran 2001). Paradise in Queensland is a recurring cultural trope since its inception as a state in 1859. The settings for myths and counter-myths of paradise in the films discussed in Part 2 are in North Queensland, although the north is not always exclusively associated with the myth of paradise in Queensland. Bruce Molloy (1990b) identifies the paradise myth in films shot in or set in Queensland from World War II to the 1980s. He cites films in which Queensland serves as an 'exotic background to conventional stories', or 'a site of rich resources for the taking [...] through hard work', and sometimes a destination of an epic journey (Molloy 1990b, 66–68). His examples are *The Overlanders* and *Sons of Matthew* (Chauvel 1949), which 'celebrate the spirit of enterprise and the virtues of hard work' (70). He points out that whereas there is usually pessimism in encounters between pioneers and the bush, in Queensland settings, there is a contrasting success for the protagonists. *Sons of Matthew*, which was made around Lamington National Park and the Numinbah Valley in Southeast Queensland, is exemplary, with its biblical framework for the story of a pastoral dynasty which succeeds in establishing its place in paradise after overcoming all forms of natural challenges (cyclone, bushfire and flood) on the journey.

A much later example of Molloy's, in an outback setting, is *Buddies* (Nicholson 1983), which was shot on the gem fields of Central Queensland, and where a spirit of larrikinism is also to be observed in the hard-working ethic. Another of his examples is the Eden-like setting of *Age of Consent*, which was filmed mostly on Dunk Island in North Queensland. As these films testify, locations all around the state have been co-opted as versions of the paradise myth, such that paradise in Queensland seems less of a spiritual destination than an allusion to Queensland's difference from other states within the settler nation. Pertinent to this difference, too, is Molloy's noting of the 'depiction of eccentricity or excess' in feature films shot in or set in Queensland since the silent era, notably *On Our Selection* (Longford 1920) (Molloy 1990b, 72). Such types are found in literature as well (Craven 2013).

Chapter 3, 'Tropical Gothic', takes up the mythology of paradise, but in a contrasting perspective. The 'shock, recognition and trauma' Collins and Davis (2004, 9) associate with the confrontation of the fiction of *terra nullius* is registered in *Radiance*, the first feature film directed by Rachel Perkins, in which idyllic, prosperous, settler Queensland and its holiday tropics are contested and subverted. Image, sound and music contest the space of paradise in the story of three women who reunite at their family home in North Queensland for the funeral of their mother. Pregnant Nona (Deborah Mailman) hopes to raise her child in the family home and also longs to deliver her mother's ashes to her ancestral Nora Island, seen across the water. But her idealism is contested by Mae (Trisha Morton-Thomas) and Cressy (Rachel Maza), who reveal the history of trauma and violence that has occurred in the house, from which they are about to be evicted. Collins and Davis argue that *Radiance* is a definitively post-Mabo film because of the resonances of Native Title and the Stolen Generations in Nona's quest to return her mother's ashes to Nora Island. Whereas the prevailing debate until the early 1990s concerned the representation of Indigenous people in cinema, and the critique of exotic stereotyping (Jennings 1993), more recently, film, as Nicholas Rothwell suggests, has become a 'frontier' of subjectivity in the hands of Indigenous film-makers (Rothwell 2007a, 31). *Radiance* was a groundbreaking film in this direction.

Paradise returns in the films discussed in Chapter 4, 'Island Girls Friday', where films set on islands in Queensland are linked to the myths of the South Seas. In terms of feminine myths, paradise island settings often stereotype the 'doomed erotic figure of the dusky maiden' (Pearson 2013, 154). This figure stems from imperial accounts of South Seas women and influences portrayals of Pacific women in imperial literatures and Hollywood films. Patty O'Brien argues that not only assumptions about the sexuality of Pacific women but also the 'environs determined [their] erotic potential' (2006, 51). The warm weather–inspired assumptions of heightened libido combined with perception of the feminine lack of reason to suggest sexual insatiability (54). Historical personages, such as the Tahitian Queen Oberea, who is named in the journals of the *Endeavour* voyages, 'launched the myth of Pacific women', according to O'Brien (63), and became counterparts of the masculinised myth of the noble savage (172). In Hollywood films after World War I, O'Brien argues, 'white women began to appropriate what they considered desirable in the Pacific exotica', and this tendency was also influenced by taboos on cross-cultural sexual relations (235). The Pacific siren becomes a racially crossed figure, she claims, with white or South American women playing the roles (235). Sometimes termed 'sarong girls' (Jericho 2005), these women are named by O'Brien as the '"Hollynesian", a Hollywood-styled Pacific muse of no consequential geographical location' and who was whitened to 'ease race anxieties' (235).

There is a detour from this narrative in Chapter 4 in the three films made on islands in North Queensland: *Age of Consent*; *Nim's Island* (Levin and Flackett 2008), a children's fantasy; and *Uninhabited* (Bennett 2010), a supernatural thriller. As 'island' women the heroines of these films are seen to adapt the 'bush woman' of an earlier cinematic era in Australia (the 1920s and 1930s) to the mythic spaces of the holiday tropics and the South Seas, and with variable cultural politics towards Indigenous presences in these spaces. *Age of Consent*, which generated controversy in its day, resembles the island paradise of Claude's fantasy (in *Will the Great Barrier Reef Cure Claude Clough?*). In *Nim's Island*, the South Seas literature of masculine adventure shapes the narrative place which Nim defends against invasion by 'Queenslanders'. *Uninhabited* is the only film of the three in which an Indigenous character is figured, who is Coral (Tasia Zalar), the ghost of an islander woman who was brutalised during her much earlier lifetime. Where *Age of Consent* is an Edenic paradise, in which the innocence of the pleasures are unallusive to any past, its heroine wants to get away. *Nim's Island* and *Uninhabited*, on the other hand, are cognisant of the racial histories, and Europeans are incorporated as intruders, if in parodic and uncanny scenarios.

O'Brien's classical framework for deriving the origin of Pacific exoticism poses the corresponding myth of the 'unfettered sexual freedom of voyaging men', a key myth of the South Seas (2006, 68). The 'Odyssean temptresses' (9), the likes of Circe, Calypso and the sirens, figure a 'central theme of the Odyssean myth, which became core to Occidental colonisation, of the travelling man's exposure to sexual danger' (41). Their inability 'to withstand temptation was the great paradox within constructions of [...] civilised, Occidental masculinity' which was partly justified as the effect of the greater seductive power of South Seas women compared to those at home (75). This was influenced, she argues, by classical associations of water and ocean with goddesses like Aphrodite (or Venus in Roman tradition), and in legends of sirens and nymphs (see 47–49). The association of nakedness with the assumption of sexual readiness and availability was also deemed a 'virtuous lack of shame about sexuality' that '"reminded" the Occidental mariner[s] of their own classical past' (79). This has implications for Bradley in *Age of Consent* and Harry in *Uninhabited*, who have something in common with the men in Part 3.

Paradise to Neverland: Masculine Dramas of the Coast in Part 3

The settings of the films are diverse in this section, and the focus is derived from the lately established hub of film production, the Gold Coast in Queensland. The emergence of the Gold Coast as a centre of film production and the presence there of Village Roadshow Studios has been accompanied by increased activity around the state, notably in Southeast and Far North Queensland (see Chapters 4, 5, 6 and 7). The presence of the Village Roadshow Studios has both attracted and stimulated domestic and international productions, aided by production offset incentives, and supported by the film entrpreneurship of Screen Australia and Screen Queensland. The films discussed in this section represent times before and since these developments.

Chapter 5, 'The Sunshine Boys', is an account of the myth of Peter Pan as it emerges in two films made on the Gold Coast nearly 20 years apart – *The Coolangatta Gold* (Auzin 1984) and *Peter Pan* (Hogan 2003). *The Coolangatta Gold* was one of the first feature films made on the Gold Coast, as part of a larger goal of state and private interests to establish a film production infrastructure, as the chapter relays. The main spectacle of the film was an international beach-athletic event, the inaugural Coolangatta Gold

Iron Man Marathon, around which the family drama of the film is built. In spite of aspirations, it is not a highly regarded film but survives as a forward-looking enterprise that indirectly contributed to the present era of film production on the Gold Coast. In comparison, *Peter Pan*, a nostalgic fantasy production of J.M. Barrie's story of 'Peter Pan' – in which, coincidentally, Neverland is also an island fantasy – was produced in the (then) recently established Village Roadshow Studios on the Gold Coast. The mythic narrative of Peter Pan suggests how this history is underpinned by an ethos of adventure celebrated in the production ideology of film-friendliness (as defined by Goldsmith et al. 2010).

In Chapter 6, the myths of the South Seas are reintegrated in the diving drama of *Sanctum* (Grierson 2011a), for which the offshore setting of a cave in Papua New Guinea was created in the Gold Coast studio. The cave-diving team members are compared as late examples of the travelling man in the Pacific. This is not to suggest that the travelling men of *Sanctum* are 'unfettered', quite the opposite. Their chastity is attributed to the aura of the cave, another site of classical association through Plato's parable of the cave, and their attraction to extreme sport. The spirit of risky adventure is also linked to the transnational creative and production interests of *Sanctum* in the comparable pull of the film and commodity industries in Queensland towards markets in Asia, where *Sanctum* had its most successful release.

The imagining of Papua New Guinea in *Sanctum* is also contextualised with Jane Landman's (2006) account of the 'South Seas' films in Australian cinema history, a rival construction to the Hollywood South Seas imaginary O'Brien described. Landman identifies a crop of 13 films, putatively Australian, made from the 1930s to the 1950s. The films were set on the fringes of northern Australia in the Torres Strait Islands and Papua New Guinea, and involved a significant amount of location production, either in the places named, or elsewhere, including islands of the Great Barrier Reef. This corpus of South Seas films, Landman argues, presents masculine narratives of adventure and imperial romance within a spectacle of 'scenic melodrama' in which the places are exotic backdrops, and the Indigenous people are marginalised, or even disavowed. Moreover, this marginality is reiterated in the histories of distribution of the films, and in colonial censorship and control of Indigenous participation in and spectatorship of these films. The implications in Chapter 6 are for the evocation of the narrative place, and the masculinities performed in *Sanctum*. But the relevance of Landman's analysis of the racialised order of the scenic melodrama of the Australian South Seas films carries forward to the final section, in which, in the films discussed, scenic melodrama and the marginality of Indigenous people are contested.

Regional Rewind in Part 4

Chapter 7, 'Unknown Queensland in Torres Strait Television', considers two television mini-series set in the Torres Strait Islands – *RAN: Remote Area Nurse* (Caesar and McKenzie 2006) and *The Straits* (Andrikis, Ward and Woods 2012). The congruence between narrative place and locations of production is high in these series. Both are notable for their culturally collaborative location production in Far North Queensland and the Torres Strait. These series present Indigenous perspectives but in quite different genres, and utilise diverse approaches to representing the regional environment and registering the frontier of subjectivity. Where *RAN* is a test case of a collaborative venture that gives recognition to Torres Strait Islander culture and perspectives, *The Straits* deploys its tropical setting to excess in evoking an international genre, the crime family drama. A sense of tropical difference emerges in both series in settings that are presented initially to the (non-Indigenous) audience as 'unknown' places. The drama and spectacle is constrained to one island in *RAN* in a series that has attracted praise for its collaborative production and recognition of Indigenous perspectives. *The Straits*, in comparison, poses the wider region as a space of movement and action of the central family such that tropical difference becomes, arguably, a kind of parody of the scenic melodrama of the South Seas films.

In departing from the tropical, coastal regions to the inland zone, Chapter 8, 'Back to the Back', concerns two films made in the emerging hub of film production activity in arid landscapes of Western Queensland and centred in the town of Winton. The region has attracted a number of productions modelled on the American Western, and the examples discussed are *The Proposition* (Hillcoat 2005), which commenced this production trend, and *Mystery Road* (Sen 2013). These films return the gaze to the outback in Queensland spaces and register the continued aftershock of Mabo. The character types and use of genre re-impose the colonial sense of the place as frontier, but with knowing deployment of the genre tropes in contesting historical and contemporary racism. Performances of gender types from the Western transform the iconicity of the landscape and enable reflections on historical violence in the region.

The approach to these films is informed by Peter Limbrick's (2007, 2010) discussion of the Western as a mode of settler cinema, and Priya Jaikumar's (2001, 2006) account of the colonial place in (British) imperial films. Jaikumar's account of what she calls the 'modernist mode' of imperial film is defined in distinction to the 'realist' and 'romantic' modes, and 'gives primacy to the crisis of empire during decolonisation' and the concomitant 'breakdown of imperialism's categories of "self" and "other" through the sympathetic enactment of Western trauma' (58). In the modernist mode she notes the 'operation of the colonial "place"' whereby the 'coherence of the narrative is predicated on the continuation of the colonial place as an unproblematic backdrop' (58). Coherence, in the realistic or romantic mode, she argues, is maintained by 'ignor[ing] the place' which would otherwise have to become a site of 'crisis' itself (59). In the modernist mode, 'the coherence of the imperial self' is 'broken' and this occurs through forms of recognition of the place. There is comparison in the decolonising narratives of *The Proposition* and *Mystery Road*, and the sense in which the 'backdrop' is looked into, and the landscape, gains some form of subjectivity as it is investigated by the protagonists. It is 'backtracking' of a purposeful kind.

In the simplest sense, this book is a story of the bush to the beach and back. The chapters suggest some dimensions in the way Queensland, the narrative place, or places near or within it are imagined and rendered through the films made in its locations, which invoke and imbibe the mythic, formal and local knowledges of the place, the people and the times in which the films are set or made. All are subject to the contingent and sometimes contrived methods of production, and the influences of the interests that support the practices.

Cinematic Queensland, like real Queensland, is syncretistic, and its variable elements suggest that what is known of it is contingent and interdependent with other identity constructions. In the films discussed in the chapters, the differences of region, race and gender emerge in the utterances of an art form overlain with institutional, industrial and cultural frameworks that extend within and beyond the state and in the transnational flows of cinema.

Part 1

BACKTRACKS: LANDSCAPE AND IDENTITY

Chapter 1

PERIOD FEATURES, HERITAGE CINEMA: REGION, GENDER AND RACE IN *THE IRISHMAN*

> For those who aspire to respectability, finding suitable clothing in which to dress up the past has long been part of what being Australian means. (Flanagan 1998, 16–17)

Period Pains

The Irishman was one of a crop of period drama films produced in the late 1970s that formed the second stage of the revival of Australian cinema. The period genre was also dubbed the 'AFC genre' (Dermody and Jacka 1987, 1988; Elliott 2010). Susan Dermody and Elizabeth Jacka (1988) define the genre in terms of the aesthetic influences generated by the role of the Australian Film Commission (AFC) in driving cultural and commercial aims in the Australian film industry at the time, even though the AFC did not directly fund these films. The period genre has also been seen as reflecting policy initiatives to do with 'culture and quality' as a reaction against the so-called ocker comedies of the first stage of the revival (O'Regan 1989, 77). There was also an agenda to represent Australian history, and it is for this in particular that the period genre gained distinction, but not without criticism. Visually impressive, the stories told were often criticised for their inconclusive endings and lack of historical depth, history being more a source of 'imagery' and 'design' (Dermody and Jacka 1988, 33). This emphasis, furthermore, descended to a romantic, uncritical view of Australian history that in Graeme Turner's words was 'too *decorous*', considering the historical events of 'armed class conflict, a brutal legal system, and genocide' (Turner 1989, 110, emphasis added). The period genre, he argues, 'retrojected' Australian 'nationhood' to the colonial past, mythologising Australia in a way that was divorced from the 'complex contemporary realities of an urban [...] "multicultural" society' (115). Nevertheless, the genre played a role in the emerging national consciousness of the 1970s, insofar as 'the preoccupation with historical drama seemed designed to demonstrate that Australia *had* a history and therefore *was* a culture' (103). The genteel aesthetics of the period genre are also attributed partly to a 'literariness' that was traceable to the origins of some AFC-genre films as novels. This quality, Dermody and Jacka suggest, 'inhere[s] in their gently descriptive and evocative creation of period' and in 'character rather than action-based narratives' (1988, 32).

With the passage of time, and the transition of film industry models and practices, the era of the period genre now resembles a 'period' in Australian film-making that is marked by the style of the works produced, in much the same way as the films provide decorous images of an imagined national history. The 'decorous' aesthetic Turner ascribes to the period genre is examined in this chapter, using *The Irishman* as an example. Decorousness is exhibited in more than mise-en-scène. It influences the performances of principal characters, especially gender and racial values, which seem incorporated as period features in much the same way as the set and costumes. Furthermore, the decorous aesthetic emerges most clearly when these elements of the film are compared with the novel on which it is based, Elizabeth O'Conner's Miles Franklin Award–winning *The Irishman: A Novel of Northern Australia* (1960). Epic in scope and sometimes rollicking, the novel is associated with the 'masculine frontier tradition' (Taylor 2003, 28), and it belies the assumed 'literariness' of the period genre, cited earlier. While nostalgic, the novel is less sentimentally so than the film that appeared 18 years later. A focus on the production of the film, filtered through the adaption of the novel, therefore brings to light the role of region in the nationalist tendencies of the period genre. While *The Irishman* was received as a product of a national cinema, its genesis can be traced to North Queensland, where the novel was written and set, and where the film was largely made. It was also partially funded by Queensland interests. Attention to *The Irishman* has resonances for the continuing production of Australian period films in Queensland locations, notably *Australia* (Luhrmann 2008), *The Proposition* and *Beneath Hill 60* (Sims 2010).

Aside from the period conventions of mise-en-scène, *The Irishman*, and the period genre and its recent examples, are also distinguished by their location production, especially in small towns. *The Irishman* was made on location in the North Queensland town of Charters Towers, 130 kilometres west of Townsville. Apart from the making over of the main street, Gill Street, *The Irishman* featured a livestock spectacle in the form of crossings of the nearby Burdekin River by horse teams driven by the titular Irishman, Paddy Doolan (Michael Craig). The character of the town and the performances and labour of the residents are incorporated into mise-en-scène so that it is not only bodies but the region and town that are 'dressed' to resemble the national period depicted. These practices conform to Eckart Voigts-Virchow's description of 'heritage films' (2007, 123), a category he bases on British examples and contexts, and describes as 'crucially determined by creating heritage space through location hunting' and through '"authentifying" [sic] period settings [...] and [...] lavish but "correct" costumes' (129). Heritage is not historical in the sense of 'seek[ing] knowledge about the past'; instead, it exhibits a 'modern-day use of elements of the past' that projects 'a shared cultural memory' and an 'imaginary identity', which is utopian and 'prone to be abused for nationalist or ethnocentrist purposes' (124). Heritage privileges 'diachronic' cultural memory, whereby a 'desirable past' is preserved; and it is also 'metonymic' in that 'only part of a given space is loaded with the defining features of a community's heritage' (124).

The utopian feeling was generated beyond the films, in the aura of Hollywood that settled around the towns. In Charters Towers, to this day, relics of the film shoot are exhibited in a local museum and gallery. Ironically, the utopian heritage aura neutralises the film's regional distinctiveness, which is transformed into a generic heritage setting, in which ideas of a period and a region converge. The ways region and locations are simultaneously featured and diffused in *The Irishman* are discussed in this chapter, and the influence of the decorous nostalgic codes on the adaptation of the novel, and the performances of gender and race in the film. In the conclusion of this chapter, the insights are compared with *Australia* to suggest how heritage and literariness are deployed and commoditised in the production and marketing of this more recent film and how the regional dimensions of its production are similarly overwritten by the discourse of nation.

Queensland Time: Period and Place in Novel and Film

O'Conner's novel *The Irishman* concerns the Doolan family – Paddy, Jenny and their sons, Will and Michael – the mining town and the various stations in the surrounding district, in which they live, in a time that seems to be the 1920s. Paddy's haulage horse team is under threat from both the emerging motorised industry and the decline of mining. The story is epic and takes place against the background of social change figured by the town, and Paddy's demise.

The author, Elizabeth O'Conner, the pseudonymous Barbara McNamara, was the wife of a station manager at Forest Home Station in the Gulf Country of Queensland, and the novel was based on her husband's relationship with his father, who ran a horse team between Georgetown and Croydon during the gold boom years. Crombie tells of reading the book as a teenager and of how it 'resonated with me as a Queenslander from a rural background' in Central – not North – Queensland, in that the issues 'seemed real' (Crombie 2002;

and all comments attributed hereafter to Crombie are from Crombie 2002). Crombie tells that he wrote the script for the film while working for the South Australian Film Corporation (SAFC), adapting it from the novel and using much of the original dialogue. It was after his involvement in the production of *Caddie* (Crombie 1976) that he offered the script to the producer, Anthony Buckley, who was looking to follow up the success of *Caddie*.

In spite of the biographical genesis of the novel, Cheryl Taylor sees it as resisting 'technological change by reverting to a romanticised pioneering past' (Taylor 2003, 28). It is therefore prescient of the retrojective tendencies Turner attributed to the period film genre. These tendencies were subject to some ridicule, typically, as Turner comments, because '[a]t their most formulaic, our period dramas rehearsed a simple, even silly, ritual of the loss of innocence within an exotic and lusciously photographed setting' (1989, 108). This is fair criticism, and Crombie himself refers to *The Irishman* as one of the last 'nostalgia' films. But the loss of innocence theme is perhaps due to the provenance of the novel since, as Gillian Whitlock suggests, writing about Queensland often concerns 'childhood or adolescence and the past' and frequently casts Queensland 'in terms of a retrospective' and 'a wilderness space which cannot be recaptured' (Whitlock 1994, 75).

Queensland, however, is barely referred to in the film *The Irishman*, nor is the diegetic place named, in spite of a couple of fleeting references to local place names, Croydon and Georgetown. An author's note in the novel states that the main place setting 'could be any of the old gold mining towns of North Queensland' (O'Conner 1960, n.p.), although the town is said to be Georgetown, in the Gulf Country (Crombie 2002; Taylor 2003) and the setting for the timber camp in the latter stages of the novel is most likely the Atherton Tableland (Cheryl Taylor, personal communication). In the film, the action moves between a dusty hinterland town and a coastal rainforest. Charters Towers was chosen for the first location, according to Crombie, because of its proximity to the regional city of Townsville, which was a suitably near supply point for film stock and other resources, while a rainforest near Cardwell, around 160 kilometres to the north of Townsville, became the second setting. The film's credits acknowledge Charters Towers and the Kennedy Valley, North Queensland.

Beyond locations, however, Crombie recollects that many of the actors were from Queensland, especially Brisbane, and some were Charters Towers locals, who acted as extras, and in at least one of the principal roles. In addition, the authentic dressing of the sets in period relics and décor and even the vintage vehicles were sourced, Crombie says, from North Queensland stations and private owners. The township and the local properties used as sets were the main heritage features. Crombie recalls that local politicians, especially

Bob Katter Jr (then a state government minister and later federal member of Parliament), with the then mayor of Charters Towers, Thomas 'Tiger' Titley,[1] persuaded the local business people in Gill Street to be involved in dressing and painting the street in heritage colours. Local properties were the sets for the Doolan family's dwellings, Clarke's Timbooran Homestead and Dalgleish's Huntingdon Station. While the film streetscape exhibits a generic heritage appearance, the images of the Doolans' house, in particular, evoke the distinct architecture of the Queenslander house, of which there are many in Charters Towers, a building style that Jennifer Craik says 'feeds into a collective fantasy about the past and heritage' and the 'uniqueness of Queensland' (Craik 1990, 211–12).

In his commentary, Crombie refers to the simplicity of using these ready-made heritage sites. He remembers how views of landscape needed only to be framed; and how it was necessary only to paint and dress the town and dwellings, and to 'populate' and 'art-direct' the bush racecourse, as if the town and surrounding district were a living film studio. While Dermody and Jacka attribute production quality in the period genre to good lighting, 'fine photography' and 'attention to detail' (Dermody and Jacka 1987, 176), design in *The Irishman*, especially interior scenes, was inspired, according to Crombie, by the paintings of the distinguished North Queensland artist Ray Crooke. Crombie also recalls how many scenes were captured in generous takes, and how the set-up allowed space for actors to move around. He reflects that the desire to create a feeling of space also made the film seem slow, but observes that this quality seemed more unsatisfactory at the time than it does today. Some praise *The Irishman*, such as Scott Murray, who writes of its 'beautiful images, fine performances' (1994, 89); and David Stratton, who has commented that it is an 'underrated' film (see Turner 1989). Still, Crombie's comments resonate with earlier generalised criticisms of the period genre, such as Turner's description of the tendency to 'aesthetic mannerisms such as fondness for long atmospheric shots' (Turner 1989, 100).

Some of Crombie's comments also suggest mildly disingenuous attempts to excuse the stagy action and occasional ham acting in *The Irishman*, which now appear as period features of 1970s Australian film. However, his remarks reveal a greater depth of purpose in this individual film project than is accorded by its association with the period/AFC genre. In spite of the apparently nationalist cultural politics associated with the AFC, and the production influences of the SAFC, *The Irishman* appears to have been conceived and produced largely as a Queensland project, even though the distinctive signs of Queensland architecture and landscape merge with a general pioneer mythology and heritage mythos in keeping with putative AFC aims. In the following sections, I examine the screen adaptation of the novel more closely, and suggest that, through the influence of the period genre, the characters seem to have been adapted into the film's decorous heritage discourse, in much the same way as the houses and cars.

Restyling the Frontier: Heritage Masculinities

Briefly, O'Conner's story of the Doolans commences with the situation of the family as economic change threatens Paddy's teamster business. Also addled by drink and conflict with his elder son, Will, Paddy leaves, never to return home, and the family is then dependent on Will, who eventually also leaves town, taking his mother with him, while Michael gains work with Dalgleish, the manager of Huntingdon Station. On the rise to seniority, Michael is severely injured in an accident partly caused by Paula, Dalgleish's mixed-race lover and assistant manager. Michael recovers but is permanently disabled, and, seeking to be reconciled with his father, heads off on a droving stint, in search of Paddy. They are briefly reunited before Paddy is killed in an accident. The story concludes with Michael intending to return to the employment of Dalgleish.

The compression of the narrative for screen retained the family melodrama but diminished the epic quality, and in a manner that privileged the heritage aura. A coming of age occurs for Michael (Simon Burke), but his accident, its aftermath and the related subplots are omitted from the film. Whereas the focus and perspectives of the novel are largely shared between Will and Michael, albeit relayed in a third (narrator's) voice, the central focus of the film is on Paddy (Michael Craig). The theme of technology and social change is emblematic in the film in the manner of his death, which occurs when a truck overtakes his wagon on a bridge, whereas in the novel Paddy dies when his horses bolt. Arguably, the shift of focus from the sons to the father simplifies a level of intrigue in the male power relationships of the novel as a number of 'father substitutes' to Michael (Taylor 2003, 29) are diminished or trimmed. This results in the suppression of a covert theme of the novel concerning masculine succession, whereby biological sons are alienated from fathers and pursue their fortunes from station owners and managers. The most notable casualty of this reduction is the liminal character, Chad Logan, a white nomad and outcast, who has a prolonged and critical role in Michael's odyssey in search of his father, and who propels Michael to return to the employment of Dalgleish after Paddy's death. Logan has had similar benefactors in Mr and Mrs Swan (they do not appear in the film), who employed him after his release from a jail term that he innocently incurred on behalf of his own father, a murderer. In the film, however, Logan (Gerard Kennedy) is treated as a benevolent drifter, whose position in the bush patrilineage is irrelevant, so that his influence on Michael appears instrumental rather than thematic. This contraction of Logan, and the concentration in the film on Paddy's fate rather than Michael's, has the effect of idealising Michael as a (p)lucky hero, whose relationships are filtered through sentiment and mateship rather than the more ritualised codes of station patriarchates.

The heritage aura of the film particularly impacted the characterisation of Paddy. The period genre is now seen partly as reaction to the perceived vulgarity of the ocker films of the revival, a loose cycle of films that were an 'unabashed celebration of the "Australian"' (O'Regan 1989, 76), and with strong, male-centred sexual themes. In contrast, Dermody and Jacka observe, the male characters of the AFC genre are on the whole 'recessive, sensitive in temperament and doomed to failure', partly due to 'withdrawal [...] from the comically offensive masculinity of the ocker comedies' (1988, 33). The most acute irony of this no doubt appropriate reflection is that the Paddy of the film *The Irishman* is a noticeably more refined, less vulgar character than the Paddy of the earlier, pre-ocker novel. The Irishman of O'Conner's novel is known as 'Black Paddy' or 'Big Paddy Doolan'. While he is not in the ocker league, he is not genteel, in spite of humour and occasional witty charm. Nicknamed for his 'black hair and moustache, and the short strong hairs that grew on his broad chest and thick arms' (O'Conner 1960, 5), which gain him racist taunts of 'black Irish', Black Paddy is a forbidding and volatile figure, given to boozing, violence and Irish profanity. Black Paddy is far from the whimsical, lanky gentleman in the film, about whom Turner complains that it is 'hard to sustain interest in Michael Craig's Irishman' as he 'indicates his complexity of character by getting drunk and playing the harmonica' (Turner 1989, 109). Turner sees this as a 'fashion' in Australian cinema of the time for 'explicitly "colourful", eccentric characters [...] using drunkenness and other rituals of mateship as the indices of originality of character' (109). It must be said, however, that boozing and harmonica-playing are true to the characterisation of Paddy in O'Conner's novel. But Craig's film Paddy is hardly the fearsome character who dominates Michael's youth in the novel, and is more akin to vaudeville Irishmen found elsewhere in the AFC genre.

Omitted in the film is an Aboriginal character, Split Nose Alec. Reflecting on Split Nose Alec's role in the novel, Taylor suggests that, in O'Connor's works, Aborigines feature either 'as the homestead workforce or as unhappy wanderers existing on the fringes' (Taylor 2003, 22). O'Conner's works, including *The Irishman*, 'implicitly advocate integration' of Aborigines 'at a lower level within white society', while they 'elide the possibility of any thoughtful or accurate representation of Aboriginal culture' (24). Yet Taylor suggests that O'Conner sometimes 'invites compassion for individuals, while elaborating a racial disempowerment and denial of culture' (27). This is apparent in the depiction of Split Nose Alec in *The Irishman*, who, O'Conner says in a note, is based on a real character known in her district (O'Conner, Author's Note: n.p.). Aside from an Aboriginal stockman on Dalgleish's property, and Bo-Bo, who is discussed hereafter, Split Nose Alec is the most prominent Indigenous character in the novel. To Michael, Split Nose Alec, who is named for a facial disfigurement, at first represents fear: 'The native's chest was bare. [...] The wild disfigured face destroyed the beauty of the morning. It was there within the vision of the frightened boy as though it had materialised from a nightmare' (O'Conner 63–64). Michael's fear is allayed by Logan's friendship with Split Nose Alec and later he intervenes when other boys harass Alec. It is not difficult to recognise Split Nose Alec's bush gothic associations, but his omission from the film can be compared with other films of the period genre. *The Last Wave* (Weir 1977), *Manganinnie* (Honey 1980), *Storm Boy* (Safran 1976) and *The Chant of Jimmie Blacksmith* (Schepisi 1978) include comparable characters and, according to Turner (1987), portray a romantic, exotic view of Aborigines (138).

North Queensland Noras: Dressing Houses, Gazing on Women

The treatment of the female roles in the film *The Irishman* is a more obvious instance of heritage construction, in ways that can be seen as derived from the novel and influences of the period genre. All of the female roles are written out by halfway through the novel. A few are retained and limited in the film: Mrs Clarke (Roberta Grant) makes a brief appearance, Mrs Dalgleish (Marcella Burgoyne) is reduced to almost a non-speaking part, and the brief role of Bo-Bo (Tina McMahon) is directly transposed. The principal role of Jenny (Robyn Nevin), on the other hand, is extended to the duration of the film narrative, but in a manner that brings little more than melodramatic atmosphere to the tale of Paddy and Michael.

The film adaptations of these female roles are also affected by the diminution of the homestead settings of the novel, which, as Taylor argues, are significant to women's roles, in that O'Conner's fiction typically creates a web of homesteads in which social power is arranged. O'Conner's homesteads, Taylor says, hegemonise subjectivity and operate not only as logistical centres but also to 'preserv[e] class and racial distinctions' by enforcing the 'subordinate status of women and non-European[s]' (Taylor 2003, 20). O'Conner's homesteads are 'conditional matriarchies', in which an overlay of female domestic rule conceals an 'unhappy substratum' of disaffection among the women (Taylor 2003, 29). In the film narrative, however, the homesteads play less of a structural role, and the characters are reduced in number, thus clipping out depth elements of the narrative and visually making way for the township and properties to appear as the heritage spectacle.

There is also an intriguing adaptation of O'Conner's coding of social differences between women, who are compared, in the novel, through images of their plants and gardens. A comparison is established, for instance, between Jenny, a battler, who is first seen in her kitchen with no electricity, 'hurry[ing] about the hot room like a moth' (O'Conner 1960, 6), and Mrs Clarke of Timbooran Station, a graceful new bride from the south, who lolls around her marital home wearing a tussore silk dress. Will observes that this is the same fabric as Jenny's *best* dress (27). Mrs Clarke is mostly found on her veranda – another motif of Queensland literature (see Whitlock 1994) – a site of 'ferns and broad-leafed califas, standing sedately in painted pots along the veranda's edge' (27). The painted pots are elegantly contrasted with Jenny's plants in 'tins' that she 'tended with pride [...] carrying [...] water in a bucket from a well', and a 'vine' that 'grew about the front of the house' (6). The fine women of the novel, Mrs Clarke and Mrs Swan, have beautiful gardens, while tragic Mrs Dalgleish has 'no garden', and the only tree marks the grave of her only child (156). Plants, vines and trees signal female domiciles, and as miniaturised allusions to the bush these suggest pioneer legend, in which women are associated with cultivation and civilising effects (Robson and Zalcock 1997, 10). But they suffer and duly depart from the homestead economies through migration, death or removal, thus resembling Kay Schaffer's description of women in earlier bush fiction, who are both idealised and 'objectified into figures of defeat' (Schaffer 1988, 118). It is perhaps not surprising that the women's roles are mostly trimmed from the film. Moreover, the novelistic gaze on plants, vines, gardens and women seems to be displaced in the film onto the depiction of the women within heritage dwellings, whereby, as Neil Rattigan comments, 'even the rather dingy houses [...] are made to look pretty' (Rattigan 1991, 160).

The Doolans' house is realised in the film in an authentic Charters Towers miner's cottage, composed of timber and galvanised, with a latticed veranda at the front. Faithful to the novel, the Doolan family is seen mostly in the kitchen. Jenny tends Paddy's wounds from brawling in a memorable outdoor laundry, dressed with antique roller and galvanised iron cupola. Iconically placed before a doorway, greeting Michael, in framing scenes, Jenny resembles mothers in Australian films of the 1920s and 1930s whom Routt describes as 'good' mothers and infinitely giving, but who do not 'project much power' (Routt 1989, 47). Mrs Clarke is also idealised and objectified within a heritage setting as the location for Mrs Clarke's abode, Timbooran Station, was the colonial homestead of Bluff Downs, with the film action taking place mostly on the veranda and sleepout. On the veranda, Mrs Clarke utters her longest speech: 'It's a man's world in the bush. There's nothing here for a woman except submission. My only purpose is to produce heirs for all this. Sometimes I feel just like another of his broodmares.' Mrs Clarke's speech has no source in the novel, except in the vague sense that Black Paddy is thought to prefer horses to women, although none of the novel's women directly identify with livestock.

While Jenny gains greater presence in the film than the novel, all the women's roles become absorbed by the heritage settings as period features, as spectacle rather than as subjects of action. It seems more than a coincidence that Crombie in his commentary consistently refers to the production labour on the dwellings as 'dressing' them. In other words, while Dermody and Jacka (1988) attribute little mise-en-scène to the AFC genre, apart from 'picturesque landscape' and 'beautifully dressed interiors' (34), *The Irishman* seems to typify the way 'the representational system of the film [...] privileges women "only" as spectacle'; 'women's power is textual (iconographic [...] aligned with the *mise-en-scène*) rather than physical or performative' (Verhoeven 2006, 104). The dwellings' importance signals the women's role and presence in *The Irishman*, a presence fetishised through the art heritage discourse of 'period', in which women are living décor. The setting is not simply subordinated as background but woman *is* setting through association with women's 'natural' or ideological place in house and home, irrespective of social level, from cottage to homestead.

A coda to this heritage treatment of gender is the adaptation of Aboriginal characters from O'Conner's novel. It was written during the era of assimilation policy towards Aboriginal people, but is set in the earlier period of so-called protection. O'Conner's approaches are overridden by the adaptation as most aspects of race seem to have been handled by omission. Racist language and sentiments of some characters in the novel, including Michael, which undoubtedly reflect the times and the region in which the novel is set, were not adapted to the film. This may have been on grounds of racial sensitivity, or because these elements were deemed incongruous in a nostalgic heritage film. Of several Indigenous characters – Bo-Bo, Paula, the black stockman of Swan's homestead and Split Nose Alec – only Bo-Bo is transposed to the film. Indeed, many characters were cut in the adaptation, not only Aboriginal characters, and this was likely dictated by budget and scale of production as in any film. In fact, Bo-Bo's brief role, unlike other female roles, was largely unchanged from book to film. One overlooked detail in the transposition is that, like Jedda, in *Jedda*, Bo-Bo was a foundling child, who was adopted into station life. Bo-Bo works as Mrs Clarke's maid at Timbooran, where she meets and becomes pregnant by Will (Lou Brown). Will leaves Timbooran, abandoning Bo-Bo, who dies of a haemorrhage, apparently caused by either a suicide attempt or an attempt to bring on a miscarriage. This tragic incident ultimately propels Will's conflict with Paddy.

In production, however, Crombie says that the role of Bo-Bo was difficult to cast because Aboriginal actors were few 'back in that era', although they auditioned 'vigorously'. Eventually a local woman, Tina McMahon, gained the part, but according to Crombie she proved vocally unsatisfactory and the part was therefore 're-voiced' – a euphemism for dubbed – by the (uncredited) Brisbane actress Judy Morris. The implications in any era of 're-voicing' an Aboriginal speaking part might be seen as comparable to 'blacking up', which is how Casey and Syron (2005, 101) characterise the casting of non-Indigenous actors in Aboriginal roles. It is a practice, they say, that has been claimed as justified in the past by the non-availability of Indigenous actors, reinforcing the silence that they argue is a 'consistent feature' of Indigenous film characters (104). Not only silence (which is discussed further in Chapter 2), but the re-voicing of Bo-Bo also contributes to the predominant alignment of female roles with visual spectacle in *The Irishman* as Bo-Bo is, in a sense, seen but not heard.

Beyond the Homestead: Baz Luhrmann's *Australia*

In summary, aspects of the production of *The Irishman* mark it as a heritage film of the late 1970s, subject to the proto-nationalist cultural politics of the then AFC. A layer of nostalgia in the director's recollections reveals that the film was born of a personal and regional identification with the source novel. The film imposes a superficial gentility, thereby transforming a story of homestead cultures of a specific North Queensland region into a family melodrama about battler whitefolks and a stage Irishman. If this view seems like a reissuing of the 'which is better, book or movie?' variety, which Voigts-Virchow warns models literature as 'cultural norm' (Voigts-Virchow 2007, 123), its relevance is more to the continuing production of period films in which regional Queensland is seen through a national lens.

Parallel with nostalgic rendering of region for a past national cinema audience, *Australia* packages racial and political histories for a global audience in the present. The recreation of the main street of the North Queensland town of Bowen as a set for *Australia*, and the incorporation of a livestock feature, a drove through the town, is reminiscent of the making of *The Irishman* in Charters Towers. More than merely decorous, *Australia* presents racism and the abuse of Indigenous people as spectacles of melodrama (and even comedy) within a fantasy blockbuster that both exposes and forgives the nation metonymised in the title. But the strategy in *Australia* seems to be more of intervention than of retrojection. The racist language, until now taboo in a film of this kind – although not in social realist films about Indigenous poverty – echoes the language trimmed from *The Irishman*. While it is a transnational film of an original screenplay, *Australia* is also heritage in a number of senses. The homestead, Faraway Downs, is a central spectacle, along with the Darwin pub and Mission Island, and it is overseen by a Blytonesque memsahib in the form of Nicole Kidman's Missus Boss, who in her innocence and instinctual humanity overthrows the bush patriarchy – something a more traditional homestead matriarch might not have achieved. She is helped by the Drover, an itinerant horseman not dissimilar to Chad Logan, and echoes of *Jedda* also resonate around vivid landscapes and in the figure of another surrogate Indigenous child, Nullah (Brandon Walters). A heritage aura was also imposed through HarperCollins's re-publication of Xavier Herbert's *Capricornia* (Herbert 2008), and promoted as having 'inspired' *Australia*. This superimposition of a literary work onto *Australia*, apparently to forge depth and value, seems ironic in light of the past criticism of AFC-genre films for their decorous incorporation of a literary ambience.

Like *The Irishman* in Charters Towers, *Australia* is celebrated in and for the places of its making, Bowen – nicknamed 'Bowenwood' during the making of *Australia* – and Darwin. More attention has been drawn to Darwin because of the recreation of its war-time history and the bombing raids featured in the film. Moreover, partly thanks to digital technology, Bowen's participation verges on anonymity, not only because Luhrmann's film is a fantasy that transforms its diegetic territories into worlds beyond the rainbow, but also because, when the film alludes to real places, Bowen plays Darwin. Even though the red carpet at the Bowen premiere of *Australia* did not receive the stars, who attended the main event in Sydney, Bowen audiences poured undeterred into showings of *Australia*, which reputedly recorded a better box office in Bowen than *Titanic* (Cameron 1997).

It seems that the disparate production ecologies of transnational film in the 2000s are as prone to exploit the aura of Hollywood in seducing town loyalties as was the case in the 1970s, and to impose heritage values through period drama. This is the case, even though the dominant model of the cinemagoer is not associated with small town or rural populations but is modelled on 'specifically urban modernity' (Bowles 2008, 87). But the practice of using small towns as film sets today has more prospect of economic benefit for filmmakers because of Screen Australia's location offset incentives. The practice also benefits the towns in terms of tourism, fostered by the greater success of Australian players in the international film industry, a situation much changed since the 1970s. The potential of benefits to local film-makers is also more likely today than in the AFC period, and this was alluded to in local coverage of the post-*Australia* effect in North Queensland (see Ryan 2008a), as well as a promised boom in Bowen real estate (see Ryan 2008b).

However, only the townspeople in Bowen and Charters Towers, and the casts and crews, now recall the productions of *Australia* and *The Irishman*. It is like the lands near Winton in *The Proposition* (see Chapter 8), or Townsville (albeit, not a small town) in *Beneath Hill 60*,[2] places that are not realised, but diffusely depicted, using methods long since conventionalised in costume dramas. These methods become more illusory as the digital age progresses, resisting and enshrouding rather than manifesting the presence of a place. Heritage affects a synthesis of identification by masking the local and dressing up the more abstract signs of nation, and creating a spectacle of curiosity for audiences who know the places where the action was filmed. In the cinemas of nation and trans-nation, everything – region, history, race and gender – is framed and art-directed, and all the voices are dubbed, so to speak.

In turning again to *The Irishman* in the next chapter, and comparison with *Jedda*, the element of dubbing is highlighted as a dimension of the identity discourses of both films, and the colonial and nationalist resonances and precedence of images over voices in these films.

Chapter 2

HERITAGE ENIGMATIC: THE SILENCE OF THE DUBBED IN *JEDDA* AND *THE IRISHMAN*

The Dub Economy in Cinema

The post-synchronisation of sound and voices has been a widespread practice throughout the history of cinema. Limited critical attention has been paid to these practices, and this is no doubt an aspect of the continued predominance of visual over aural regimes in film production and reception, a hierarchy that persists, arguably due to the historic primacy of silent over sound cinema (see Chion 1994). However, *dubbing* is a term applied to 'any copying process that may occur in audio or video recording' (Holman 2002, 199). The extensive post-production of voices, sounds and dialogue in cinema is curiously subversive of cinematic spectacle, and this perhaps partly accounts for the carnivalesque associations of dubbed cinema. Moreover, Ian Penman argues that a 'certain dub effect can be heard everywhere in modern sonics' (2001, 110), giving rise to a condition that we now inhabit, a dub economy of 'echo logic'; and 'echoellipsis' (107).

Penman likens 'dub' to a haunting, the sonic uncanny, and speaks of dub as the death of language; as 'tone, reverberating, never ending – and never fully present – echo' (111). In dub: 'the song *rings* as if it has come through [...] from the other side' (110). Penman is writing of dub effects in music but his echologic may well apply to various settings. The haunted and haunting associations of dub explored in this chapter concern the roles of Bo-Bo in *The Irishman*, discussed in the previous chapter, and Jedda (played by Rosalie Kunoth, credited as Ngarla Kunoth) in *Jedda* (see Introduction). Probing the decisions to dub these roles draws attention to shifts in cinematic practice and meaning over time. Bo-Bo and Jedda, the dubbed, also reference changes in the performance of identity in Australian cinema then and now. First, this preamble provides some context for the current status of reception of dubbed voices in cinema.

Dubbing, or 're-voicing', is popularly associated with B-Cinema and especially with comic and carnivalesque inversion of drama. The prevalent association of dub with distortion, play and subversion belies that post-synchronisation of sound and dialogue is long-standing practice in film production, and that post- and pro-synchronisation have long influenced auteur practices. Francois Thomas suggests how this is sometimes incorporated creatively because post-synced sound is neither 'enslaved to the spatial environment [...] nor to a concern for verisimilitude' (2000, 186).[1] Vocal or dialogue dubbing or post-synchronisation is typically marked in montage by uneven lipsync where added voices are aurally plastered over utterances of on-screen speakers, and it is this visual dissonance that lends to the carnivalesque uses of dub, and has perhaps created the sense of dub as 'sight gag', and in a manner in which the non-visual is re-appropriated to a visual discourse. Dubbing therefore has become associated with language and linguistic play, the conventions of which also mask the economics of production, as dub is an inexpensive technology of adaptation in cultures that depend on imported film product.

The vernacular association of dubbing with B cinema is largely due to the post-war American importation of 'so-called "B-grade" foreign movies to be cut-up and repackaged' as local product, a practice Philip Brophy sees as implicitly xenophobic (2001, 233–34). Brophy views the adaptation of *Godzilla: King of the Monsters!* (Honda and Morse 1956) from the originally titled Japanese film, *Gojira* (Honda 1954), and the treatment of a number of European films from the same period as prototypical of dubbing as cultural vandalism, where there is no attempt to interpret, or even wilful disregard of the earlier, cultural thematics. The B-ness of these films was acquired, he argues, through the importation of B-genres (sci-fi, horror and fantasy, martial arts) from supposedly B-sources ('European and Pan-Pacific countries') as an 'economical' way to create product for domestic (Western) markets because it was deemed that 'the original language of these foreign films rendered them ripe for recoding and reformatting' for American/Western conventions (Brophy 2001, 233). The carnivalesque meanings of dub have been exploited, as Brophy also points out, by numerous comedians who have compiled gags from 'post-dubbed configurations' of any number of A- and B-list films and television shows – *The Samurai* (Funatoko and Toyama 1962–65), *Beavis and Butt-Head* (Judge 1993–2011), *Double Take*'s 'talking over' of *Hercules Returns* (Parker 1993) – in what Brophy describes as 'flip dismissal of "Otherness"' (2001, 237).

In the current era, however, the surging dub economy is persistently invested in both carnivalesque and dramatic modes. Carnival dubbing persists in the use of celebrities to 'voice' the principal roles in animated features. Mike Myers's voicing of Shrek in *Shrek* (Adamson and Jenson 2001) and all the follow-up films of the series is a touchstone of such roles in the digitally animated era. The humour, charm and bankability of the aural 'spectacle' of a celebrity voice in a digital 'body' owes to the long history of human voices in animated films. The carnivalesque conventions of B cinema dubbing gain new meanings in the context of the current appetite for avatars in virtual worlds and voice fonts in computer-generated environments. The dramatic reaches of the dub economy, however, are widely apparent in realist mode, in particular, in forms of special features packages and audio commentary that are ubiquitously included with feature films in domestic release. Digital Versatile Disc (DVD) packaging with commentary makes going 'behind the scenes' of film production a standard format, exposing production processes and anecdotes and bringing the intimacy of a chat show while demystifying the feature film but distancing the industrial apparatus of film marketing and production. The technology is not quite so much mixing and dubbing as talking over the feature, and the effect is of 'de-dramatisation', to borrow a term Stuart Cunningham (1987b) coined to describe the aesthetics of documentary. Through the suppression of film sound the commentary involves unseen (often expert or celebrity) commentators reviewing the visuals and talking over the scenes, thus transforming the packaged spectacle from fiction to documentary. The simulation of audience proximity to production derives an aura quite separate to that of the feature film, and has the additional effect of 'personifying' the technology of film through the commentary and interviews with film-makers, stars, writers and producers (make-up artists and gofers are rarely included). These bonus extras are frequently presented as sub-productions or mini-documentaries that incorporate scenes from the feature, thereby duplicating the spectacle of the feature film. The ambience of a director's commentary, in particular, invokes the aura of the auteur, whether the commentator is Scorsese, or a first-timer, or a little-known old-timer. This aura is intensified in the proliferation of DVD sets of particular film-makers' works (Kubrick, Lynch, Cronenberg, Jarmusch and Hitchcock, to mention a few), which revive the mystique of the auteur, especially when accompanied by interviews or pieces to camera by historians or academics that simultaneously praise and analyse the feature (I am yet to see one that critiques the featured films). These practices result in the echo-logical effects of both expanding and subordinating the spectacle of the featured film, and increasing the variations on dubbed productions, and hence of the fetishistic economies of cinema.

This preamble has been posed thus far to blurrily illuminate the myriad of uses of post-synchronisation in the past and in the expanding digital economy today, and the implications for contemporary views of past practices of dubbing. In the remainder of this chapter, the dubbing of Bo-Bo and Jedda is juxtaposed with this contemporary reception of dub to consider the lingering silence that emanates from the voices of these characters. From a contemporary perspective, their silence is comparable to Chris Healy's view of the use of voice-over narration in television documentaries on Aboriginal people (in the 1960s) whereby the silence (of the Aboriginal subjects) 'understands indigenous people as colonised' (Healy 2008, 38). But an investigation of the circumstances – both of the original dubbing in each film, and the manner in which, subsequently, these interventions have been accounted for – reveals some complexity and uncertainty in the ideas of both the 'silent' and the 'colonised' that raise some questions as to how this might be viewed from a contemporary perspective. In the case of Bo-Bo, in *The Irishman*, the director unambiguously discloses the reasons within the audio commentary released on DVD, more than 20 years after the release of the film. In *Jedda*, the motivation is more obscure as the voice of Jedda was not the only dubbed voice in the film, and this has been a source of contention that is discussed hereafter. I do not wish to form conclusions but to suggest that – notwithstanding the history of discrimination regarding Indigenous actors – the dubbed voices of Bo-Bo and Jedda resonate discretely, first, because of the sparse distinction of these characters as principal female Indigenous roles in Australian films until the 1970s; and, second, because of the perceived dissonance of the dub with the technological prowess these films reputedly represent. The larger implications, however, are for the place of Aboriginal people in Australian culture signified by their marginality within representational media. Struggling to be seen, in these rare instances in which they are shown, they are effectively silenced by the process of dub and thus also subject to lasting implication in the carnivalesque reception of this practice.

Decorously Dubbed: Bo-Bo in *The Irishman*

In the previous chapter, I discussed the place of *The Irishman* in the revival and the heritage treatment of history and mise-en-scène in this film, a tendency which, in Graeme Turner's view, resulted in a an uncritical view of Australian history as 'too decorous' (1989, 110). I argued that the decorousness of *The Irishman* can be seen as a cinematic code of gentrification that is not limited to setting and décor but also affects the performances of gender and race, and that this is most apparent when compared to the novel on which it is based. Only one of several Indigenous characters in that novel is adapted to the film, namely Bo-Bo, a servant in one of the key households in the drama, whose brief but critical role of only a few scenes is transposed almost directly from the novel to film. I commented on the circumstances of the casting of Tina McMahon in the role of Bo-Bo, and how the vocal dubbing of the role appears to silence the voice of this actor. There are further reflections to add, as not only is Bo-Bo the sole principal Aboriginal character in *The Irishman*, but she also appears to be one of very few principal female Indigenous roles in any of the films of the period genre, with the notable exception of the title role of *Manganinnie* played by Mawayul Yanthalawuy – who also appeared in *We of the Never Never* (Auzin 1982) and *Bedevil* (Moffatt 1993) – and in comparison to a number of male Indigenous characters in contemporaneous films (see Chapter 1).

Bo-Bo's main antecedent, therefore, appears to be the eponymous Jedda – the only lead role played by an Indigenous woman for decades – with whom she shares several characteristics, and whose appearance in 1955 was roughly contemporary with the publication of O'Conner's novel, *The Irishman*, in 1960, and, hence, with the genesis of Bo-Bo. While Jedda is a central, lead character, Bo-Bo appears only briefly in *The Irishman*, but there are similarities in the dramaturgy of the characters as both Bo-Bo and Jedda are foundling children adopted as the protégés of their respective mistresses. Bo-Bo becomes the servant of Mrs Clarke, the mistress of Timbooran Station, in *The Irishman*, while Jedda, orphaned by the death of her tribal mother, is handed to Mrs McMann, the station mistress in *Jedda* (see Cunningham 1987a; Molloy 1990a). Both characters suffer tragic fates. Jedda is abducted by Marbuk (Robert Tudawali), which leads to her death; Bo-Bo dies from an apparent miscarriage after becoming pregnant to a white man who leaves her. In spite of, or perhaps because of, the relative uniqueness of these characters in Australian cinema the sensitivity of the reception of their performances is apparent from the accounts of the vocal dubbing.

The disclosure that Bo-Bo was dubbed in post-production is made by Crombie, in – an already echo-logical medium – the Audio Commentary, where he is joined by leading cast members Simon Burke and Michael Craig. Their de-dramatisation is in the style of nostalgic reminiscence, especially Crombie's recollections. Burke and Craig's comments are faintly larrikin in tone but do not distract from Crombie's efforts to justify the artistic aims of the production and minimise the shortcomings of the film, which remains a respected example of the period genre. As the scenes involving Bo-Bo slide by, Burke prompts Crombie to reveal that it is not the voice of Tina McMahon heard in the film, and Crombie agrees to tell that the part was 're-voiced' by the Brisbane actor Judy Morris, who was uncredited in the film. (Indeed, it is usually, although not always, the convention not to acknowledge dubbed voices except in forms such as animation where the human voices acquire star or performer billing.) In accounting for the decision to 're-voice' the part, Crombie speaks of McMahon's inexperience, saying that she was not a professional actor and had no training, and he comments that: 'She looks nice but she just didn't have a voice that […] [breaks off] […] and her performance was extremely flat. […] It's always slightly embarrassing when you have to revoice somebody but in that case we had no choice really' (Crombie 2002).

Objectively, McMahon's performance appears creditable, and not out of place with other roles in the film, especially as Simon Burke humorously reflects on his own inexperience as a child actor and admits to 'bad acting' in places (Crombie 2002). Crombie also reflects on his inexperience as a director, with only one other feature film behind him at the time. The comments about McMahon therefore seem uneasy, and perhaps this is also symptomatic of the risks of the impromptu (unscripted) commentary format. More considered information might have suggested the integrity of the decision to dub, or indicated whether any other voices in the film were also dubbed. It might be presumed that there were no other dubbed voices, in light of Crombie's further comments on the speech of another female actor in *The Irishman*, Roberta Grant, who plays Mrs Clarke, Bo-Bo's mentor. Grant's Mrs Clarke speaks in refined, received-pronunciation tones, in the style of many Australian actors of the pre-revival era. Crombie justifies this in *The Irishman* by commenting on the squatter classes 'of the era' (presumably referring to the period of the film's setting), who, he says, spoke in English accents, and dressed for dinner in an English aristocratic way. This explanation seems improbable while Cheryl Taylor's view of O'Conner's fictional homesteads is that they are essentially 'middle-class rather than aristocratic' (2003, 20). In other words, while there is an effort to justify the incongruous vocal tones of Mrs Clarke, the authentic voice of Tina McMahon's Bo-Bo was removed, albeit with such skill as to be undetectable to the inexpert viewer, and therefore with apparently respectful regard for McMahon's performance, and, no doubt, for the rarity of an Aboriginal actor in a principal role at the time.

Crombie's justification for the dubbing of Bo-Bo alludes to production quality, and the faint aura of the auteur, which is no doubt deserved for Crombie's long and distinguished career, and his vanguard role in the revival. The production standards, cinematography and acknowledged splendour of the visual aesthetics of several of the period films, including *The Irishman*, have sustained a reputation for technical distinction in Australian cinema since. Yet the calibre of production makes – even skilful – dubbing appear anachronistic, especially due to the carnival associations of this practice outlined earlier in this chapter, and, especially, as it seems to have occurred in the service of the decorous aura of the period genre, an aura Crombie references in his characterisation of the 'nostalgia' film, and in the tone of reminiscence in the shared commentary with Burke and Craig. The accounts of the two actors' voices, McMahon's and Clarke's, however, give pause to reflect on how the same voices might be handled today, in an era of the much greater presence of Aboriginal actors in film and television, and when the colonial associations of Mrs Clarke's cultivated accent might seem too confronting or absurd. It is not far-fetched to speculate that the one to be re-voiced might not be Bo-Bo.

The Many Voices of *Jedda*

In contrast, there is a degree of mystery attached to the use of vocal post-synchronisation in *Jedda*. The film is said to have been made, in a sense, to feature Indigenous people as the story is told that it was Chauvel's reputed response to American journalists' challenge to make an 'indisputably' Australian film (Cunningham 1987a, 29). Equally, a number of accounts of the production of *Jedda* refer to Chauvel's desire to exhibit the Australian outback, and Cunningham associates the exotic treatment of the landscape with what he calls Chauvel's 'locationism'. It is therefore also ineffably associated with the novelty of cinema technology in remote Australia, especially as the production featured several technological innovations, including the use of colour, and, it is claimed, the first use of magnetic sound in an Australian film. The speech of Jedda, however, bears the obvious signs of uneven lipsync that betray the dub. This has provoked some stern commentary by, for instance, Benjamin Miller (2007), who sees it as an unambiguous instance of aural 'blackface'. But there is somewhat more query attached to the history of the dubbing of Jedda than Miller's (albeit sympathetic) account suggests, not least in that several actors' voices were dubbed in *Jedda*.

A number of accounts of the production (Chauvel 1973; Cunningham 1987a, 1991; Carlsson 1989; Kunoth-Monks 1995) make no allusion to dubbing or manipulation of Jedda's voice, even though there has been critical commentary on the undisputed voicing-over of Joe (Paul Clarke), the 'half-caste' stockman and fiancé of Jedda. This technique has been seen as an aspect of the quasi-documentarism of the format of *Jedda* by Cunningham (1987a), and associated with (anti-)assimilationist rhetoric by Karen Jennings (1993). Referring to the re-voicing of Joe (played, incidentally, by an actor identified as third-generation Italian rather than Aboriginal) in *Jedda*, Jennings says: 'there are two Joes in *Jedda* – the diegetic character, Joe, whose dialogue and actions personify the perfectly assimilated "half-caste", and the Joe of the (very cultivated) voice-over narration whose discourse veers strongly towards Doug McMann's anti-assimilationist views' (1993, 35). Cunningham sees the device of re-voicing as symptomatic of the project of *Jedda*, and of the simultaneously progressive and regressive representation of Indigenous characters whereby 'the extremes of ethnographic realism and Hollywood signifying practices meet: untrained social actors [are] nevertheless constructed as stars in terms of narrative centrality, composition and spectatorial activity' (1987a, 36). But the comments as they pertain to voice are directed towards the role of Joe rather than Jedda.

In an interview with Paul Clarke (aka Paul Reynell, the actor, credited as Paul Reynall, who played Joe in *Jedda*), dated since Cunningham's research,

Gino Moliterno (Clarke 2005) asks Clarke whether he did the voice-over attributed to Joe because, Moliterno says, 'it's hard to tell now whether it's your voice or not' (26). Clarke responds by explaining that he recorded the voice-over 'in three styles', that is, '[i]n my best stage voice; in my ordinary voice; and with a bit of an ocker accent' (27). He reflects that his youth and inexperience might have made the results unsuitable, but he attributes the final voice-over to the 'pressure' Chauvel was under 'in relationship to the narration, because his backers were not very happy that there was an Australian accent introducing the film, because Australian accents in those days were not very popular in the industry around the world, except for an Australian character' (27). He mentions a number of voices that seem to have been changed, but indicates that the precise status is unclear:

> [W]hen I see the film, in the dialogue sections I can hear myself, and in other parts, not. And I know that Jedda was voiceovered [*sic*]; Hugh Wason Byers was also dubbed; and the narration was changed and voiceover [*sic*]. And [...] I think Tas Fitzer the police officer. Now I don't know why all this was done. And [...] it wasn't done in Australia, it was done in England. The girl who did the voiceover [*sic*] for Jedda was a South African. I don't know who the English chap was who did the part of the narration there. And I [...] recognise the voice of Grant Taylor who did Hugh Wason Myers [*sic*]. I don't know who did Tas Fitzer. [...] But it's a great mystery. All I know is that the backers were giving Chauvel a bad time about Australian accents and the whole production. (27)

In further comments, Clarke alludes to other (unsourced) criticisms made of *Jedda*, notably the incongruity of the voice of Joe or moreover that 'one of the greatest criticisms [...] at the time was [...] how would a half-caste Aboriginal have an English Oxford accent' (28). He also questions why an Australian actor was not employed to do the voice-over narration, noting that many Australian actors worked in England in the 1950s (28). Ken Berryman observes that accounts of the production of the film 'steer right away from the notion that there was a problem with the accents' and instead 'talk about [...] the problem with the location sound, and that was what required the dubbing in post production [...] in the UK' and it 'wasn't logistically possible to get the actors who had done the original lines [...] to do them' (29). Berryman's explanation is the generally accepted one, and is also supported by Susanne Chauvel Carlsson, who records the problems of using recording equipment in the more challenging locations of Chauvel's films and in spite of the reputed distinction of *Jedda* as the first Australian-made feature film to use magnetic sound (1989, 168). In fact, Carlsson's (albeit very) brief account of the post-production of *Jedda* in England includes no reference to sound-related interventions at all. But Cunningham refers to post-production at Avondale Studios in Sydney, and then to 'the sound mix' as well as 'colour processing and final editing at Denham Studios in London' as taking up 'most of 1954' (1987a, 32).

Other evidence suggests that dubbed voices may have been intended from the outset as some sources indicate that there was limited use of a script in shooting *Jedda*. For instance, Clarke says that '[n]obody to my knowledge ever saw a full script. [...] The morning of or the day before if you were lucky, you were handed a page of script' (2005, 9). This is supported by Rosalie Kunoth-Monks's recollections that when she was chosen for the role of Jedda she 'wasn't given a script or anything' (1995, Tape 2). Kunoth-Monks has also spoken of her audition by appearance in a line-up of girls at her school (Thornton 2003); vocal auditioning does not appear to have occurred at all. She has also commented at length on the uneasiness of her relationship with Elsa Chauvel during the production (see Kunoth-Monks 1995). Elsa Chauvel is credited in *Jedda* as the 'dialogue director', a vague term which might mean something like voice coach or refers to what Carlsson says was Elsa's 'usual role on set' in Chauvel's films as 'scriptgirl' (1989, 168). Furthermore, Carlsson mentions that Elsa Chauvel's voice was used at times in post-production to 'sob, scream or laugh for actresses who were unable to make these sounds convincingly', but does not refer to specific instances or films (168).

A further layer of explanation for the apparent incongruence of the lipsync in the montage is available in the National Film and Sound Archive's digital restoration of *Jedda*, in which it is noted that sound restoration was required due to the deterioration of the film, and that this resulted in some mis-sync of voices (see Chauvel 1955/2004). In spite of these several and various accounts, the source of Jedda's voice (or the actor whose voice was dubbed) is not revealed, nor is it credited in the film.

Uncertain Reflections

Irrespective of the disclosures and mysteries attached to these accounts of *The Irishman* and *Jedda*, ongoing sensitivities surround these decisions to dub. These concerns are related to the silence said to be a consistent feature of Indigenous film characters (Casey and Syron 2005, 101), as noted in Chapter 1. Moreover, in both *Jedda* and *The Irishman*, the decision to dub appears to have been associated with a certain discourse of uncertainty about Aboriginal actors. This is apparent in Cunningham's reportage of the Chauvels' explanations for the extremely lengthy period of pre-production of *Jedda* partly due to the 'time taken to coach "untrained and primitive aborigines"' (1987a, 32) (the internal quoted comments are from Elsa Chauvel's autobiography). A faint echo of this discourse of uncertainty appears in Crombie's commentary on Bo-Bo in *The Irishman*, an echo that also sounds across the discussion I alluded to earlier of the surrounding inexperience of the cast and crew of *The Irishman*.

More diffuse influences derive from the broader national context as it is well known that the scenario of pressure on Chauvel to which Clark alludes is corroborated by past and contemporary practices. Australian films have been and are often adapted through post-synchronisation to render voices and accents more accessible to international audiences, and this situation has been accepted as an industry imperative and deemed unproblematically to apply to white Australian voices as a relatively uncontested aspect of the performativity of (national) identity abroad. This has occurred even as related practices have contested the mediation of Australian voices within national settings such as, for instance, the concerns raised towards the voices of community radio announcers on early FM radio (Molnar 1997, 218–19). Rebecca Coyle has noted that Australia, unlike the United States and the United Kingdom, did not have formal codes of standard pronunciation, in spite of the hegemony of broadcasting protocols and policies such as the ABC's Standard Committee on Spoken English of the 1970s (2001, 207–9). Beyond broadcasting, other vocal and speech conventions have been formulated in national institutional contexts, such as for teachers in school-based education. As prefaces to any conclusions, these histories suggest a wider context for the reception of the dub in *Jedda* and *The Irishman*, and thus temper the uneasy implications of the dubbing of Aboriginal voices, which might otherwise be automatically received now in the aura of the haunted and sometimes perverse associations that accrue in postmodern audio-vision.

To dub, as Penman says, 'undoes the pretence that recording is just the re-presentation of a natural act' (2001, 112). In *The Irishman*, auteur practice is obliquely cited to justify the silence of Bo-Bo, while in *Jedda*, dubbing imposes certain foreignness on the Indigenous actors and less obviously on the non-Indigenous actors, distancing them all visually and aurally as other to the actors who speak in their own voices. The visual spectacle of the dub is more apparent in *Jedda* than *The Irishman*, but justification is evaded through multiple accounts of the conditions of place, production and post-production. In each film the dub is both an echoing signal and a masking of the history of incorporation of Indigenous bodies and voices in the national cinema, processes further muffled in the discourses of explanation surrounding the dub. Both instances perhaps reveal a tension between the perceived 'prowess' (to adapt a term from Alice Maurice 2002) of the medium and the aspirational nature of Australian national cinema of the past. These practices also resonate hauntingly in comparison to the contemporary post-national politics of voice and language in films about Indigenous cultures, notably in *Ten Canoes* (de Heer

2006), where cultural languages are dominant and require translation or subtitling for non-Indigenous audiences, and the device of voice-over narration (by David Gulpilil) is used overtly to position – with humour and some irony – non-Indigenous audiences in deficit towards the discourse of culture in *Ten Canoes*. *Samson and Delilah* (Thornton 2009), on the other hand, draws attention to language and culture largely through the device of silence, as narration is mostly visual and musical. While Delilah (Marissa Gibson) and Nana (Mitjili Napanangka Gibson) speak language, Samson (Rowan McNamara) utters only one word – his name, 'S-s-s-Samson' – and English is spoken mainly by white actors (although Samson writes to Delilah in English, on the wall of a building). These practices reference the continuing histories of silence of Aboriginal people, even if explicit practices of discrimination (in the film industry and elsewhere) are now more readily challenged than in the past. The instances of the dub in *Jedda* and *The Irishman*, therefore, do not belong to the past but subtend an understanding of the ongoing ways industry and culture collude in rendering identity and difference in the (post-)colonised nation.

The resonance of this account of the voices of Bo-Bo and Jedda lingers in the echo-logics of the next section, and, in particular, the next chapter, on *Radiance*, in which the voices of Aboriginal and Torres Strait Islander women are plainly heard. In *Radiance*, image, voice and the intercultural discourse of the music of the film transform the frontier of subjectivity and rend the silence. The tropics, its coast and islands, is the regional space in which this is set, and which challenges the stereotypes and national myths of Indigenous and settler identities and landscapes.

Part 2

SILENCES IN PARADISE

Chapter 3

TROPICAL GOTHIC AND THE MUSIC OF THE CANE FIELDS IN *RADIANCE*

Radiance was the first feature film Rachel Perkins directed, and she co-wrote the screenplay with Louis Nowra, the author of the play *Radiance* (1993) on which the film is based. Marcia Langton has noted the significance of familial narrative in Indigenous women's film-making, and she places *Radiance* in this context, describing the film as 'melodramatic' and 'redolent with its theatrical origins' (2003, 53). These qualities are apparent in this chapter, but are approached through the relationship between locations, setting and narration, as well as the process of transposition from play to film. It is a film that readily draws the local gaze, and North Queensland audiences fall for its recreation of the setting in North Queensland. The house, the sugar cane fields, the beach and the island are regional sign systems, to use Whitlock's phrase; some audiences experience these features as familiar. The director, Rachel Perkins, who grew up in Canberra and trained as a filmmaker in Alice Springs, tells how she set the film in Queensland to honour the original setting of the play, and she speaks of travelling to Queensland to gain the 'atmosphere' of the place, and to choose locations ('Interviews' 2003). In fact, the locations chosen were far from North Queensland, and closer to Central Queensland: Agnes Water, Rosedale, Childers, Bundaberg and Hervey Bay, as well as Max Film Studios in Sydney. Nora Island, a key location in the fiction that is seen in the distance in some scenes, was 'a fabrication although some people swear they recognise it,' says Nowra (2000, xiii). *Radiance* therefore comes to stand for the power of film to suggest a reality, and for the sometimes uncanny role of settings in film narrative.[1]

Little in the dialogue of *Radiance* explicitly anchors the setting, apart from Nona chiding Cressy for not referring to Queensland in publicity about her origins: '[N]o mention of Queensland. Here. Mum. Mae. Me' (Perkins 1998). This is incidental to the illusion of North Queensland in *Radiance*, except for the way it is homologous with the illusion of home around which the drama is constructed. *Radiance* curls through gothic passageways that evoke the disturbing history of the region of North Queensland. It challenges the pre-Mabo cinema myth of Queensland as paradise. As a post-Mabo film (Collins and

Davis 2004; Kelly 1998), *Radiance* rewrites the mythology of paradise so that Queensland becomes an anti-Eden, a dystopia. Fields of sugar cane that surround their house and district figure the wealth and prosperity of the region. But the sugar cane becomes a gothic figure at the climax of the film with the burning of the house amidst the seasonal burning of the sugar cane. The evocation of home as gothic and dystopian in the tropical setting in *Radiance* is discussed at length in this chapter, and how its uncanniness is also linked to Nona's inner performance of *Madam Butterfly*, and in the role of sugar cane in the visual discourse of film. Cultural allusions in *Radiance*, and the intercultural channel of the film music, are threaded with the gothic drama, and encounters between the women in more optimistic spaces away from the house and the cane: on the road and on the beach.

Myths of Home

Ideals of home are linked to 'childhood memories and feelings of [...] "the security of a private enclave where one can be free and in control of one's life"' (O'Hanlon 2002,3). It is an ideal, Seamus O'Hanlon argues, inextricably associated with colonial traditions, originating from class practices in Britain and Europe, and 'transplanted through colonialism [...] to the English-speaking world, firstly to North America and later to the Antipodes' (7). In colonial Australia, he says, home 'was a symbol of the freedoms and opportunities available, at least theoretically, to the colonist' (11). In *Radiance*, home represents not an ideal but a dystopia, a site of violence and discrimination. This emerges gradually as the three sisters, Nona, Cressy and Mae, reunite initially for the funeral of their mother in the family home. The women are the entire focus of the action, apart from the priest (Russell Kiefel) who conducts the funeral, some minor male characters who appear briefly, and two characters who do not appear on screen at all, Harry, the landlord, and the Black Prince.

Nona, the youngest sister, has been drawn homewards from the southern states by the discovery that she is pregnant, and arrives unaware that her mother has just died. As the story progresses, her desire for her mother becomes directed towards returning the mother's ashes to her 'true home' on Nora Island, which is seen across the water. The middle sister, Cressy, an international opera star, arrives from London. It is quickly clear that she is anxious not to stay long, but her desire to escape the house and memories of her mother is tempered by her desire to see Nona for reasons made apparent only in the final stages of the film. Meanwhile, Mae, the eldest sister, has been there all along, nursing their dying mother. Resentments deepen as a tortured family history emerges. Cressy and Mae do not share Nona's affection for the house or the late mother. They admonish Nona as the 'lucky one' who was not removed by authorities, signalling their connection to the Stolen Generations. Their tensions ignite in a dispute over how to dispose of the mother's ashes. Their conflicting desires combust when Mae reveals that the house, in fact, was never theirs and that they are about to be evicted by the landlord, Harry, their mother's lover. In revenge, they decide to burn the house to the ground, and in this heightened state, a powerful family secret is revealed concerning Nona's birth. The destruction of the house therefore forms a spectacular background to the destruction of a more profound illusion in their relationships and sense of home.

The familial paradigm of returning home is subverted by the spectre of colonial dispossession and of loss of land and ancestry that looms over the story of the women. Even so, Nowra and Perkins say that the film is about 'any three sisters reuniting for their mother's funeral, where the past is an issue but the women's Aboriginal identity is not' (Collins and Davis 2004, 127), an approach that emerged in the original workshopping of the play (Nowra 2000, ix). Perkins speaks of wanting to make a movie to which 'everyone' could relate ('Interviews' 2003). Collins and Davis suggest that *Radiance* 'grants Aboriginality the status of an unmarked identity', a status, they point out, 'usually confined to white masculinity in Australian cinema' (2004, 127). Even so, *Radiance* is an 'explicitly post-Mabo film' in its attention to 'the original act of dispossession of Indigenous land and identity, signified by Nona's desire to return her mother's ashes to the island of her grandparents' as well as the additional dispossession of assimilation (127). This gives rise to the 'painful absence' of the 'nameless, dead mother', and is complicated by her 'perceived compliance with imposed power' (Kelly 1998, 96, referring to the play).

Maternity is at the heart of *Radiance* and its myth of home, although a shift occurs between play and film from a focus on Cressy's quest to Nona's. Kelly describes *Radiance* the play as 'the story of a mother's homecoming to heal her estrangement from the daughter she has not been allowed to know or acknowledge' (Kelly 1998, 163). The addition to the film of Nona's pregnancy intensifies the focus on Nona's quest, in that she desires to give birth in the house in which she was born.[2] In either case, the sisters' destruction of the house at the conclusion is a de-mythologising act, against home and against mythic, Edenic Queensland. It is emphasised through the inner parody of *Madam Butterfly* performed by Nona, a narrative that evokes the complex displacement of colonised maternity in the gothic setting of the dead mother's house.

Retelling Madam Butterfly

Radiance takes shape as a kind of ghost story, as a number of characters are invisible, dead or mythical: Harry, the Mother, the Black Prince (who Nona believes to be her father) and Madam Butterfly. A mythical Oriental woman abandoned by her lover, Butterfly materialises in Nona's performance of Cressy's recordings of her signature role in Puccini's *Madam Butterfly*. By candlelight and dressed in a kimono, Nona performs a burlesque of Cressy's aria, Butterfly's death scene. This performance is one of several 'costume changes', as Mae dresses up in their mother's unworn wedding dress, and Cressy changes out of her elegant suit into a sundress, all of which Kelly interprets as 'theatricalisations of the enigmas of identity and of the mother's sexual and moral roles' (1998, 168). Nona's performance of Butterfly is also an Oriental theatrical metaphor for the sisters' stories. But it is not a straightforward retelling of Butterfly's story. Its meanings are illuminated by Marina Heung's (1997) study of the myth of Madam Butterfly, as it was adapted in the stage musical, *Miss Saigon* (by Claude-Michel Schönberg and Alain Boublil, first produced in 1989), and in *Indochine* (Wargnier 1992), works contemporary with the genesis of *Radiance*.

In Puccini's opera, *Madam Butterfly*, the geisha Cio-Cio San commits suicide after giving her child to the American wife of her lover, Lieutenant Pinkerton. Not only is Cio-Cio San the exemplary 'expendable' Asian woman, according to Heung, but *Madam Butterfly* is a 'foundational narrative' of 'the Orient' figured as 'sexualised' and 'sexually compliant' (1997, 160). *Madam Butterfly* is an 'exemplary text extolling the female virtues of domestic duty and self-sacrifice' figured through the 'travails of an Asian woman', and thus it is an orientalisation of Western feminine ideals (164). As both 'displaced wife/mistress and the non-European, [Puccini's] Butterfly is [...] doubly Other, and her rivalry with an Anglo-American woman only underscores her marginality in relation to both family and culture' (164–65). In *Miss Saigon* the myth becomes a 'restorative drama paradigmatic of the post-Vietnam era' that transforms from an interracial romance to a trope that Heung calls 'the family romance of Orientalism', or a 'saga of recovering lost fathers' (161). In Heung's reading of *Indochine*, the story of Madam Butterfly is recast from one of a mother's loss of her son to a mother/daughter melodrama (172).

Madam Butterfly enters *Radiance* as a layered figure of the otherness of the dead mother. The Japanese nationality of Butterfly is obliquely referenced through the sisters' banter about Nora Island, their mother's ancestral home, which has become the site of a Japanese tourist resort. Later Nona playacts Cressy's signature operatic role of Puccini's Madam Butterfly. This 'playlet', as Kelly calls it, is a lampoon of exoticism, as Nona 'hams' the performance, perhaps because the myth seems farcical when applied to their situation. Not only does their demented mother seem an unexotic replica of Butterfly, but the recovery of fathers is all but futile, so many were the boyfriends who visited the mother. While the original Cio-Cio San was in conflict with Pinkerton's wife, there was no estrangement between herself and her child. However, in *Radiance* and *Indochine* the betrayal breaks out in relationships between mothers and daughters, through the dead mother's handing over of her two elder daughters to institutions, and through Cressy concealing that she is Nona's biological mother.

Kelly comments on the slip in *Radiance* whereby this recasting of the story occurs. She describes how in Puccini's opera, the 'powerless, colonised mother of a mixed-race child contemplates killing him rather than surrendering him to his white father; but instead of killing the child (as Nona misremembers) Butterfly kills herself, preserving honour in the face of defeat and shame' (Kelly 1998, 169). This has the effect of both 'reversing the sacrifice Cressy's mother made of her, and reflecting what Cressy herself has had to do by killing her maternal identity to spare Nona the truth' (169). While neither the dead mother nor Cressy have literally suicided, the repression of their maternity has the same effect. Cressy's choice of 'a career of performance' (170) as an opera singer is emblematic of her dissimulation. Her offer of money to Nona in the film (which does not occur in the play), Nona later realises, is to finance an abortion (Nowra 2000, 109), an offer that seems to further echo Butterfly's plight. Nona's charade of Butterfly is a kind of haunted trio: performed by candlelight in the house in the cane fields while Nona is still unaware of Cressy's secret, it gives a voice of sorts to the deceased mother through Nona singing to the recording of Cressy as Butterfly.

Dys-tropic Home and the Road Out

There can be no more powerful metaphor for home than a house. The house, a ramshackle old Queenslander with lattice, verandahs and tongue-in-groove walls, forms a significant presence in the film. Collins and Davis describe it as 'a far cry from the suburban dream. […] A shack in the canefields, rather than a haven at the beach, the mother's house is a piece of evidence in a long history of perfidy', and it is 'alive with unreconciled memories' (2004, 127). Referring to the film, Nowra says: 'We saw the house as Gothic, haunted by ghosts and the burden of the past,' and he explains how '[w]ith slow pans through the house that revealed kitsch images of Aborigines and even a picture of Christ with a burning heart, Rachel was determined to show the potency of the [dead] mother's presence' (2000, xi–xii). The shabby, claustrophobic house suggests the agonies associated with home in the family, and the scenes within it are filmed as if the interiors intrude on the sisters' tense reunion, the walls, windows and wallhangings figured strongly in close-ups and medium shots on the sisters, suggesting Perkins's vision of the claustrophobia of the house. Tensions are lessened between all three women on the verandah, a transitional site closer to Nora Island, where, unlike in the interior, the light is amber and nostalgic.

For Nona, this nostalgic sense of the house resembles what Gillian Whitlock calls a 'child-in-the-house' narrative, which she argues is a feature of regional Queensland discourses (Whitlock 1994, 79) (although Whitlock is not referring to *Radiance*). Whitlock notes the abundance of examples in Queensland literature, where the 'child-in-the-house narrative makes its way from verandah, through the rooms and down to "under the house"', a space of the 'irrational' that is mythologised as a fairytale forest 'as dark as anything in Grimm' (78). In a similar pattern, Nona journeys from upstairs, where she revels in raunchily recollecting the mother's sexual history in the rooms, beds and sheets (while Mae associates her mother with the chair in which she died), to under the house where her 'spooky wailing' and 'maniacal laughter' upset her sisters who demand that she 'get back here'. In the play these associations are created off-stage by Nona and the under-house is not seen, but Nowra tells how as film-makers they saw under the house as 'the cellar of a gothic film' (2000, xii). Under the house, Nona finds a relic, the Black Prince's hat, which she adopts into her fantasy of her parentage, provoking the first of Cressy's disclosures about the past.

The torching of the house is pure gothic melodrama.[3] But the cinematic spectacle – apart from the fact that a real house was burned down for the scene (see 'Featurette' 2003) – is emphasised musically. As they throw kerosene around, Cressy says: 'this is so operatic', and plays *Madam Butterfly* on the stereo. The soaring arias accompany the destruction, and the revelations of Cressy's rape and her conception of Nona. While the house burns, a juxtaposition of elemental forces occurs as Nona desperately plunges across the water to Nora Island with the 'Radiance' urn containing the mother's ashes. As morning comes, and Nona is seen depositing the ashes and returning to the mainland by boat, the strains of *Butterfly* give way to non-diegetic chords of 'My Island Home' sung by the Indigenous female vocal group, Tiddas, the same song that Nona has earlier sung to Cressy. The song continues over the end of the film as the apparently homeless women drive away, with Mae and Cressy wearing Nona's wigs. Nona grudgingly acknowledges Cressy as her mother, but the new family relationships born in the tensions of the previous night remain to be explored. As Collins and Davis observe, while the 'shame of being the daughters of the anonymous men who visited that hidden house in the canefields is gone forever [...] the differences between the sisters/ daughters remain' (2004, 128).

The burning of the house is a climax to both play and film. It is also a statement about *terra nullius*, if it is considered that the first settlement by Europeans equated the absence of permanent architecture with an absence of culture

(Ferrier 1987, 42). However, *Radiance* the play does not show Nona spreading the mother's ashes on Nora Island as in the film – although Nowra mentions that a Queensland Theatre Company production directed by Wesley Enoch did conclude with Nona scattering the ashes (2000, ix) – nor are the women seen reunited in the morning. Instead, the play ends with Mae and Cressy watching the house burn. Kelly concedes that strong closure might be expected to elude a play such as *Radiance* was in 1993, when 'aboriginal right to "home" yet remain[ed] provisional and dependent on the goodwill of powerful whites' (1998, 164). While not much has changed since, the film makes a stronger symbolic statement as the women are seen reunited in the morning and then heading away up the road. In this closing sequence the film skips genres and leads into a road movie.

Fiona Probyn-Rapsey (2006) details discourses of the road in feature films about Indigenous people, such as *Backroads* (Noyce 1977), *The Wrong Side of the Road* (Lander 1981), *Bush Mechanics* (Batty and Kelly 1998), *Backlash* (Bennett 1986) and *Beneath Clouds* (Sen 2002), to mention a few. She suggests that the road movie genre carries images of *terra nullius*, and that the genre mythologises '"freedom on the road to nowhere"' (Corrigan quoted in Probyn-Rapsey 2006, 97). She also notes the presence of road trips in a number of human rights actions on behalf of Indigenous Australians over several decades, such as the Charlie Perkins–led Freedom Ride of the 1960s, modelled on the US Freedom Ride; and Michael Long's 'Long Walk' of 2006. Probyn-Rapsey argues therefore that the road is a contested site in postcolonial discourse, associated with dystopian and poetic narratives, and that it has been adopted at times as a metaphor for reconciliation, even though in many films she says, 'Aboriginal mobility appears as a threat to whites, in particular to the State' as it is represented by a white police force (109). Most positively, though, she suggests that the road movie often exhibits the 'poetics of "interval"' as being more powerful than journey or destination (108). It is this sense of 'interval' that emanates from the closing vision of *Radiance* as the women take to the road in Mae's car. Neither conclusive nor pessimistic, their future is given simply as unknown.

The Music of the Cane Fields

The burning of the house merges with another spectacle that is distinctly evocative of region: plantations of sugar cane. It is one of the effects of the play's transformation to film that cane becomes a more visible element of setting. In the play, cane and burning of cane are referred to, and the villain Harry Wells is said by Nona to have 'the biggest sugar plantation' (Nowra 2000, 23). In both play and film, the women plot to torch the house during the seasonal cane burn so it will not be noticed except by Harry, a plan that also defuses audience anxieties about arson. But while the setting for the play is clearly given as 'North Queensland' (Nowra 1993, vi; 2000, 4), Act 1 is entirely set in 'the large living room of a wooden house on stilts' with 'many shutters' (Nowra 1993, 1; 2000, 5); and Act 2 is located on 'the mud flats' (Nowra 1993, 35; 2000, 59). Cane is therefore talked about but not seen. Adapted to film cane has visual presence, and Nowra says that the vision of canefields was crucial to the authenticity of a North Queensland setting: 'I [...] wanted to make sure we portrayed North Queensland, especially the sugarcane fields, because people always associate Aborigines with the outback rather than the tropics' (2000, x). He adds: '[w]e wanted *Radiance* not only to *be* different but to look different' (x, emphasis in original).

Nowra's preference for a non-native plantation crop rather than, say, a rainforest as metonym for the 'tropics' has potent implications. The towering cane plantations double as a metaphor for the plantation economy and colonial culture that has determined the women's lives, and views of cane are allied with musical motifs in evoking a sense of dystopia. Cane signifies the plantation economy of Queensland that was underpinned for many years by indentured labour. Cane symbolises the alienation of the women from this economy: not residents, not tenants, not progeny or possessors, they are evictees from a home that was a false one anyway. Cane therefore looms as a symbol of Aboriginal dispossession. It is as gothic a symbol as the house. First seen through Nona's eyes through the window of a semi-trailer as she wends her way north, cane recurs as a visual motif that frames the narrative. High, abundant cane plantations surround the house and the roads. An early view of a burning cane field is followed by the sea at sunrise, and by a morning view of the house, with the access road passing through a towering cane plantation. In the closing scenes, the cane fields are razed. Traditional songs (sung by the Saibai Islander Community of the Torres Strait) accompany views of the women driving through cane fields on the road to the funeral of their mother. Traditional song in these short sequences is in contrast with the music of *Butterfly*, which is the music of the house, heard diegetically on the stereo and in a non-diegetic piano score over several sequences.

On the way to the church, the objective view of a cane plantation is followed by footage of the car proceeding through tracks in the cane, which becomes a blurred rush of green. A cutaway to a close-up of a pristine floral bouquet on the coffin indicates the sisters' arrival at the funeral at the same moment as the non-diegetic traditional song abates and the dreary voice of the priest replaces it. The church is a musically uninspiring place: Nona wails loudly through the service; Cressy, the opera singer, refuses the priest's request to lead the hymn; and the dull strains of 'Amazing Grace' are played on a tinny organ, before the jingle of cicadas is heard as the women leave the church after the service. In the car, following the church service, metal music is heard on the car radio, and accompanies Mae's vengeful whim when she drives to Harry's house to return his wreath. The camera frames her in close profile against the car window and cane is seen behind her. Later, traditional drumming is heard while the women travel back through cane fields, taking Cressy to the airstrip to catch her plane. The drums suggest Nona's playful sabotage of Cressy's escape from their reunion. When her ploy fails and Cressy decides to wait for the next plane home, Nona and Mae air their tensions in the car by arguing over Mae's choice of metal music on the radio. This pattern of subordination of the music of the cane fields to the noise of family angst adumbrates the theme of dystopian home and counters the white settler myth of Edenic Queensland.

On the Beach

According to Kelly, Nowra was inspired to write the play not by cane but by the 'tidal mangrove mudflats at Emu Park' during 1987 when he was a writer in residence at Central Queensland University in Rockhampton. Asked some time later to develop a play for Indigenous women actors, he wrote *Radiance*, which was first performed at the Belvoir Street Theatre in Sydney in 1993. With funding from the Aboriginal Arts Board, the play was workshopped with Indigenous actors, who, along with an early director of *Radiance*, and Nowra's partner at the time, Justine Saunders, influenced Nowra's writing of these characters (Kelly 1998, 30; Nowra 2000, viii–ix). Nowra tells of an early inspiration for *Radiance* when he stayed at Kinka Beach near Yeppoon (because he 'wasn't keen' on Rockhampton), and how he was 'intrigued' by the tidal mud flats 'that seemed to stretch all the way to Great Keppel Island' (vii). The sight one evening 'of an unknown woman walking across the nocturnal mud flats, as they glistened in the moonlight', stirred his imagination (vii). He relates that some years later, 'a friend from Queensland' had told him of caring for her dying mother, and of the funeral that ensued with a 'strange and awkward [...] reunion of girls who didn't really know each other' as each was the child of a different father (vii). Nowra attributes the genesis of the play to a meeting of 'the image from the mudflats' with 'the story of my friend' (vii).

Those mudflats figure in *Radiance* as the beach (which becomes mudflats at low tide). The sisters seem most reconciled in scenes on the beach, where Mae vents her sadness that her mother did not love her; Nona sings to Cressy; and the idea to burn the house is unfurled. The beach is also the habitat of another character first introduced in the film – a turtle that washes in on the tide and is caught by Cressy and Nona. For Nona the turtle represents a way to commemorate their mother traditionally, if only she knew how to perform the rituals and roast the turtle. It languishes in the kitchen, until, with the burning of the house imminent, Nona returns it to the beach. First-time viewers often query the fate of the turtle, not noticing what becomes of it, and not understanding its cultural role in the drama. Presumably few non-Australian or non–North Queensland viewers would know that federal law authorises only Indigenous people to take turtle. For those unfamiliar with this law, the story of the turtle is something of an ellipsis, and it became a point of contention in the making of the film. Nowra relates an anecdote about a meeting with a funding agency when (presumably in an earlier version of the script) the turtle did not survive:

> I felt as if I were caught in a Monty Python sketch as a bureaucrat argued at considerable length about the treatment of the turtle. I argued that Aborigines kill turtles up north (and turtle is delicious), but the woman, who prided herself on her small-L-liberal devotion to 'getting Aborigines right', kept on saying she thought it was gruesome. Finally I gave in – the turtle wouldn't be killed and it would escape the fire. (Later at a preview a woman came up to me and said, 'Oh, I'm so pleased the turtle lived.') (2000, xii)

Nona's rescue of the turtle by returning it to the sea is comparable to the rescue of her mother's ashes, and both the turtle and Nora Island are strong allusions to culture. But the subtlety of these allusions in the context of the unmarked presentation of these characters is comparable to the way the setting of the film is unmarked as North Queensland; and to the way home seems like home, but it is not; and to the way the mother seems like Nona's mother but is not. This poetic of similarity between the illusion and the hidden real is also threaded in the diffuse metaphor of the title, 'Radiance'. Its allusions are not limited to the spectacles of the burning house and cane fires, or to the luminous courage of the sisters, and 'Radiance' is explicit in the name on the liquorice tin that Nona finds under the house and uses to store the mother's ashes. Nona likes the smell of the tin, but after Cressy tells her the story of the mother's rape, the first fictional version of Nona's origin, she finds that the tin has 'lost the smell of licorice' (Nowra 1993, 34; 2000, 42 and 115). The Radiance tin comes to signify the sensual, affective experience of loss that prefigures Nona's total loss of her illusory mother, and the illusion of home that dissolves in the burning of the house.

Revisiting *Radiance*

The gothic elements of the narrative, so concentrated in the old Queenslander house with its literary motif of the 'child-in-the-house', and its enclosure of the burlesque Orientalism of Nona's pantomime of Madam Butterfly, and its complex dramaturgy of maternity, are burned away in *Radiance*. But the landscapes linger, the cane fields and the mud flats, and the counterpointed aural world of Indigenous and operatic song. *Radiance*, with its deceiving locations, is a study in the unanchored regionality of meaning, and this does not diminish the evocation of the dystopian histories of the women and the region that contests the ideals of colonial home, and of paradise in the holiday tropics of North Queensland. The fate of Mae, Cressy and Nona, as they head off up the road in their car, is a mystery that begs for a sequel.

In reflecting on this possibility, the fictional circumstances of the sisters become uncanny again. While *Radiance* is set in the contemporary present, the seasonal cane burn is an anachronism that adds to the uncanniness of the story. The historical practice of burning sugar cane before harvesting, in the past, was a routine process long replaced by more sophisticated harvesting techniques. Burning of the cane was done to kill off vermin and dangerous creatures in the fields, and remove detritus, to facilitate the safety and efficiency of the task of felling the ripened cane crop. The documentary (referred to in the Introduction), *The Cane Cutters*, shows this spectacle of the burning of cane fields in North Queensland. While knowledge of this history adds, in one sense, to the hidden layers in *Radiance*, in that the destruction of the house can be seen as part of the rubbish and detritus in the cane fields, it cannot be construed similarly that the challenges for some Indigenous people of the region are simply, like the burning of cane, consigned to the past. *Radiance* therefore continues to speak to contemporary audiences with a sense of place informed by present realities and the past.

Chapter 4

ISLAND GIRLS FRIDAY: WOMEN, ADVENTURE AND THE TROPICS

The dystopian Queensland of *Radiance*, discussed in the previous chapter, has not allayed or discouraged the persistence of the trope of Queensland as paradise in other fictions. The mythic island of the mother of the sisters, that vista that Nowra reveals as a 'fabrication', has resonances in the setting or sites of production of three fantasies of the holiday tropics in this chapter. *Age of Consent*, *Nim's Island*, a children's fantasy, and *Uninhabited*, a supernatural thriller, were all set and largely made on islands in North Queensland. The fictions extol the islands as remote, and sparsely settled or – eponymously – uninhabited. Island settings in Australian films potentially allegorise the nation through the figure of island geography, especially *Uninhabited* with its Indigenous ghost, Coral, and its titular resonance with *terra nullius*. This does not preclude resonances with the literary and cinematic archive of the Pacific region and the South Seas.

The island fantasy in these archives often stereotypes 'either the doomed erotic figure of the dusky maiden […] or the prelapsarian paradisiacal island and often both' (Pearson 2013, 154). The maiden becomes a racially crossed figure in mid-century Hollywood films, according to Patty O'Brien (2006; and see Introduction). These tropes figure variously in each of the films. However, this chapter extends earlier work with Chris Mann (Craven and Mann 2009), in which we compared *Age of Consent* and *Nim's Island* as films that used locations on the Hinchinbrook coast in Queensland to fictionalise settings in or towards Queensland, and which adapted the symbology of Eden, paradise and epic journey. Both films were made by visiting international interests and represent minor milestones in Australian cinema in periods of change. *Age of Consent*, made in 1969, has a reputation as a stimulant of the revival film-making of the following decade, while *Nim's Island* signifies Queensland's more autonomous engagements in the twenty-first century in international runaway production. The contexts of change were signified, we suggested, by the tropical locations and settings, to which we drew attention in difference from the more mythologised bush and desert landscapes of Australian mise-en-scène. In *Age of Consent* this occurs through the figure of the island resident, Cora (Helen Mirren), in a film with mature themes that generated controversy about sex and nudity. Cora is emblematically associated with the forces of nature through her nude immersion in the waters of the Great Barrier Reef. But armed with her coral knife, harvesting the waters for income, Cora is more bush woman, we argued, as these qualities have affiliations with the young woman character found in Australian cinema of the 1920s and 1930s. The bush 'woman' of *Nim's Island* is an heroic little girl, Nim (Abigail Breslin). The tropical setting was deployed in Nim's Robinsonade,[1] we suggested, to naturalise the heroism of the child, and parodically draw attention to the context of production in Queensland.

In the present chapter, comparison of these heroines with Beth (Geraldine Hakewill) and Coral (Tasia Zalar) in *Uninhabited* suggests their alignment or identification with the environment, in films that utilise or rework genre and mythic tropes from the literature and popular culture of islands and the South Seas. Cora, Nim and Beth exhibit traces of the bush woman, although not the idealised and objectified type of Schaffer's melancholy bush (see Chapter 1), but the spirited, resourceful type of the early cinema. These traces are markers of their difference, too, from the femininities of South Seas fiction, and uncanny Coral figures the dusky maiden, a return of the repressed. The idea of Queensland as paradise becomes unstable through these figures, who experience it ambivalently (Cora), parodically (Nim), uncannily (Beth) or vengefully (Coral). A further motif is their connection to those mythic figures of island life and imperial romance, Robinson Crusoe and his native offsider, Friday. The motif occurs in Michael Powell's observation that *Age of Consent* was a 'girl Friday' film (1992, 502) and in the helping exploits of young Nim towards her hero, Alexandra Rover, in *Nim's Island*. Beth's encounter with the footprints of the ghost, Coral, on the haunted island of *Uninhabited* recalls Crusoe's first fearful encounter with the footprint of Friday, which, in spite of his longing to see another 'of his own species', fills him with dread.

Cora, a Bush Woman on the Barrier Reef

In the Australian feature films of the 1920s and 1930s when 'independent leading women are common', according to Routt (1989, 31), a young 'bush woman' type is identified, who works in the stockyard where she dominates the men (Tulloch cited in Routt 1989, 31). Routt notes that this 'bush woman' type is not so common, for example, in American Westerns of the same period (31). An example of such a character is in *The Squatter's Daughter* (Hall 1933). Of the casting of the role, Ken Hall says: 'We began looking for a girl who could be the daughter of a squatter. Naturally she had to be very attractive, used to animals and had to be able to ride a horse as if born to the saddle' (1977, 76). The heroine may be a squatter's daughter, but she fights successfully and virtually unaided to save her inherited property. The tradition of the independent woman is also evident beyond the 1930s, in *The Overlanders* and *Bitter Springs*. The heroine of *The Overlanders* is shown several times riding a horse at speed and is contrasted with her would-be romantic interest, who falls off his horse and is trampled by a stampede which she succeeds in stopping. The heroine in *Bitter Springs* is more in control of her rifle than her brother: where her brother kills an Aborigine who was threatening the group, she shoots the spear out of the hand of another potential assailant.

A long period intervened between these films and *Age of Consent*, a period in which relatively few feature films were made in Australia, either by local or international interests (see Introduction). Like *Age of Consent*, *The Overlanders* and *Bitter Springs* resulted from visitations to Australia by international studios, but whereas these earlier films and the period films of the AFC genre (see Chapter 1) typify the colonial view of Australia as *terra nullius*, featuring desert and bush landscapes, the setting of *Age of Consent* in tropical North Queensland on Dunk Island represented a departure from that norm. Cora, who emerges initially from the sea in *Age of Consent*, has qualities that align her with the traditional bush woman style of heroine. Her domain is the waters of the Great Barrier Reef, where she swims underwater with a spear, harvesting crustaceans. The relationship of Cora to the reef is therefore one of dominance and exploitation. No one else in the film actually works the marine environment. The men, if they venture onto the water, stay in a boat (except for one aggressive suitor whom Cora expels from the boat and half drowns). Cora is rarely seen in the interior of the island, and when she is there, she is not blending with the landscape but stealing chickens or fighting with her grandmother. Cora's favoured environment is mainly the beach, the foreshore and the sea, and her relationship to it is comparable to the traditional bush woman.

Evidently, Cora does not completely align with the pattern of the bush woman, not least because she is in her element when she is underwater. While she swims underwater with her spear, she is not in fact spearing fish – her catch is gathered, not shot. This relationship is taken further from that of the hunter when she agrees to swim around underwater naked so that Bradley Morahan (James Mason), the artist who has settled on her island, can paint her. David Thomson sees this as an aspect of Michael Powell's films that offers 'an unsettling mixture of emotional reticence and splurging fantasy', and thus *Age of Consent* is 'a mild beachcombing anecdote [...] lit up by baroque passages of Helen Mirren, naked and underwater' (2003, 695). Stafford speaks of 'a striking juxtaposition of the human form against the natural beauty of the Great Barrier Reef' (Stafford 2010). Anyone with local knowledge of North

Queensland waters would find improbable this naked body brushing past scratching coral branches and risking the marine stingers.

Cora has an aspirational side that is ambiguously associated with the bush woman. Cora has a plan to go to Brisbane and train as a hairdresser. She can be compared with Kate of *On Our Selection* (Hall 1932), who Routt sees as a quality '"bush woman"' and Dad's pride (Routt 1989, 30–31). Kate is training to be a primary schoolteacher. Although the bush woman might not be expected to leave the land, and despite her ability to take independent action, the bush woman has ties to the land through her family, and her aim is to perpetuate those ties. As Routt says, 'Quite a number of Australian films made from 1919 to 1939 can be described as stressing family relationships,' and, in nearly 150 films that he viewed from the 1920s and 1930s, father/daughter relationships were privileged in more than one third (30). Cora unambiguously falls outside the pattern of family loyalty. She has no father or mother and is at odds with her exploitative grandmother, whom she ends up unintentionally killing after wrestling with her to retrieve her savings. Not only is she not bound by emotional attachments as a daughter, for Cora the bush is part of what oppresses her. It does seem as though Cora the bush woman would rather be in Brisbane than in the tropics.

Cora is usually seen as a nature child, as in Meaghan Morris's description of an 'apple-munching nature girl' who signifies an 'affinity' between nature and 'the feminine' (quoted in Murray 2009); or a 'wild child' (Cashill 2009); or 'sprawled petulantly on her bed chewing at a plastic comb', a relative of Lolita (Combs 1969, 256). Cora's 'wild' innocence has been imbued retrospectively through Mirren's own recollections of herself in the role. Interviewed in 2005, she commented that not only was it her first movie, she had 'hardly been on an aeroplane' and 'never seen a palm tree' (Maddox 2005). Powell himself, in referring to *Age of Consent* as a 'Girl Friday' story, commented on the casting of the lead role and that the obvious choice of the day was Helen Mirren (1992, 502). Powell does not explain what he means by 'Girl Friday' story – whether some island version of an urban romantic comedy, or a nod to Cora's emergence as the hero's 'native' companion on his island retreat. If the latter was his thought, then the 'bush woman' affinity has another dissonance through an illusion of her indigenousness, or at least unconsciousness of Europeans as settlers. Whatever was intended, the film is remembered for its doubled spectacle of the heroine and the island idyll.

Freedom and the Island Maiden

Age of Consent was a risqué film in its time. It was based on the novel of the same name by Norman Lindsay, published in 1938, which was a 'scandalous evocation of an island utopia that celebrated artistic and sexual freedom at a time when the dominant wowserish culture rejected both' (Hoorn 2005, 74). It was banned, according to Jeanette Hoorn, until 1962. *Age of Consent* came about, initially, through collaboration between the Australian actor Michael Pate and the star James Mason that led to the production funded by Columbia Pictures, and to Michael Powell's involvement. Hoorn compares *Age of Consent* to Powell's other Australian film, made a few years earlier, *They're a Weird Mob* (Powell 1966), because both films, she argues, centre on 'the experience of alienated, denationalised [male] subjects' (Hoorn 2005, 74). Both films, she says, 'celebrate manly independence: the right to sexual freedom, drinking and an independent lifestyle away from family' (74). The freedom that Cora desires is not identical with that pursued by Bradley, but in the sense that both pursue freedom of a kind, Hoorn links these characters, while making the point that the 'libertarianism' of *Age of Consent* 'was more directed towards extending the freedoms of men than women' (83). Hoorn observes that 'Powell knowingly exploits an "innocent" image of free love on the Great Barrier Reef' through his 'lushly evocative filming of Helen Mirren' (74). Hoorn associates this quality with what she calls 'naturalism' in the portrayal of the heroine, her relationship with the hero and the island landscape.

The setting in Norman Lindsay's novel was Bateman's Bay, on the south coast of New South Wales. It is not clear precisely what led to the choice of North Queensland for the film locations, although Powell later regarded it as a kind of 'fate' that brought him to Dunk Island (1992, 508). According to Powell's autobiography, he 'discovered' Dunk Island during a holiday in North Queensland during the filming of *They're a Weird Mob* (which was shot on location in Sydney) when he and some colleagues went to Cairns and sailed on the Reef and around the islands, including Dunk (475–508). In his memoir, Powell wrote that 'Norman Lindsay's book had been a bit of a romp', but 'my film belonged to the age of innocence' (508), so it might be assumed that Dunk Island provided an Eden-like setting and a sense of innocence. *Age of Consent* was '90 percent made on the coast opposite Dunk Island and on the island itself' (507). In *Age of Consent*, there are explicit references to 'Queensland' and to 'Brisbane', which is shown along with New York. Brisbane and Dunk Island would have been obscure destinations to international audiences in 1969. Powell plays with the audience's perception of the authenticity of the setting: near the start of the film underwater shots of the Reef merge into the interior of a fish tank in New York as part of an advertisement for the durability of a Swiss watch. Hoorn suggests that this scene is meant to imply the 'fake world of the New York art scene' which Bradley rejects in turning to island life in Australia (2005, 81). Cora seems to embody something of what he seeks there.

The production sojourn on Dunk also seemed to catch the spirit of Bradley's quest.

Mirren recalls how the crew enjoyed its time on Dunk Island and how 'the cast and crew [...] arrived barefoot [in Townsville] after three months filming on Dunk Island' (Maddox 2005). '"We'd gone completely native, the lot of us. [...] [W]e were all in our sarongs and blissed-out Dunk Island state"' (quoted in Maddox 2005). In spite of this reflection, the production presented challenges for Mirren. The underwater scenes were staged and shot by Rod and Valerie Taylor, who took Mirren out with them, Powell recalls in his autobiography. She followed all their demands even though, he says, she admitted later to great fear (1992, 508). Hoorn, quoting an interview with Mirren, reports on her discomfort with the nude scenes, where the 'crew were fully clothed', and in which Cora is the only naked figure (2005, 81). Hoorn suggests how these feelings of discomfort and resentment are carried into the fiction of Cora's experience, who agrees to pose naked for the artist for a 'ticket out of her unhappy home with her demented grandmother, her escape to the bright lights of Brisbane' (81). Mirren/Cora appears to 'take no personal delight in her task, squinting at the camera at times and giving the impression that she might prefer the scene to be over' (82). As Bradley's attention is more to the canvas than her body, the 'relationship conveyed is one that appears to be "innocent"' (82). Hoorn praises the film for its 'naturalism', a quality imputed to the relationship between Cora and Bradley, and the filming of the island setting (82).

The 'naturalism' does not, on the whole, extend to the minor roles, played by Australian performers. Shades of the 'romp' are evident in the low comedy elements that have been criticised from time to time (see, for instance, Bourne 2005). Hoorn observes a number of 'anachronisms' in the film that emerge, she suggests, through the conflation of the 1960s setting (unambiguous through the use of John Coburn's paintings) and the screenplay that was closely based on Lindsay's novel, published in the 1930s. Some of the supporting roles of 'familiar types' were played by 'veteran' actors and seem 'incongruous' and 'throwback' in the context of the 'sixties' (2005, 76). In addition, some of the Australian components of the film suffered cuts in the versions that were released internationally, including the musical score by Peter Sculthorpe, which was replaced, and, according to Hoorn, had 'emphasis[ed] Australia's Asian geography with its Balinese references' (76). Also cut was an opening scene in which Bradley is 'seen in bed with a girlfriend from the Brisbane art scene' (76).[2] It is not clear if it was cut because it was a bedroom scene, or because it was in Brisbane, or because the naturalism of the girlfriend's (Clarissa Kaye) broadly Australian accent gave offence. In any case, these aspects did not eclipse the enduring spectacle of the leads, the island or

Mirren's adventurous performance, in production sites now more regularly commodified in the international industry.

Adventurous: Locations and the Girl on *Nim's Island*

If compared to the 'naturalism' of *Age of Consent*, paradise in Queensland was more fully realised as simulacra in the children's fantasy *Nim's Island*, based on Wendy Orr's (2008) children's novel of the same name. It was one of two American films made in Far North Queensland in 2008. The other, *Fool's Gold* (Tennant 2008), in which the Far North, Port Douglas and some locations in Brisbane stood in for Florida and the Caribbean, tapped into the imperial romance theme of treasure hunting. Imperial romance is the narrative of adventure into unknown places that allegorises imperial quest (Pierce 1998). *Nim's Island* shares the connection to imperial romance in its fictional setting in the South Seas, but minus the treasure hunt, and without the erotic associations of South Seas women, and more of the masculine adventure riffs.

The adventure tradition of roving and the Robinson Crusoe myth instil the idea of islands as spaces in which '[b]oy heroes can act as the natural masters of these controllable environments' (Bristow 1991, 94). In *Nim's Island*, the Robinsonade concerns the adventures of a girl, Nim, who lives on a remote island in the South Seas, and is alone during the absence of her marine scientist father, Jack Rusoe (Gerard Butler). The action develops through Nim's correspondence with Alexandra Rover (Jodie Foster), a San Franciscan author who traverses the globe in an effort to support Nim in her isolation. Created on Hinchinbrook Island, North Queensland, and in the Village Roadshow Studios on the Gold Coast, *Nim's Island* also features the effect of an erupting volcano, a feature Queensland cannot naturally provide. It makes Hinchinbrook seem more like Hawai'i, a place in which Hollywood island fantasies were once more typically created (Landman 2006, 10). Hawai'i is also alluded to through the white hula dancers who land on the island with a grotesque group of tourists, who are Queenslanders.

Nim, by virtue of her age, can barely qualify as a bush woman even though she has some commonalities in her environmental competence and attachment to her father, a characteristic of the bush woman of earlier. But, compared to Cora, Nim collocates various masculine myths of the South Seas, divulging her literary antecedents as she dare-devils about her island with bush knife, spyglass and lizard (not parrot) on her shoulder. She is rover and castaway, islander and settler all in one. Like earlier male adventurers of imperial romance fiction, Nim is the offspring of a seafarer father, Jack Rusoe (with allusions to both Crusoe and Jean-Jacques Rousseau in his name), a marine biologist in search of a species of nanoplankton which he eventually finds and names after Nim (Protozoa Nim). Nim's island as the setting for Rusoe's scientific outpost borrows the centuries-old idea of the island as (social) laboratory, and myths of Robinson Crusoe surround Nim's high-tech solitude during her father's absences at sea. In comparison to Cora's economic relationship to the Reef, Nim's labours on her island are turned to maintaining the settlement, and doing research for her favourite author, Alexandra Rover, tasks at which Nim proves as resourceful as Crusoe and as faithful as Friday. For all her masculine prototypes, Nim's relationship to nature, especially her close association with animals, disambiguates her femininity through conventions derived from folk tales, 'where animal helpers feature persistently as guides or magical aids to protagonists' (Whitley 2008, 19). Nim's postmodern Robinsonade is an androgynous bricolage of rover, bush woman and other tropes from children's fiction (absent mothers, talking-to-animals) and folklore (including seal legends, except that the aquatic mammal is a sealion, named 'Selkie', supplied by Sea World on the Gold Coast).

Roving, the nineteenth-century trope of the imperial romance, is playfully ironised in the diverse routes of the journeys of first Nim and her father, then Alexandra Rover to the island. The location is known only by map coordinates: '20 degrees south and 162 degrees west'. Nim and her father have sailed to the island via Patagonia, Singapore and the Cook Islands. Rover, an agoraphobic San Franciscan author, journeys to Nim, after a travel adviser locates the island in the 'South Asiatic Sea' and Rover arrives via Borneo, Rarotonga and Tuvalu. The place names are authentic, but the fictionalised places are oriental. Rover's encounters in these exotic outposts are a hint that her perspective on the southern hemisphere may parallel that of the producer's on Queensland, and there are further hints of the adventure of transnational film production in the antipodes.

Within the pastiche setting created on Hinchinbrook Island, Nim repels a visitation by the unwelcome Queenslander tourists. These characters are adapted from the 'Troppo Tourists' of Orr's novel, and revive the tropes of eccentricity and excess in films of Queensland. If '[e]very Eden may have its serpent' (Maher 1988, 172), then in *Nim's Island* it appears in the form of the grotesque Queenslanders[3] who represent the local workforce comically incorporated as intruders, and who Nim repels from her island in a carnival reprisal of an invasion narrative. In the shadow of the volcano, Nim assaults the tourists with lizards in catapults before she accidentally triggers the eruption of the volcano, from which the tourists flee. The allusions to Queensland seem to have been devised in production of the film (they do not appear in the novel), and Nim, the heroine, is not a Queenslander. This is comically emphasised when, in an ironised drama-of-first-contact, Nim meets a little boy who strays from the tourists, and Nim is persuaded that he is no threat when he explains that he is from Brisbane.

There is a twist in the sequel, *Return to Nim's Island* (Maher 2013), an Australian production. It did not star Breslin, but was the debut film performance of the nation's best-known adolescent bush woman, Bindi Irwin, daughter of Steve Irwin, the late crocodile handler and icon of Queensland wildlife tourism and the founder of Australia Zoo. Bindi plays in the sequel an older Nim who experiences her first romance. The plot is still consumed in the adventures of children's fiction, animal rescues and pirate drama, and there is an environmental bent, as the purchase of the island by the Buccaneer Resort Company threatens the natural paradise and some of the species in it, which Nim and her erstwhile companion, Edmund (Toby Wallace), save. Although Nim is not a threatened species herself, the spectacle of Nim's far-flung narrative place is diminished, as this production did not visit Hinchinbrook Island, and was made entirely on the Gold Coast.

Haunted and Hunted: The Fatal Bush Woman of *Uninhabited*

The tropical bush woman becomes a haunted figure in *Uninhabited*, one of a spate of horror-styled Australian films that utilise novel settings. *Uninhabited* adapts the landscape tradition to genre conventions in the pristine beach and bush setting of Masthead Island, a coral cay off the Capricornia Coast of Queensland, although the narrative place is not named. *Uninhabited* develops its haunted narrative knowingly. The Australian accents and tones of the didgeridoo in the musical score suggest an Australian setting, and anyone familiar with the distinctive scrub vegetation of the islands of the Great Barrier Reef will recognise it. *Uninhabited* makes no palm-fringed spectacle of the haunted place. The naturalism of the island setting is more comparable to *Age of Consent* than the pastiche of *Nim's Island*. The heritage-preserved island of Masthead is filmed generously, in aerial view and in depth, for its natural spectacle. The signature establishing shot which captures the whole island, initially suggests the clichéd 'deserted island paradise'. As the narrative proceeds, and the haunting progresses, the whole-island view becomes allied with the ghost's omnipotent perspective and her control of those who land on its shores, and thus the natural spectacle of the island becomes uncanny.

Prima facie, *Uninhabited* is a version of a Robinsonade or castaway narrative, but features a couple, Beth and Harry (Henry James), rather than a solo voyager. A genre double-dip emerges as the adapted castaway patterning incorporates horror tropes: the haunted shack/house of the ghost, the grave of the ghost, the episodes of nocturnal haunting and haunted technology – the videocamera with mysterious footage filmed by the ghost, and the ghostly phone that conveys the voice of the ghost. This awaits the couple who settle in for their 10-day holiday, equipped with state-of-the-art camping gear. A private launch operator, Jackson (Bob Baines), delivers the couple and the gear to the site. He leaves a satellite phone with them and a promise that, if they wish to leave early, he can be there in 'five hours'. Harry refers to the isolation and the beach-camping scenario as like 'reality TV'. He shows no such reflexive recognition of what is shared with his literary forebear, Crusoe, perhaps because it is not the drama of a solo voyager, so not among their privations is Crusoe's longing '"to have seen one of my own Species"' (Defoe cited in Seidel 1981, 369). Beth and Harry relish their privacy, rapidly moving from their first submersion in the pristine waters to sex on the beach.

No detail is given of Harry's means of livelihood, but it is quickly established that Beth is a marine biologist who is very acquainted with the environment and who has expert knowledge of its marine and terrestrial wildlife, a tropical bush woman of an educated kind. She skilfully identifies a deadly stonefish, holding it up to show Harry and carefully replacing it in the water. Like Nim, Beth is a preserver of the environment, rather than an exploiter, but Harry still seeks assurance that she will not be 'working' while they are on the island. Beth, whose abundant wardrobe of couture bikinis is elegantly combined with her spear-fishing gear, assures him that she is there for a holiday. But the haunting begins as soon as they partake of the pleasures of the flesh. Coral's first 'appearance' occurs in daylight in the line of footprints leading from the camp to where the post-coital couple have been sleeping.

How Coral, a ghost, manifests footprints, is not explained, and only suggests what type of ghost she is, thus, less of a poltergeist, more of an elemental spirit, as her environmentally referenced name suggests. Nor does Harry, when he awakes before Beth, recognise the mythic origin of the haunted footprints he finds beside them. Puzzled, he asks Beth if these are her footprints. Whereas Crusoe's encounter with the mysterious footprint was at first alarming because the print was too large to be his own, Beth demurs, and the threat is diminished because the prints are 'too small'. Unlike Crusoe, whose whole life on the island was transformed by the footprint, and although Beth is uneasy and wants to leave, Harry persuades her that they are not alone due to the presence of 'kids' or others. The plot is infested with more relics of the Crusoe narrative, including (Greek) pirates from whom they are rescued by the ghost, and the fatal hut, where the facts of life and death of Coral, the ghostly islander, are stored in an ancient visitors' book Beth reads aloud to Harry, to his great scepticism.

Coral is more than a gothic echo of Friday; she is a reappearance of the dusky maiden, an islander whose uncanny quest is rape-revenge. Coral's history, detailed in the visitors' book, reveals that she once worked on the reef and suffered a fatal stonefish sting while working, only to be raped by the company men on the site as she lay dying. The ghostly phone call that summons Harry to the shack replays the sounds of the gang-sexual assault on Coral as she lay dying nearly 100 years earlier. Lured to the shack by the ringing phone, Harry is confronted by the ghost and bloodily despatched with her bush knife. Her vengeful afterlife is thus mythically blended with classical temptresses, as she earlier visited Harry by night in a sexual foreshadowing of his fate as her victim. Harry, the travelling man, falls victim to sexual danger of a ghostly kind, while Beth, the bush-woman-worker, becomes a ghost, too, after she dies from a stonefish sting of her own when she is summoned into the water by the enigmatic ghost.

Perhaps this is some variation on Gaia's revenge, a pattern of Australian horror Catherine Simpson (2010) identified in which tourists are killed as punishment by deadly wildlife. In Simpson's examples, white women, with the greater knowledge of the protocols of the place, gain a sense of belonging over the tourist by evading the risks, while their knowledge displaces Indigenous knowledge of the environment. If so, in this instance, Beth is both tourist and knowledgeable white woman, who falls victim to a combination of Indigenous ghost and marine beast. If adventure tourism is also seen as resource development, then it represents another fatal outcome to enterprise and the plot of the foregoing South Seas films, as Jackson, too, is taken by the ghost of Beth, who now works for Coral in a vengeful afterlife.

Coral's story potentially has power because it arises from the history of violence perpetrated towards Indigenous women, a history so skilfully represented in *Radiance* (see Chapter 3). The very least *Uninhabited* shares with *Radiance* is disturbance of the myth of paradise in Queensland from the perspective of an Indigenous woman, but beyond that its power is limited. While a popular genre like a supernatural thriller has the potential to suggest the ongoing implications of history in contemporary settings, it is equally prone to the quality of its script and the handling of the conventions of the genre, especially when, like *Uninhabited*, it is constructed of more than one. The castaway story and the haunted house story are merged, and the unifying element is the setting of the island. Coral is barely seen in *Uninhabited*, appearing briefly in embodied form only a few times, but her presence is ubiquitous in the various uncanny happenings. The lingering uncanniness of the film is in the image of the island, Coral's dominion, its vegetation and halo of surrounding sea so starkly posed as a singular haunted natural spectacle. Unlike the islands of the other films, where vision of shorelines marks its presence, Coral's island is seen in whole, in the opening and closing vision of the film, a symbol of a place imagined as uninhabited. The haunted irony of the title gains resonance in the conclusion when Beth joins Coral in eternal residence and in pursuit of Coral's revenge, but this does nothing to transform the fate of Coral, who remains essentially the stereotype of the doomed dusky maiden.

Heading Back to Shore

The lingering symbols of each of these three films are the island settings and the heroines. Their mythic allusions are more arbitrarily discerned. These films also represent different approaches in terms of location or studio production, and address audiences of different age groups and tastes. The naturalism of the island setting seems more pronounced in *Age of Consent* and *Uninhabited*, both films for broadly adult audiences. *Nim's Island* and its sequel are more obviously adventure fantasies for children's entertainment. They also owe much to the production infrastructure that has grown in times more recent than those in which *Age of Consent* was made. In turning, in the next two chapters, to films produced in the main hub of this growth on the Gold Coast, in south-east Queensland, and the masculine dramas that its history entails, the mythic discourse is traced to yet another island dweller, a fantasy figure in the fairy tale form of Peter Pan.

Part 3

MASCULINE DRAMAS OF THE COAST

Chapter 5

THE SUNSHINE BOYS: PETER PAN AND THE IRON MAN IN THE COASTAL CINEMA OF QUEENSLAND

> Peter was not quite like other boys; but he was afraid at last. Next moment he was standing erect on the rock again, with that smile on his face and a drum beating within him. It was saying, 'To die will be an awfully big adventure.'
> (From *Peter and Wendy* by J. M. Barrie 1996, 96)

Peter and Wendy is a novelisation of J. M. Barrie's play *Peter Pan*. The excerpt (above) occurs when, in a confrontation with Captain Hook at Marooner's Rock in Mermaid Lagoon, Peter Pan is wounded and left alone on the rock as the tide rises (96). In the inner thrill of this rare moment of fear, Peter hears the oft-quoted words, 'to die will be [...] an adventure'. In dramatisations of the story, typically, Peter utters the words to signify his defiance of Hook and his indomitable optimism. Also overlooked in many adaptations of the Marooner's Rock episode is the Never Bird, who rescues Peter by desperately paddling her nest to him and abandoning her two eggs. Peter manages to raise a flag on the nest and shift the eggs to a pirate's hat so that he sails away and the eggs are saved (Barrie 1996, 100). The Never Bird rejoices and Peter crows and more adventures ensue. An unlikely bridge to the film industry in Queensland it might seem, yet Peter's survival is no more remarkable than the industry that now flourishes.

The story of Peter Pan, a touchstone myth of adult masculinity, is filtered in this chapter in accounts of two films made on Queensland's Gold Coast, namely *The Coolangatta Gold* (Auzin 1984) and *Peter Pan* (Hogan 2003). The fortunes of the productions and the quests of heroes, both, like Peter, near-naked boys, and of their mentors and enemies, are compared as fables of adventure and choice. *The Coolangatta Gold* dates from the shady years of industry start-up under the later disgraced state government led by Joh Bjelke-Petersen. The film was conceived with the aim to showcase the Gold Coast to the world. *Peter Pan* was produced in the sunshine years of the Gold Coast as a 'local

Hollywood', as the term is coined (Goldsmith et al. 2010). The production was something of a coming-of-age for the era of 'film friendliness' on the Gold Coast, showcasing the production capabilities of the Warner Bros Movieworld Studios (now Village Roadshow Studios[1]), and it received a Sunset Boulevard premiere.

A local Hollywood is understood as an outpost of 'global Hollywood', a hub for domestic and outsourced (American or other) international film production, characterised by 'film friendliness' (Goldsmith et al. 2010). 'Film-friendliness' is engineered in the hub through government policy and alliances with industry to favour film production through incentives and project management facilities. Goldsmith, Ward and O'Regan compare the film-friendly Gold Coast with, among other places, Wilmington, USA, and Vancouver, Canada, all 'greenfield locations', or sites once lacking in existing film production infrastructure and history but rich in potential for the same. On the Gold Coast, the potential culminated in the building of the Village Roadshow Studios. Its sources are traced to the establishment of resort and theme park developments on the Gold Coast in the 1970s, and state government legislation in 1977 in support of a film industry as a synergistic adjunct to entertainments and tourism (Goldsmith et al. 2010, 61). Film friendliness was therefore pioneered on the Gold Coast 25 years before other Australian states, and gained impetus with the various state film bodies that were established (163).[2] A Never Bird emerged in the form of one Dino de Laurentiis[3] and his alliance with the Bjelke-Petersen state government in an unlikely plan to build a film studio on the Gold Coast. *The Coolangatta Gold* was one of only two feature films made on the Gold Coast before de Laurentiis's arrival, and it involved the leader of de Laurentiis's Australian business, Terry Jackman, who was an executive producer of *The Coolangatta Gold*, and also was appointed as a director of the Queensland Film Corporation[4] (54). De Laurentiis began work on the studio a few years later, but when his international business fell into crisis through other ventures, he eventually resigned and Village Roadshow stepped in to take over De Laurentiis's Australian company (71). It subsequently formed an alliance with Warner Brothers whereby the studio complex and its operations eventually took flight. Goldsmith, Ward and O'Regan point out that an economic rationale was the main one for the Gold Coast film industry, and suggest that the federal government was relatively less supportive of these initiatives compared to studios established roughly contemporarily interstate, which also gained some national cultural policy remit; and that, on the local front, in Queensland there was some in-state resentments, too, towards the Gold Coast developments. But the studios that grew through Warner-Roadshow's alliances with the state government could make Peter crow, or he might grimace with the memory of the earlier history of feature film production on the Gold Coast.

Low Tide in the Land of Gold

'All children, except one, grow up.' (Barrie 1996, 7)

The Coolangatta Gold has been described as an 'attempt at a blockbuster' (Goldsmith et al. 2010, 54). It had 'the biggest budget ever in Australia at the time', according to Terry Jackman; and Michael Edgley claims he saw the 'world appeal' of its script on a first reading (BP Australia 1984). The titular 'Coolangatta Gold' was an Iron-Man beach marathon staged for public participation and fictionalised within the film narrative. The race attracted more than 50 contestants and crowds of spectators, creating the appearance of a cast of thousands. The idea for the race is attributed to Peter Schreck, who devised it as a spectacular climax to the 'sporting love story' (BP Australia 1984). The alliances formed around the production of the race and the movie included Michael Edgley International, then the major events promoter in Australia, the Queensland Film Corporation, the Australian Film Commission, the Gold Coast City Council, Kellogg's (who sponsored the race), 4GG (the local Gold Coast radio station) and Australian United Foods. Di Morrisey, reporting for *Good Morning Australia* on the day of the race, signed off saying that 'long after the movie is forgotten, the Coolangatta Gold will live on' (Morrisey 1984) (Figure 5.1). Indeed, the race continues to the present,[5] while the film resides with memories of Queensland's dimmer days in the cinematic sun, and now goes under the title of its release in the United States, *The Gold and the Glory*. A believable slice of 1980s Gold Coast life and the reverence for beach and sport, the aura of Queensland as 'the sunshine state' is background in the film to tensions between youth and elders.

Descriptions of the film's plot range from a 'melodramatic tale of stage fathers, neglected and favoured sons, and personal transcendence' (Goldsmith et al. 2010, 200), to a 'Cane and Abel story' (Terry Jackman quoted in BP Australia 1984). It concerns a father, Joe (Nick Tate), and his vicarious ambition for his son, Adam (Colin Friels), to contest the Coolangatta Gold ostensibly for the prize of cash and sponsorship, but more for Joe to avenge his own loss in the race years earlier to Hayden Kenny, the father of the present champion, Grant Kenny. The second, unfavoured son, Steve (Joss McWilliam), longs to upbraid his father by competing in the race and upstaging Adam by winning. In a chopper's-eye view of the coastline marathon course, Joe proclaims it the 'toughest damn race [...] in the world', a full 'natural course marathon' of 26 miles, equating the beach and landscape with the classical athleticism of the marathon, nature becoming culture. Emblematic was the appearance of Grant Kenny, the real-life state Iron Man champion and golden boy of the day, a redoubtable athlete, who played himself. He was 'very disappointed', he said, that acting in the film prevented him from competing in the race (Morrisey 1984).

Figure 5.1 The day of the race: Surfers Paradise and the cast of thousands in *The Coolangatta Gold* (1984). Image provided courtesy and with kind permission of John Weiley and Heliograph Pty Ltd.

Adam eventually wins, but is not the hero of the film. The hero, Steve, is loosely drawn from the pantheon of teenage dreamers and rebels adapted to a Queensland milieu. He is the manager of a fledgling rock band, seen auditioning for its first gig, singing a song titled, 'We are the Kids' (*'we are the kids with the sun in our eyes [...] hard to see with the sun in your eyes'*). Steve's father disparages the gig as 'background music to a bunch of drunks', and issues Steve with that enduring challenge to youth in the adult world: 'when are you gunna grow up?' Undeterred, Steve's band makes the gig, and at the nightclub Adam is induced to break his race plan of no consumption of alcohol.

He becomes drunk and lands in hospital, provoking a further confrontation between Steve and his father. The tensions play out in the family home, an old and ungentrified Queenslander house on a banana farm well out of town, a marker less of wealth than paternal incumbency. Steve is eventually motivated to contest the Iron Man marathon by his mother (Robyn Nevin), and aided by the zen counsel of his martial arts teacher, Gary (Paul Starling), who warns of the risks of competing 'for the wrong reasons; even if you win there'll be nothing in it for you' (Figure 5.2). The race is shown with Adam victorious, Steve second and Kenny third, but only because Steve, after leading, elects to fall over near the finish line after sighting the look of horror (at the prospect of him winning) on his father's face in the crowd. At the end of the race Kerry (Josephine Smulders), Steve's girlfriend waits in the sand dunes on a motorbike with Surfers' Paradise as a backdrop as the lovers unite (although no locations are named in the film's credits).

Steve's adventure in self-effacing loss – or the adventure of failure – might be couched in the boy-to-man myth of coming of age, or a view that Steve grew up while Adam stayed in Neverland with his father, or vice versa, or that Steve learned more from martial arts than from beach-marathon running. But in the larger project of *The Coolangatta Gold*, the defeat of both the real-life hero, Kenny,

Figure 5.2 Steve (Joss McWilliam) takes counsel with his mother (Robyn Nevin) outside the family home in *The Coolangatta Gold* (1984). Image provided courtesy and with kind permission of John Weiley and Heliograph Pty Ltd.

and the fictional hero, Steve, suggests conflicted aims of this film that sought to elevate Queensland by dramatising a noble loss within an international sporting spectacle. It is at once worldly and homey, and suggests Queensland in its development era, championed by aspirational locals, whose methods and means of imposing progress were often churning with desires both parochial and flamboyant. The production team, who were not all locals, had more romantic aims, as Schreck speaks of their desire to show contemporary Australia as 'glamorous' and 'glossy', and as a 'South Pacific paradise' (BP Australia 1984).

The Coolangatta Gold was something of a Marooner's Rock episode, running over its large budget. There are no individual credits in the film to a director, writer or producer, only a corporate credit, which includes Igor Auzin, the director (then known for the period film, *We of the Never Never*).[6] Just as the wise man of the film, Gary, warns of the risks of competing for the wrong reasons, the multiple parties in the production suggest that it was too weighted as a commercial rather than an artistic venture. In an interview on the day, Michael Edgley mentions that the race-day shoot alone cost $350,000, albeit a modest sum by today's standard. When Morrisey asked him if it is better to make a film that 'you liked' or because it is 'commercial', Edgely replies, 'I like to do both' (Morrisey 1984). It did not succeed, commercially or otherwise, at the time. But today the film recognizably portrays a time and place, and delivers a lingering reflection on heroism and the wiles of competition, if at odds with the aspirations of the project. The inaugural race was won by a surf-lifesaver from New South Wales.

It was a long time before a successful feature film was made on the Gold Coast. It came in the form of P. J. Hogan's debut feature, *Muriel's Wedding* (1994), which was made in a range of locations on the Gold Coast (including Surfers' Paradise, SeaWorld and Coolangatta) and New South Wales. If *The Coolangatta Gold* had tried to offer an 'obverse vision' of the Gold Coast as a 'dystopia populated by corrupt politicians [and] unfettered developers' (Goldsmith et al. 2010, 199), ironically, the story of Muriel is of the heroine's escape from such a dystopia. A camp and penetrating satire, *Muriel's Wedding* is set in fictional Porpoise Spit, which, with its wilting garden palms and sandy verges, could be any of the suburban havens of 'a thinly disguised Gold Coast' (200). Antigone on the Gold Coast, all Muriel's hurt, suffering and defiance is attributed to the social conditions there, her shady-local-politician father and her denounce-able girlfriends. Muriel leaves this (fictional) dystopia for (actual) Sydney, and transitions from an aspirational adolescent to a well-groomed heroine of a post-feminist fable (see Collins 2002). Aside from Muriel's employment in a video store in Sydney, there is no obvious connection in her story to the film industry. Yet Muriel's transformation could be an allegory of the turn-around in the film industry on the Gold Coast with the arrival of the Village

Roadshow Studios. Its production capabilities were showcased in Hogan's next film, *Peter Pan*, nearly 10 years later.

A Place in the Sun: Moving to Neverland

'You just think lovely, wonderful thoughts [...] and they lift you up in the air.'
(Peter's words in Barrie 1996, 40)

Peter Pan is a nostalgic adaptation of Barrie's story, co-written by Hogan and Michael Goldenberg. A screen credit acknowledges that the production is based on the 'original stage play and books written by J. M. Barrie' (Hogan 2003). Barrie's *Peter Pan* has an elusive textual history, having emerged as a play in 1904 that other writers reproduced before Barrie himself eventually penned it as *Peter and Wendy* (published in 1911; see Rose 1994). Hogan's film seems largely based on Barrie's writings, and there are embellishments and additional characters (Aunt Millicent); and omissions such as the Never Bird. The production reinstates a theatrical tradition of doubling the role of Hook and Mr Darling (the children's father) as these character parts are 'almost invariably' doubled in performance, according to Rose (35). It featured an international cast: an American Peter (Jeremy Sumpter), an Australian Wendy (Rachel Hurd-Wood), and British actors play Mrs Darling (Olivia Williams), Aunt Milicent (Lyn Redgrave), and Mr Darling/Hook (Jason Isaacs). It is an ornate and nostalgic production in period style; fairy tale as an antique novelty in all but the digital animation and animatronics. Hook's parrot – an intertextual escapee from R. L. Stevenson's *Treasure Island* – and the crocodile (its head, at least) were created in John Cox's Creature Workshop on the Gold Coast.

Nostalgia abides, too, in the imperial romance of Barrie's island setting of Neverland. *Peter and Wendy* (and its stage antecedents) is a quintessential island fantasy, created on the cusp of the late Victorian and Edwardian eras. Neverland, '[o]f all the delectable islands', is said to be the 'snuggest and most compact; not large and sprawly [...] but nicely crammed' (Barrie 1996, 12). For Hogan's production the 'fairy tale Neverland of grottos, verdant jungle, coastal landscapes and storybook Victorian London' were all created in studios (Goldsmith et al. 2010, 193). The infrastructure of fantasy production was well endowed and supported by proximity to nearby Sea World with its 'permanent cadre of stunt professionals', the site of some earlier mermaid-themed productions (192).[7] The illusion of flight, a key element of the fantasy of Peter Pan, was well accommodated, and even Hook becomes airborne in this version. The challenges of the flying scenes and the need for the child actors to work in harnesses for much of the shooting time apparently contributed to the decision to shoot in studios, rather than to follow earlier plans to shoot on locations and on ships (Murray 2014a). The role of Tiger Lily was revived in the production, and the Redskin camp, a key setting in Barrie's story, gained a makeover with deference to Native American culture. The production "'scoured the world for an actual Native American girl to play Tiger Lily'" (Lucy Fisher, producer, quoted in Universal 2003). Carsen Gray was cast. A speaker of Iroquois, she improvised a few lines for the role (which she translates in the short, 'Princess Tiger Lily', but which are not subtitled in the feature).[8] The Redskin camp thus becomes an oddly authentic spot in the trans-regional fantasy of Neverland.

Through the veil of period and nostalgia, Neverland references Queensland in Barrie's metaphor of childhood (Neverland) as a beach, or 'these magic shores' where 'children at play are for ever beaching their coracles' (Barrie 1996, 12). The place is figured as a site of memory for the adult subject enclosed in the address, as '[w]e too have been there; we can still hear the sound of the surf, though we shall land no more' (12). It gains more connection to Queensland through the figure of the crocodile that dispatches Peter's arch enemy, Captain Hook, as crocodiles have become iconic symbols of northern Australia and its masculinised myths of adventure in the tropics. Crocodiles also represent uncanny oral sadism (Simpson 2010), a quality of perennial relevance to the myth of Peter Pan. The crocodile lusts for Hook's flesh, having sampled one of his hands, cut off in a fight with Peter. A ticking clock consumed by the crocodile warns Hook of its approach, and Peter Pan mimics the ticking to terrorise Hook (Barrie 1996, 141). The Walt Disney Studio's animated feature film of *Peter Pan* (Geronimi et al. 1953) incorporated the orally uncanny ticking in the crocodile's signature tune with a ticktock beat, 'Never smile at a crocodile.' The ticking signifies Hook's mortality and Peter's antipathy to time in his righteous quest to remain young. But, as Hogan's production shows, the performativity of the myth is subject to realist purpose because a key revision in Hogan's production was the casting of a boy (Sumpter) in the traditionally cross-dressed role of Peter.

On stage, Peter is played, in a Victorian convention, by a 'principal boy' (a girl). An early silent film version[9] maintained the cross-dressing of Peter Pan, and even well into the twentieth century, among its many stage productions, was the celebrated Broadway production in the 1950s, in which Peter was triumphantly performed by Mary Martin, one of the grand dames of the American stage. Disney's *Peter Pan* broke the convention. With the production of *Hook* (Spielberg 1991), the gender game changed course as *Hook* is a kind of sequel and parable of adult manhood in which Peter Pan has grown up and become a father. Peter Banning (Robin Williams), a corporate executive in the toy industry, revisits Neverland to regain his kidnapped children from Hook

(Dustin Hoffman). The myth has since had several sideways film productions in *Finding Neverland* (Foster 2004), and various film manifestations of 'lost boys' are entertainments that, if not exclusively addressed to adult men, suggest amnesia about the cross-dressed history of the role of Peter Pan.

In post-production publicity, Hogan commented that 'Peter Pan's never been played by a real boy before' (Otto 2003); and he is said to have been 'delighted to have the opportunity to cast a boy in the role' (Murray 2014c). He refers to the emerging masculinity of Peter Pan in the twentieth century, saying that: 'Peter Pan has been a cartoon character, and onstage he's mainly been played by women. In the silent film version, he was played by a woman, and in *Hook* he was 40 years old. Now a kid is finally getting to do the greatest role ever written for a kid' (Hogan quoted in Murray 2014c). (But he does not explain why he elected to resume the old code of the doubling of Hook/Mr Darling.) This act of casting a boy as Peter highlights the pastiche effect of quotation of Barrie's story in Hogan's *Peter Pan*, if quotation is accepted, to adapt Susan Stewart, as 'mak[ing] present what can only be experienced abstractly' (1984, 19). In an opening title, Barrie's words are adapted to: 'All children grow up except one,' with the central clause moved to the end of the sentence. The line is spoken again at the end of the film by the narrator, who is belatedly revealed as adult Wendy, who now tells the story to her 'own children' (Hogan 2003). Wendy grows up, of course, and Peter remains a boy, yet the performance of the ageless mythic subject posed a challenge in the casting, as Barrie portrays Peter as quite a young child with his baby teeth intact.

Ageless

> He was a lovely boy, clad in skeleton leaves and the juices that ooze out of trees; but the most entrancing thing about him was that he had all his first teeth. When he saw [Mrs Darling] was a grown-up, he gnashed the little pearls at her. (Barrie 1996, 16)

Barrie gives few clues as to Peter's age, although Wendy says that 'he is just my size', which 'meant that he was her size in both mind and body' (1996, 14). Hogan overcame the riddle through speculation on the author's life. He says:

> Barrie always fudged the age a little bit. […] It was between the lines. I went back into Barrie's life, and the inspiration for Peter Pan, to me, was obviously the brother that Barrie had, who died at the age of 12. And I thought 12 seemed to be the age for Peter, so I looked for a 12-year-old boy to play the part. (Hogan quoted in Otto 2003)

Ironically, the model for the casting was neither child nor adolescent but the legendary Australian actor Errol Flynn. 'I always said to the producers that for the part of Peter Pan, we are looking for Errol Flynn age 12 years old' (Hogan quoted in Murray 2014b). Why Flynn is the model is not stated, although Flynn played various swashbucklers and fairy tale types, notably Fletcher Christian and Robin Hood, in his early career. The boy chosen, Sumpter, makes no reference to Flynn but mentions, in an interview, that Disney's Peter Pan is one of his favourite characters (Otto 2003). Costume-wise Hogan's Peter is less swashbuckler (a la Flynn) or uniformed elf (a la Disney) and more green man, in his off-shoulder jumpsuit of sewn leaves. Perhaps this suggests period (Edwardian) or Barrie's description of Peter quoted earlier ('clad in skeleton leaves'), which is suggestive of the classical myth of Pan. Whatever design influences were invoked, Sumpter's age posed a challenge as he claims he grew eight inches during the production and the window size (in the nursery) had to be altered four times (Murray 2014c).

The motivation for the casting of a biologically male actor in the role of Peter is more suggested by the embellishments on the subplot of attraction between Peter and Wendy that originates as their 'kiss' in the nursery, the exchange of a thimble for an acorn button. The kiss is a motif of attraction between Peter and Wendy that is played out in their Neverland roles as mother and father to the Lost Boys. The adaptation of this desire in Hogan's *Peter Pan* suggests a tween romance scenario, supported by the age and gender of the players:

> When you cast an actual 12-year-old boy to play the part of Peter Pan and cast a 12-year-old girl to play the part of Wendy, something that I think never happens on stage [...] because the part, traditionally on stage, is played by a middle-aged woman [... ,] you've got a boy and girl opposite each other, they're 12 years old [...] they had their chemistry. But, it had nothing to do with us. Sometimes, I just felt like I was recording what was happening between the two of them and it's pretty interesting. (Hogan quoted in Otto 2003)

However, some scripting seems to have occurred as Hogan's Peter first appears hovering over sleeping Wendy and touching her lips. Wendy relays this scene in her schoolwork and is punished by her teacher, which leads to her father telling her to 'grow up'. (There is no schoolroom in Barrie's novel.) Peter and Wendy duly exchange the thimble and the acorn button and the almost-kiss is disrupted by Tinker Bell before Wendy and the boys take flight with Peter to Neverland – all much as in Barrie's story, but the proto-love plot is taken further. Wendy speaks of 'feelings' and – hesitantly – of 'love', to which Peter reacts like any trapped boyfriend: 'Why do you have to spoil everything – we have fun don't we?' (Hogan 2003). The budding romance is manipulated by Hook, visibly double-cast as Mr Darling, when he seduces Wendy into piracy where she masquerades as 'Red Handed Jill' (in a crossing of 'Red-Handed Jack', which is the name the pirates give to her brother John in Neverland (Barrie 138)). She compares Peter unfavourably with Hook, saying he is 'deficient' because he is 'just a boy'. Hook wounds Peter by telling him that Wendy is leaving because Peter can't 'offer' her anything; that he is 'incomplete', and that she would rather grow up than stay in Neverland with Peter, and that a future 'husband' will replace him in her affection. Peter is so affected that he loses his power of flight until it is restored by Wendy's kiss ('it's a powerful thing', says one Lost Boy), precipitating the final destruction of Hook mid-battle with Peter, when he plummets into the mouth of the giant crocodile.

Hooks and Fathers

> He was determined to show who was master in that house, and [...] he lured [Nana] out [...] with honeyed words, and [...] dragged her from the nursery. [...] When he had tied her up [...] the wretched father went and sat in the passage, with his knuckles to his eyes. (Barrie 1996, 24)

The doubling of Mr Darling and Hook makes father figures omnipresent in the children's adventure in *Peter Pan*. Barrie wrote the father as an anxious softie who craves attention in a child-like way. After the children fly off to Neverland, Mr Darling 'went down on all fours and crawled into the kennel' and would not come out (158). In contrast, Hook is a malign patriarch and misanthrope, artfully written by Barrie as a witty gent who prides himself perversely on 'good form'. Peter is all subversion of Hook, mimicking him, defeating him, then dressing up as Hook and imitating the hook with his finger (156). This subversion often gives rise to the cavalier dramatisations of 'to die will be an awfully big adventure,' as Peter's defiant response to Hook's warning, 'prepare to die, Peter Pan' (as in *Hook* and *Peter Pan*). The novelisation of the story bears no obvious trace of the character doubling of Hook and the father, unless it is coded in Mr Darling's exile in the kennel for the duration of the children's absence in Neverland. It is apparent in dramatisations, and Rose sees the doubling of Hook and the father as enabling the children to 'symbolically murder him through Peter Pan' (1994, 35). The final fight between Hook and Peter is part of a 'retaliation fantasy, the completion of the Oedipal circuit for John and Michael with Peter Pan [...] the "avenger"' (35). It unravels in various ways in adaptations.

In Spielberg's *Hook*, the father is Peter and his quest is to affirm his choice to grow up and leave Neverland to become a father. So the paradigm of retaliation is either null or hyper-narcissistic. Peter becomes an idealised father, and when Rufio (Dante Basco), the chief Lost Boy, is killed by Hook, he dies wishing he had a dad like Peter. Peter's concluding declaration on his return home from Neverland that 'to live will be an awfully big adventure' affirms the adventure and pleasure of fatherhood. In Hogan's *Peter Pan*, the nostalgic doubling of Mr Darling/Hook plays to the gender casting of Peter in the tween romance scenario. Hook is sinister and grotesque and much less than the artful spoof on an educated gent. He is first seen half-naked with his hand stump visible, rather like some metal-rocker amputee. Hook's erotic threat towards Wendy, the marriageable wench, brings down Peter Pan. But there is no gain for Hook, as doubled or not, the crocodile stalks him.

Of Iron Men and Crocodiles

> The redskins disappear [...] and soon their place is taken by the beasts [...] lions, tigers, bears. [...] When they have passed, comes the last figure of all, a gigantic crocodile. We shall see for whom she is looking presently. (Barrie 1996, 58)

The crocodile conclusively ends the conflict between Hook and Peter Pan and the sojourn of the Darling children in Neverland. In Hogan's version this occurs with a wildlife flourish that befits a Queensland-based adaptation where the animatronic crocodile also stands for the fantastic endowments of the place of production, its natural and production assets and capacities. Disney's Hook is not seen taken by the crocodile but swimming for his life away from it. Spielberg's (already dead) crocodile in *Hook* kills Hook by falling on him (and he disappears into its jaws). Hogan's Hook is unambiguously swallowed whole, with vision of the crocodile hungrily lunging upwards, and fleeting point-of-view from the airborne Hook's gaze down on the inner jaws.

The spectacle of a man-eating crocodile gains local context in Queensland due to the male-dominated history of crocodile hunting before environmental legislation curtailed it (Brennan 2013a; 2013b), and the predatory associations of crocodiles. But as the epigraph (above) suggests, less are the associations of the gender of the crocodile itself, and Barrie's is female, and Hogan's (and Spielberg's and Disney's) is/are genderless. Thus one of only four females in the lost world of Barrie's Neverland (Wendy, Tinker Bell, Tiger Lily and the Croc, assuming the mermaids are not counted; and five, if you count the Never Bird), like queer-crossed Peter, loses her gender identity. (If you consider Nanna as well, then all the animals and supernatural beings in Barrie's story, all the non-humans, that is, are female). It is likely, too, that if *The Coolangatta Gold* was remade today, it would feature a crocodile or two, not only because the golden boys of the Sunshine State, like their immortal model, Peter, are defiantly optimistic in the face of risk and the demands of overbearing fathers and their doubles. Crocodiles mean adventure in Queensland, and in so many ways it is still deeply tied to masculinity and the coastal tropics.

The story of the Gold Coast, like the crocodile, is one of nature becoming culture. Film studios, like Neverland, are all the home of Peter Pan, where making movies is an awfully big adventure, and whereby heroes prosper and fade. Another marine blockbuster has been in production on the Gold Coast (and elsewhere in Queensland), Walt Disney Studios co-production of the next instalment of *The Pirates of the Caribbean: Dead Men Tell No Tales* (Ronning and Sandberg 2017). There is no word on crocodiles, but Johnny Depp has been to town and there were issues with imported monkeys in the film, including challenges for wranglers and campaigns by animal rights activists. Beyond the production, there was a spot of bother with dogs.[10] All of this, it might be observed, resulted indirectly from a generous incentive the federal government provided to attract this production to Queensland in the first place, enabling its success against international contenders, it is said, in Mexico and South Africa. Filming since has taken place in various locations in the north and south of the state. The production was touted as promising AUD $100 million to the state's economy (Bulletin 2014). Aside from the dividends, all the players will collect the legacy of the aquatic masculinities of Queensland's coastal cinema and the days of the film-friendly pioneers. Mere connection to such a past, or its nostalgic intrigue, does little to discourage and even sustains the enduring smiles of ageless men and crocodiles.

In the next chapter, another monster, contrived in a studio on the Gold Coast, drives the quest for adventure and risk and myths of boys and iron men. It is not the wildlife but the space that is monstrous, a cave, in the offshore setting of Papua New Guinea.

Chapter 6

A PACIFIC PARABLE: CAVE AND
COASTAL MASCULINITIES
IN *SANCTUM*

Not so far from the shores of Neverland, another story of a father and son emerges in *Sanctum* (Grierson 2011a),[1] a survival thriller in which a team of cave divers becomes trapped when a cyclonic storm floods a cave in Papua New Guinea (PNG). PNG lies across the Torres Strait to the north of Far North Queensland in the Pacific region. PNG is a peripheral setting and did not supply any locations for *Sanctum*. Dive locations were scouted in Vanuatu, Puerto Rico, Yucatan, Australia and PNG, according to Andrew Wight (in Grierson 2011b), before the decision was taken to film in studio sets on the Gold Coast. Second unit footage of Mt Gambier and Narracoorte Caves, South Australia,[2] and some exteriors shot on Dunk Island, North Queensland, evokes the above-ground spectacle of the cave and the setting of PNG.

The setting of *Sanctum* is reminiscent of the South Seas films of the 1930s and 1950s discussed by Landman (2006; 2013). These films are distinguished by settings on the fringes of northern Australia in the Torres Strait Islands and PNG, and involved a significant amount of location production, either in the places named, or elsewhere, including islands of the Great Barrier Reef. Landman describes the South Seas films as '"colonial resource adventures"' where the Torres Strait Islands and PNG form an 'exotic backdrop' to the colonial masculine adventures (2013, 202–3). In the corpus of South Seas films, she argues, the spectacle is one of 'scenic melodrama' (2006, 118) and the Indigenous people are marginalised, or even disavowed. The films convey a spirit of adventure and imperial romance in the narratives and the location-ism of the productions in perceived frontier spaces. Landman discusses these films in two groups, first, the interwar films, including *Lovers and Luggers* (Hall 1937), *Jungle Woman* (Hurley 1926b) and *Hound of the Deep* (Hurley 1926a). In *Lovers and Luggers*, the setting was created with back projection of footage shot in locations. These films, she contends, present 'trials of imperial masculine identity' in narratives that reflect Australia's negotiation of its subordinate or dominion relationship with Britain (Landman 2006, 158). She compares three of the post–World War II South Seas films, including *King of the Coral Sea* (Robinson 1954) and *Walk into Paradise* (Robinson and Pagliero 1956).[3] The dramas of resource development occur in the context of a new (in the fictional present), post-war global order in which the Australian protagonists are 'at home' in the territories as 'owners, managers and workers' (Landman 2006, 158). It is not straightforward to compare *Sanctum* with these films because of the difference in era, and because location production was not pursued in *Sanctum*. But the notion of 'scenic melodrama' remains relevant to *Sanctum* through the combination of studio production and second unit footage, and the thematic focus on the quest of the white men in the formerly colonial space of PNG. 'Papua New Guinea' is represented in *Sanctum* by footage of North Queensland and South Australia, and the adventure narrative, staged in the Gold Coast studios, is concentrated in the cave such that PNG is essentially peripheral. It functions as suggested within this chapter, as the 'anachronistic' space/time of imperial adventure defined by Anne McClintock and applied to the South Seas films by Landman (2006, 205). The adventure of the labour of resource development (of the South Seas film) transmutes in *Sanctum* to the challenge of the extreme sport of cave diving, an activity discursively allied with the action of imperial quest. The coastal cave contrives a space in which masculinity is readily equated with risky behaviour, and it also poses a space in which men's emotion is legitimated and a quest for knowledge and wisdom is pursued and validated. *Sanctum* begins above ground where the second unit footage accompanies rhetoric of caving as global exploration. As the crisis develops below ground, in the cave, the quest becomes introspective and is focussed around the emotional tension between the hero, Frank (Richard Roxburgh), and his son, Josh (Rhys Wakefield), and how caving has affected their relationship. This is resolved through a notion of the wisdom of the cave that is channelled and passed from father to son in a parable of giving and getting of wisdom.

In looking at masculine adventure in *Sanctum* in this chapter, the role of the coastal settings, especially water, shore and cave, is correlated with the spectacle of masculinity and tropical mise-en-scène, such as it is condensed in the exteriors and in the world of the cave, and elaborated through the production discourse. As a dive film, *Sanctum* departs from the lifestyle aura of surfing athleticism figured in *The Coolangatta Gold* and the island fantasy of Neverland and evokes another aquatic environment. But, owing to its caving plot, *Sanctum* is a variation on a dive film. The underwater action and predominant costume (wetsuits) gives it that appearance. When the cavers dive to explore or navigate the cave, or to gain egress from it, the unique mechanics of diving forms the spectacle. But the environment of the cave encloses the action of this film in a way that distinguishes it from a typical dive feature. A subtle difference between the cinematic dynamics of ocean diving and cave diving inheres in the relationship between diver, water and surface. Submarine action in dive features attains narrative segmentation through breaks to the surface. In the cave system, the submerging/surfacing dynamic is essentially unbroken until the divers leave the cave as finally occurs for Josh only at the end of *Sanctum*.

The force of environment, figured by the deep cave, is pitted against the team masculinity of the cavers, a team that includes women cavers as well as men. But the women succumb most quickly to the cave, so that the masculine spectacle prevails. Through the aura of caves as prehistoric sites of human habitation, and frontiers of exploration, and through the quest of survival of the cave as one of knowledge and physical endurance, *Sanctum* engenders the cave as a monstrous force.

Caves, Cavers and Watery Masculinities

Victoria Nelson (2001) traces the persistence of the grotto or cave in postmodern culture to antiquity. Caves emerge in classical philosophy, notably in Plato's parable of the cave, where the cave symbolises conditions of knowledge and perception (Plato 2010). The cave is not exclusively associated with masculinity in myths of antiquity as the many sibyls and caverns of classical mythology suggest. Caves, Nelson argues, provide allegories of immersion in the unconscious. Conversely, emergence from a cave implies surfacing to consciousness and recognition and transgression of the boundaries of a world view. Irrespective of the classical legacy, a cave is an ambiguous landform, between terrestrial and marine environments, and potentially both shallow and cavernous. Plato's symbolic cave is underground, a 'cavernous cell', and 'shadows' are cast by a fire onto the walls (60–61). But the outer setting, whether it is coastal or inland, marine or terrestrial, is unknown.

The cave Chuck Nolan (Tom Hanks) inhabited, for instance, in *Cast Away* (Zemeckis 2000) is a modest inlet along the shore of the island, an unthreatening grotto. The cave provides shelter from the tropical storms, and Chuck's occupancy of it suggests his regression from company man to cave man. The heroes of *Sanctum*, on the other hand, traverse a cave system within the coastal landscape, a *mundus subterraneous* or underworld, and become entombed. Chuck's plight may resemble that of the prisoners of Plato's cave, but whatever knowledge he gains, after his rescue, Chuck distances his debt to Plato. He tells no hero's tale of his survival methods, and effectively disavows the cave dweller. Instead, he re-avows his corporate values, expressing the conviction that a 'package' saved his life, adding a moral and posting a parable of exile and return. Decorated by the sender with angel's wings, the said FedEx package has been much lampooned, most famously in a gag where the last scene is rewritten to reveal that the package contained a satellite phone.[4] Less obviously, a 'package' resonates with a corporate salary as befits a company man like Chuck. Where Chuck is ambivalent about the cave, in *Sanctum*, the cavers revere the cave. *Sanctum*, the title, bestows the sacred aura of the deep cave, an awesome mother-monster whose inhabitants are subject to its perilous passages and internal micro-climates abetted by exterior weather.

The dive team Frank leads includes his mate George (Dan Wyllie); Judes (Alison Cratchley), an expert diver; Victoria (Alice Parkinson), a mountain climber on her first dive; Carl (Ioan Gruffudd), Victoria's fiancé, a wealthy adventurer who has financed the expedition; and Luko (Cramer Cain), Frank's loyal Papuan offsider. In the watery mythos of gender in the Pacific region, the travelling man is exposed to sexual danger, confronted by Odyssean temptresses (O'Brien 2006). But, in a departure from these myths of the Pacific, the travelling men of *Sanctum* are locked in chastity, travelling in couples with women from home (Carl and Victoria), or attached in male bonds of mateship (Frank and George) or loyalty (Frank and Luko), or engaged in Oedipal hostilities (Frank and Josh). Sexual action, hetero- or homosexual, is wholly sidelined, and desire is consumed in the quest, first for exploration of the cave, and then for survival of the cave.

The adventure of cave diving is expanded into the production discourse of *Sanctum* as most of the production team are (or were) cave divers. James Cameron, the executive producer, himself a caver, says *Sanctum* offered audiences a 'unique and exotic environment' that 'most people have never seen' (Grierson 2011b). Shot in 3D, the cave environment is hyper-realised. The actors speak of the challenges of learning to dive, abseil and rock-climb for their parts, and they and Grierson comment on the 'physical' challenges of making the film (Grierson 2011b). Produced and written by cave divers John Garvin and the (now late) Andrew Wight, *Sanctum* is dedicated to the late Wes Skiles, the 'world's leading underwater cave cinematographer' in life. Skiles, along with Wight, was involved in a cave collapse in 1988 when 15 people were trapped in a cave on the Pannikin Plains in Western Australia (Grierson 2011b). Documented in *Nullabor Dreaming* (Larkin 1989), the incident resulted from a freak storm of cyclonic power which dropped two years' worth of water in 25 minutes, flooding and collapsing the cave. The rescue of the cavers took nearly two days, although there were no fatalities. These events apparently inspired *Sanctum*, which is also one of the first Australian feature films in 3D.

The fictional expedition of *Sanctum* is primed in the early stages of the film, before the descent into the cave, with allusion to caving as exploration, and the contest with nature cave diving invites. There is a trace here of Richard

Dyer's view of colonial adventure in which the 'treatment of nature is a central aspect of colonial enterprise' that is 'understood to involve mastery and ordering, but also a depredation that distances the white man from nature' (2002, 268). In *Sanctum*, flying towards the cave site (with vision of the second unit footage), Carl speaks of the 'last primeval wilderness' and of the cave as the entry to earth's crust; 'the beginning of time', in Frank's words. It is an exploratory quest coupled with a quest for identity: 'Why do we cave, Josh?' asks Carl, and later reflects 'to shine a light where no one's been before'. Frank and George are dedicated cavers, and, according to Carl, Frank is the 'most determined cave diver in the world'. Josh is more cynical about cavers due to his father's obsession with caving, and, in Josh's view, this is because 'he's got nothing else'. Carl says Frank is the 'most respected explorer of our time' like a 'Columbus or a Neil Armstrong', and that apart from 'these caves, there's nowhere else left on the planet to explore' (Grierson 2011).

The cavers' attractions to 'primeval wilderness' and the 'beginning of time' suggest the trope of '"anachronistic space"' which Landman, following McClintock, defines as an 'organising trope' of late nineteenth-century imperialism that spacialises a '"permanently anterior time within modernity"' (2006, 205). In the late nineteenth century, Africa 'served as the paradigmatic anachronistic space', and Landman argues that New Guinea plays the role in the twentieth century, at least in the region of the South Seas (205). The trope appears to persist in *Sanctum*. After they land at the cave site, momentarily (and silently) edited into the above-ground sequences, before the descent into the cave, is a Papuan man with a bone through his nose. His presence is neither explained nor highlighted, and suggests some kind of menace, perhaps a forewarning of the brewing storm 'right off the coast' and the peril of the cave.

A complex communication regime is deployed to monitor the cave environs, but Frank is sceptical of what the computers can reveal because 'a machine can't *feel* the cave', he insists. Nevertheless, the cavers descend, base-jumping and abseiling to the dive platforms within the cave, and trusting to the phalanx of technology: lamps, laptops, depth-sensing equipment and remote cameras. But the technology is ultimately ineffective in preserving them, as the deadly peril of the cave is provoked by the exterior weather system. It is an unexpected and unpredictable factor of risk, notwithstanding the ominous presence of the Papuan elder and his ancient wisdom. The fleeting vision of the Papuan man and the brief time spent with the exteriors of the cave suggest earlier iterations of adventure narrative and its historical connection to imperial quest, but the quest is doomed. The predicament of the flooded cave and the limitations of the technology in overcoming the paradigm of anachronism transform the quest from adventure to survival, and the exuberant rhetoric of exploration dissolves into the personal challenges of facing death. In this, too, the team derives strength from caving. Throughout these consecutive quests, the spectacle of the cavers is of drenched bodies and the quasi-nakedness of their diving gear.

This Sporting Life of the Cave

Dyer draws attention to the idealisation of the 'built' (muscular) body in the twentieth century 'adventure film in a colonial setting with a star possessed of a champion or built body' (2002, 262). His notable examples are the various Hollywood Tarzan movies and subsequent film cycles in classical settings or cycles featuring muscular or body-building types (262). These films, he argues, 'set terms for looking at the naked white male body' given that the white man is less likely to be seen naked than the non-white man in Hollywood cinema. A 'naked body', he points out, is a 'vulnerable body' (262), and the 'exposed white male body' is liable to pose a question about 'the legitimacy of white male power' (263). Thus, he argues, the 'built body in colonial adventures is a formula that speaks to the need for an affirmation of the white male body without the loss of legitimacy that is always risked by its exposure, while also replaying the notion that white men are distinguished above all by their spirit and enterprise' (263).

The point to highlight with respect to Dyer's theory is the absence of built bodies in *Sanctum*, and the role of wetsuits in obscuring bodies at all, even if the spirit of enterprise is active, coded as exuberance for the adventure of cave exploration. The stricken cavers in *Sanctum* are clothed skin-tight in their diving gear, their vulnerability commodified by the Neptune brand placement. Their bodies are all but bare, and their 'built-ness' is replaced or substituted by expertise in handling specialist equipment and their exuberant capacity for extreme sports. These are in lieu of more imposing bodies, which are perhaps not needed and are actually an obstacle in the tiny caving spaces. It goes, too, to the post-feminist quality of the dive team, as the women are saddled with the same excesses of equipment as the men, but succumb more rapidly than the men, each time due to some kind of mishandling of the equipment, and in spite of their competency in the action of caving.

The adventure of caving as it is performed in *Sanctum* involves multiple extreme sports aside from cave-diving: abseiling, rock-climbing, free-diving and base jumping. In practice, forms of extreme sport offer 'empowerment' through 'demonstrations of skill and strength' (Robinson 2008, 43). Victoria Robinson refers to a range of such sports, especially rock-climbing, in her research. While extreme sports are seen as individualised and non-competitive compared to commercial team sports, Robinson identifies how participants' perceptions of hierarchies of extreme sports are sometimes based on the risks to mortality that boost how 'exciting, or dangerous or special' they seem (46).

Spatiality and environment are important to some participants, such as a rock climber who relished that it is '"about environment as well [as] [...] wild, wild places"' (quoted in Robinson 46). For rock climbers, the choice of environment, whether authentic or in the relative safety of a climbing wall, contributes to a 'more or less masculine' self-image or the sense that a 'particular kind of climber' is seen as a 'particular type of man' (49). More generally, risk is sometimes seen to add authenticity and hence affect the more or less masculine self-image; so, to adapt, a particular kind of risk-taker is seen as a particular type of man. Even so, Robinson points out that research on risk yields complex findings, ranging from a 'courting' of a '"terrible sublime"' of death to the minimising of risk in order to 'climb another day' (148).

In *Sanctum* the experienced divers are highly conscious of risk and their emotional energies are directed towards both the risk and the potential wonder of the cave. But they are foiled by the sheer danger of the cave environment, and the surprise element of the external weather change. The safety consciousness of the team is neutralised in the drama, and peril gains the suspense advantage. Risk also generates the emotive sub-narrative of the tensions between Frank and Josh, in which Luko and George are implicated as mediators. George assures Josh that his father is a 'helluva fella [...] once you get to know him'. As the intense level of risk mounts it propels their emotional bonds. But all is in vain as one by one death takes its toll on the dive team. The first to perish is Judes, who becomes wedged and damages her breathing equipment and drowns, and thus the post-feminist equality of the dive team is savaged by the cave. Luko is severely injured when swamped by a surge of water and is dispatched with mercy by Frank. George 'fizzes up' with decompression sickness. Victoria dies when she defies Frank's warning not to use her knife to cut free her hair when it becomes entangled in the rigging, scalping her. Frank is fatally attacked by Carl, who becomes hysterical after the death of Victoria, and later drowns in despair.

The deaths seem to travesty any 'terrible sublime' of high-risk adventure, and Frank is provoked to observe that 'there's no god down here [...] this place doesn't give a rat's arse about [...] us [...] we're bits of dust passing through'. But, in spite of this anti-theology, a cave spirituality surrounds Frank's own fate. Emotion seeps out of Frank in poetic ways as he is fond of reciting Samuel Taylor Coleridge: '"In Xanadu did Kubla Khan / a stately pleasure dome decree: / Where Alph, the sacred river, ran, / Through caverns measureless to man / Down to a sunless sea."' This is both sentimental and nostalgic as he discloses, in teaching it to Josh, that Josh's mother, from who Frank is estranged, liked the poem. The 'sacred river' also signifies Frank's quasi-mystical wisdom in following the river out of the cave, and more mythically instils the maternal aura of the cave. His faith in caves enables reflection on himself as a caver, and is accompanied by reconciliation with Josh. In the moments before Carl attacks him, Frank confesses to Josh, 'I know I haven't been anything of a father to you. [...] I'm not much good up there full stop [...] cities, cars and mortgages [...] down here I can make sense of this [...] it's like my church. I can hold a mirror up and say this is who I am.' As he lies fatally injured, Frank begs his son to mercy-kill him, and urges him to survive: 'trust the cave, trust the cave, follow the river, it'll lead you out.'

Obeying his father, Josh takes the last rebreather and swims to safety. Aroused uncannily from the unconsciousness of near drowning, he finds an outlet into the ocean and swims to shore. His emergence seems a rendering of parturition as he surfs down a canal-like opening, reborn to understanding of Frank and the cave. Over a high shot of Josh struggling to shore after his escape from the cave, Josh, in voiceover, declares, 'George was right. I never knew my father. I found him in that cave. He was a helluva fella, once you got to know him.' The *Sanctum* team all surrender to the cave, except for Josh, who nevertheless surrenders to Frank's spiritualised view of cave-diving as source of identity and the cave as a channel of knowledge and consciousness. Josh's survival bespeaks his coming of age and the wisdom of the cave/r, and confirms Nelson's paradigm of the cave as a portal between the unconscious and consciousness. Frank's sacrifice and Josh's survival imbue the virtue of risk and masculine self-image in extreme sports – the wisdom that a particular kind of caver is a particular kind of man.

The Fast Boat to China

Sanctum has provenance as an Australian/US co-production. Its creative derivation was largely Australian, and its relationship to Queensland was largely through the place of its making on the Gold Coast.

Within a short time of its release in 2011, *Sanctum* rapidly entered the rare league of Australian films that have earned more than $US100 million (Bodey 2011, 17). This success was assisted by its release in China, where it took $US10 million within 10 days of opening, and it was 'one of only 20 international films allowed commercial release' in China in 2011 (Bodey 2011). It also succeeded in Japan, Brazil, South Korea and Russia, largely due, Michael Bodey suggests, to the value of executive producer James Cameron's 'imprimatur' in foreign markets (Bodey 2011). Its reception in China prompts reflection on how this film represents a coalescence of the interests of the creative and primary economies, because its success in Chinese cultural markets is comparable to the predominant coal production industry in Queensland, which is said to be largely harnessed to consumption by China. While mining is not caving, the endeavour of exploration is common in both practices, and technologised exploration of an inner-earth underworld bears symbolic if not literal comparison. This is not to mention the male-dominated associations of team enterprise and the health, safety and environmental risks that are known to proceed. That an economic metaphor lurks in the cave depths of *Sanctum* is only far-fetched if the investment of such films in reprising and extending the ideology of team masculinity and mateship and its potential costs are not overlooked in any transnational enterprise. Frank's sacrifice attests that any kind of man – caver, miner, filmmaker – owes his identity and relative power as much to the location and conditions of his environment as to any myth of masculinity, and that, without due care, these elements are potentially as fluid in reality as they are in the cinemas of the transnational tropics.

Part 4

REGIONAL BACKTRACKS

Chapter 7

UNKNOWN QUEENSLAND IN TORRES STRAIT TELEVISION: *RAN* AND *THE STRAITS*

The Torres Strait Islands feature in the archive of the earliest media in Queensland in A.C. Haddon's ethnographic films of Islanders in 1898 (see Introduction). Much later, the Torres Strait Islands were fictionalised in the 'South Seas' films identified by Landman (2006; 2013), and discussed in the previous chapter with respect to *Sanctum* and its comparable use of Landman's notion of scenic melodrama. The television mini-series discussed in the present chapter, the six episodes of *RAN: Remote Area Nurse* (Caesar and McKenzie 2006) and the 10 episodes of *The Straits* (Andrikidis, Ward and Woods 2012), invoke the imperial romance of exploration in unknown territories, but within a postcolonial frame and with contrasting insights on the places and people of the regions depicted. As expansive small-screen dramatisations of the Indigenous residents in contemporary settings, these productions also offer perspectives on the idea of paradise in Queensland, and reinscribe in various ways the tropes of eccentricity, excess and epic journey to diverse ends.

In *RAN* the spectacle is confined, in depth, to the location of the production, the tiny island of Masig (aka Yorke Island) in the Torres Strait. In *The Straits*, in contrast, the action moves in and out of Far North Queensland, and the (fictional) Montebello family's kinship networks and business dealings in the Torres Strait Islands and Papua New Guinea (PNG), although the production was largely filmed in and around the city of Cairns in Far North Queensland. The liminality Landman associates with the Torres Strait Island setting of some of the South Seas films is detectable in *The Straits* in the movements and modes of transport that convey the Montebello family around the narrative places, and, in *RAN*, in Helen Tremain (Susie Porter), the Gaibuis and other islanders, to and from Masig Island. While such movements are not unusual in Australian television that situates its subjects in remote locations, the liminality of the region is embedded in the numerous scenes in each series that begin or end with plane or boat landings. A signature gaze in each series, in the edit breaks and establishing views, grants a perspective on the places of action as if from a low-flying aircraft. This airborne gaze is one means whereby the sense of place in the series equates to somewhere discovered or initially unknown, a perspective explored further in this chapter with regard to each series.

Whereas scenic melodrama of the South Seas films exploited the islands and islanders as a backdrop to the action, *RAN* and *The Straits* impose a sense of the lived culture of the islands from Indigenous perspectives. *RAN* features Torres Strait Islanders in central, starring roles. Helen Tremain is the titular resident nurse and representative of the department of Queensland Health on their island, and one of only two white women and three white men. Helen, who Landman sees as 'another participant in Australia's entangled colonial legacies' (2013, 210), shows non-islander audiences a way to see the island from a legitimated and sympathetic outsider perspective, while islander audiences have engaged with *RAN* as a recognisable portrayal of home (Landman 2013). Language and cultural performances embed the 'insider' islander perspectives. The outsider view is couched through the drama of Helen's anxiety of belonging, her friendship and camaraderie with co-medical officers Nancy Gaibui (Margaret Harvey) and Paul (Luke Carroll) and her ambivalent flirtation with the family patriarch and the island's chairman, Russ Gaibui (Charles Passi). As the duration of the series encloses the time from Helen's arrival and residency to her departure, it repatriates the visitor's perspective at the conclusion (Figure 7.1).

Figure 7.1 Helen (Susie Porter, foreground) attends church on the Island with Paul Gaibui (Luke Carroll, with child in arms) in *RAN: Remote Area Nurse* (2006). Image provided courtesy and with kind permission of Penny Chapman and Matchbox Pictures.

There is no sense in which either series explicitly refers to the South Seas films. But, *The Straits* could be seen as a kind of playful take on scenic melodrama in the setting of the tropics of Far North Queensland and the Torres Strait. The series offers audiences more limited pathways (than *RAN*) into islander culture and owes more to genres from series television, family noir and gangster drama adapted to the tropical setting. Yet the patriarch of the family, Harry Montebello (Brian Cox), could be a descendent of the adventurers in the South Seas films. His backstory, on the series website, tells that he is London-born 'of Maltese extraction', arrived in 'the straits' to work on prawn trawlers and married an islander, Kitty (Rena Owen), she of Maori and Torres Strait Islander parentage ('Characters' 2015). Kitty and an unrelated character, Kingsten (Greg Kapernick), both claim relatives who worked on the pearling 'luggers' in the fictional past of the drama (Episode 10).

Compared to feature film, television is a more regionally invested medium in many senses. Public service and commercial broadcasting have historically been located in state-based and region-based activities and enterprises in Australia. The televisual archive of regional Australia is vast in terms of its documentary and public affairs content. Television drama, which is predominantly produced in metropolitan centres, typically Sydney and Melbourne, often adopts authentic and/or fictional regions and regional centres as narrative places. Until recently, Far North Queensland or its adjacent Pacific region were less visible in this corpus. This has altered with *RAN* and *The Straits* and *Sea Patrol* (McElroy and McElroy 2007–). Set on board an Australian Navy patrol boat active in the Pacific and south-east Asian region, *Sea Patrol* has had extensive production in Mission Beach and Cairns, Far North Queensland. *Sea Patrol* is less explicit in marking its narrative place, however, and its plots are much consumed in state-aligned interests of border control and security. In spite of its places of production, it is relatively low in reflecting regional or Indigenous identity, nor is it focussed on the Torres Strait.

Both *RAN* and *The Straits* were collaborative series co-produced by Penny Chapman and Helen Panckhurst in alliance with state broadcasters, *RAN* with the involvement of SBS Independent, and *The Straits* with the ABC. The largely authentic settings of both series optimise the potential of the medium of television to induce familiarity and intimacy in the address to audiences. Local allusions and colloquialisms speak to assumptions of audience knowledge of Queensland, such as the islanders hanging out maroon flags for the State of Origin Rugby League tournament in *RAN*, and Marou Montebello's (Jimi Bani) (fictional) former membership of the North Queensland Cowboys rugby league team in *The Straits*. The series diverge in the treatment of the spectacle of the places imagined and in the characterisation of the regional difference of the tropics.

RAN poses a naturalistic spectacle, evoking a sense of place in the concentrated location on Masig, and this is discussed further in the next section. *The Straits*, in comparison, is less authentically grounded in the setting due to its genre premise as crime drama, and the dark humour of the series. Cairns is the main urban mainland setting, the middle-class hub of the Montebellos' empire. The wider region of action is suggested in the movements between mainland, islands and PNG that are often marked with inter-titles of place names that imply the 'unknown' character of these territories. This sense of the unknown is extended in the series website in the invitation to interactively 'explore the region' and 'discover more', while the fiction of the regional difference is paradoxically referenced to facts and data of the 'Real Straits' ('*The Straits*' 2015), which bear limited connection. Iconography of the tropical region – flora, marine and wildlife, especially crocodiles – are embroidered into the setting and plots, evoking a sense of difference and playful irony in the portrayal of crime in the tropics. *RAN*, on the other hand, offers a more genuine sense of informed insight into life in the Torres Strait.

Community Perspectives in *RAN: Remote Area Nurse*

The designation of the title, a 'remote area nurse', is a professional one, and a significant amount of academic nursing research has drawn attention to the challenges of these appointments.[1] *RAN*, in fact, was inspired by the experiences of producer Penny Chapman's sister Peta, as Peta nursed for several years on Masig Island during the 1990s (Miller 2005). The nurse medical officer at the time of the production, Robyn White, consulted on the script. *RAN* therefore has the appearance of a medical procedural drama, but this is more of a pretext for the community drama that unfolds in the series, and various subplots focus on social issues of island life, concerning family dysfunction, domestic violence, alcohol abuse and broader political issues of self-governance (Miller 2005). The pretext, particularly in the opening episodes, justifies the presence of the state on the island, through Helen's role and the action in the clinic, the visiting doctor and peripherally in the figures of the local police and quarantine officers. But the role of the state is quickly subsumed by the discourse of island culture.

RAN has consistently attracted praise for its portrayal of the people of the community of Masig Island. Landman argues that it is a 'grassroots' production collaboration that 'enacts an exemplary cultural distancing from [...] earlier film fictions set in the Torres Strait' (2013, 202). This is the result, she contends, of the way the 'literary scripts of *RAN* intertwine colonial legacy themes (especially in relation to health) with the micropolitical personal stories' of the (fictional) Gaibui family, all played by Torres Strait Islanders. Thus

RAN elicits an 'intercultural and intracultural dialogue' which explores the 'micropolitics of Masig' (210). The colonial legacy discourse emanates in the medical sub-dramas of *RAN*, which are ultimately subordinate to more sustained discourses of place and belonging in the story of the nurse Helen and the men and women of the Gaibui family with whom she works and lives.

Some of the praise for the series came from Masig islanders themselves, who are said to have been delighted with *RAN*, and a screening of the whole series took place to great celebration in a single night on Masig in 2006. Landman comments on viewers' favourable response to *RAN*, registered in the series website, noting the 'decolonising' potential of such sites of engagement by audiences. While the site is no longer extant, Landman reports that there were more than '330 responses' in 2006, including around 10 per cent by persons identifying themselves as non-resident (mainland-dwelling) Torres Strait Islanders (2013, 201–3).[2] Landman highlights the approval of the series recorded in these posts, especially of the rarity of the 'recognition' the series affords to Island life and perspectives (203).

The sense of culture is strongly conveyed in the series through extensive use of language, Torres Kreole, which is liberally subtitled throughout the episodes. Helen does not speak the language beyond some basics. The distinctive colourful smock-style dresses of the Torres Strait women and the floral shirts and sarongs of the men are worn throughout, and Helen and her fellow non-Islanders don the dress style on festive occasions. The music of the series, 'a communicative channel' in the 'intercultural discourse of the production' (Landman 2013, 207), was produced by David Bridie, who is known for his research and composition of regional musical forms. There is extensive use of diegetic music, in scenes of festivals and weddings, and in the practices of daily life. The accompanying non-diegetic musical score, partly sung by a Torres Strait choir formed for the production, syncretises traditional and popular song that connotes the local and the global tropics.

The commitment to location production on the island was driven, according to Chapman, by a quest for 'unique authenticity' (Oc Screen 2004). Speaking in advance of the production, she describes how they would embrace '"a documentary approach"'; while being '"true to script, we'll need to go with the flow"' (Chapman quoted in Oc Screen 2004). Cast and crew camped on the island at the hospitality of the 200 islanders for three months, living in tents and rented accommodations. The challenges were intense in the heat of the year from September to December, and with limited power supply. Chapman speaks of choosing crew members carefully for their combination of technical skill and capacity to cope with the production conditions of heat, cultural sensitivity and the island's strict no-alcohol policy (Oc Screen 2004; Miller 2005). The perceived benefits to authenticity also gained reportage as benefits to islanders in terms of short-term income from the location licences, the rentals of accommodations and vehicles and the employment of locals as cast and crew and makers of traditionally styled set decorations (Miller 2005).

The fictionalisation of this authentic site is more subtle. Masig Island is the sole location in *RAN*, but the narrative place is not identified subjectively (by name) in the series. The mainland or other islands of the Torres Strait are not seen. But Thursday Island (or TI, as it is known) and Cairns form regional markers of the narrative place. TI is the location of the hospital to which residents are removed or evacuated; and Cairns enters the regional discourse towards the end, as Helen's destination for a new job for which she leaves the island. Landman sees Helen as a 'surrogate for the fly-in crew rather than for the putatively white audience' (2013, 210). This is most notable, as she points out, at the conclusion of the series with Helen's departure to Cairns. While Helen's 'point of view' frames the first episode and positions her initially as a 'cultural mediator', this is not developed because the narrative 'refocalis[es]' on the Gaibui family (208–10).

The self-contained medically related dramas of each episode are subordinated to the 'arc narratives about longing and belonging' (Landman 2013, 208). Helen's story is one of these narratives. Comparable 'belonging quests' are experienced by Nancy, who has deferred her medical studies to return home to the island, and Eddie (Aaron Fa'aoso), who is estranged from his father and seeks to regain his place in the community by successfully challenging his father for election as the island chairman. Sol (Jimi Bani), another son, is implicated in the challenges of his non-Islander wife, Lindy (Peta Brady), to cope with raising young children when she is isolated from her own family interstate. Helen is therefore positioned as one of several women characters, like Nancy, Lindy and Bernadette (Merwez Whaleboat), who experience insecurities about their place on the island, and Russ's wife, Ina (Serai Zaro) eventually leaves out of displeasure with his flirting with Helen (but she returns).

Helen nevertheless is the central figure of the series, iconic in her large straw hat that she wears outdoors and in signature images of the series. As such she is a version of the quality bushwoman (see Chapter 4) whose sense of adventure is sublimated into her desire for belonging in the community. She also embodies some of the tropes of white Queensland identity. The hat signifies her eccentricity. Her stint on the island follows an earlier one, and she has returned following the death of her mother, so that she is presented as a character in a transitional period of her life, and one whose story in Queensland is anchored by events elsewhere. Around the clinic, with her trusty clipboard, and her hair curled high in a professional top-knot, Helen is an unobtrusive and observant official, with even a touch of Florence Nightingale as she looks in on patients and oversees the clinic. The script does not demand that she is seen in complex medical activities, except at points where this is highlighted towards her sense of belonging in the community (for instance, when the death of an Uncle leads to blame and ostracism of Helen in Episode 5).

Unlike the women of the holiday tropics (in Chapter 4), Helen is professional and practical. Her island attire is typically with legs and arms covered in long sleeves and pants, sensible for a fair-skinned person under the ferocious North Queensland sun. Like the quality bushwoman, Helen finds that her life is work, as suggested by her presence on the island for employment. Work occupies Helen all day and out of hours, and eventually takes her away from the island. She takes no getaway break except in her walks and swims alone around the island. These contained interludes, and her dialogue with her love interest, the eligible whitefella Robbo (Billy Mitchell), are spaces for Helen's subjective reflections on her place in the community to occur. Robbo frequently comments on Helen's unrealistic expectations of belonging in the community. His perspective is ultimately vindicated at the point where he, too, becomes her patient during the outbreak of dengue fever in the final episode. Thus both of them are flown away at the conclusion, he on a stretcher.

If, as Landman (2013) says, this 'fly-in' surrogacy can be imputed to the central character of *RAN*, it is less obvious in *The Straits*. But at least one member of the Montebello family is almost always either air- or seaborne, in light aircraft or in a variety of luxury boats, runaround watercraft or dinghies. The implications of their movements in the liminal spaces of Far North Queensland are rather different to the more grounded sorties of Nurse Helen and her island friends. While neither *RAN* nor *The Straits*, as Graeme Blundell says, could be seen as 'didactic' (2012, 27), there is little sense in which *The Straits* comments on life in the Torres Strait in the way that *RAN* succeeded, nor is its raison d'etre as genre entertainment directly comparable. Robinsonade it is not, nor is it Neverland; the island stories of *The Straits* are from gangland. But it is a version dipped in the iconic mystique of its narrative place, mostly identified in the series as 'Far North Queensland'. The reiteration of the Far North as setting gives a darkly humorous tinge to Aaron Fa'aoso's claim that, at the end of day, it's 'all about family' ('The Inspiration' 2015).

The Oriental Tropics of *The Straits*

> '[It's] action packed with weapons, drugs, violence and crocodiles.' (Firass Dirani quoted in 'Characters' 2015)

The idea for *The Straits* was pitched to Penny Chapman by Fa'aoso, who played Eddie in *RAN*. Fa'aoso's family originated from the Torres Strait island of Saibai. He grew up in Bamaga in Cape York Peninsula, and in Cairns,

Far North Queensland. Chapman commissioned Louis Nowra to devise the outlines of the series in consultation with Fa'aoso ('The Show' 2015). The episodes were penned by various prominent Australian screenwriters, including Nick Parsons, Jaime Brown, Blake Ayshford and Kristen Dunphy. Fa'aoso played Noel Montebello, the eldest son, in the series.

The series is premised on the mixed-race origins of the adopted family Harry and Kitty raise. The scenario derives from Islander traditions of family adoption, although Kitty's infertility is given as the motivation in the series. The family comprises three sons and one daughter: Noel (Fa'aoso), Marou (Bani), Gary (Firass Dirani) and Sissi (Suzannah Bayes-Morton). Noel and Marou, as the website informs, are adopted from Kitty's 'extended family in the islands', while Gary is the 'orphan son of Harry's cousin' and Sissi the child of the family's 'PNG housemaid' ('Characters' 2015). As each child acquires a spouse, partner or love interest, the relationships all develop as cross-racial, and therefore a palpable rewriting of the miscegenation anxieties of the South Seas film corpus.

The Montebello family homestead in Cairns is the centre of the series action, an opulent beach mansion with spectacular views, filmed in a local property. Harry and his business dealings are based there. The family's activities in the Straits are based on fictional Zey Island where Kitty's ancestral links are based, and its trading partnerships, in drugs and guns, with PNG. The fictional Straits is a 'frontier society', and it's 'a little like a gangster western' (Blundell 2012). It is a tad Shakespearian, too, or the trace of King Lear is in the drama of the father testing his children for the role of successor to his criminal empire, and his particular affection for his only daughter, Sissi, which proves his own undoing.

The web of plots and subplots, and the abundance of drugs, guns, money and blood vendettas, is in the style of a mafia family drama, also suggested by the family's pastiche name of Montebello. Blundell perceives the influence of Coppola's *The Godfather* in Harry's manipulation and the 'mythic sense of equality through violence' (2012, 27). *The Godfather* films marked the domestication of the genre, Marilyn Yaquinto argues, and the more recent example of *The Sopranos* 'revels in detailing how workplace and home are [...] interdependent' in the genre (2004, 209). Viewer posts identify *The Straits* as 'Sopranos in the tropics', and a version of *Underbelly* (Various 2008) 'set in the top end'[3] ('Discussion' 2012). Blundell observes that it is 'joked about as "*The Sopranos* in thongs"' (2012, 27), alluding to that ubiquitous fact of North Queensland life, the wearing of thongs as footwear. (In the series, thongs are seen more on Zey Island than in the middle-class setting of Cairns.)

Around the family are networks of clan and communities, including Melanesian and Asian influences. Torres Strait folk are Kitty's relatives, and some form the congregation of the church where Marou, a Pentecostal Christian, occasionally preaches. Noel's 'blackfella network on The Cape' (an allusion to Cape York Peninsula) assists him in escaping from jail. The rival clan leader, Quay Lin (Sri Sacdpraseuth), said (in the website gloss) to be of 'Chinese-Lao extraction' and referred to as 'The Chinaman', operates his empire from Fly River, PNG. Various Papuan and Islander offsiders assist or abet the Montebellos in contending with Quay Lin. These include Eddie Tagobe (Cramer Cain) on Zey Island, Dizzy and Freedy (played by brothers Bill and Ray Doa Neill), who are tribal Papuans working for Quay Lin, and Kingsten, an urban Papuan aligned with the Raskol gangs. (These actors also appeared in *Sanctum*, discussed in Chapter 6, and Tasia Zalar, who plays Bridget, Gary's love interest on Zey Island, was Coral in *Uninhabited*, discussed in Chapter 4.)

The enemy of the Montebellos on the mainland is the motley 'Demon Cheaters' – or the DCs – bikie gang, who are, by and large, the main white folks. Non-Indigenous allies include Harry's old associates from his 'wideboy gang' in London, the Mafiosi-like Vince Palmero (Andy Anderson) and Paddy Brogan (Kym Gyngell), the business manager ('Characters' 2015). The family's lawyer, Natasha Denning (Rachel Blake), proves to be the mother of Harry's only biological child, Natasha's blonde son, Andrew (Finn George Newman). The disclosure of their affair and Andrew's paternity precipitates Kitty's departure from the family homestead in Cairns to Zey Island, and, eventually, the showdown that occurs with Quay Lin in the islands at the conclusion of the series.

As this cultural mix of characters suggests, initially, in the first few episodes, especially through Kitty's and Marou's community connections, the series begins to suggest something of the culture of Far North Queensland, its diversity and connectedness with places and people beyond its land borders. Bani comments accordingly, referring to the diversity as reflecting 'what Cairns is' ('Characters' 2015). While there is an effort to represent 'culture' and it is claimed that 'there is a lot of truth in *The Straits*' ('The Inspiration' 2015), 'truth' is perhaps not quite related to the 'authenticity' that characterised *RAN*. There is a knowing play with the 'truth' on the series website. A dramaturg was employed to identify stories from Far North Queensland and these are said to have been incorporated in the series. On the website, the 'Real Straits' tab details incidents purported to resemble some of those depicted in the fiction. But none pertain directly to the region portrayed. The Stories of bikie crime extend no further north than Caboolture (roughly 2,000 kilometres to the south of the Torres Strait); the 'Drugs for Guns' have some closer connection, referring to press reports from the Papua-New Guinea *Post* and the Cairns *Post* (dating from 2004–9; 'Drugs for Guns' 2015). But the nearest incident in the piece on 'Animal Smuggling' (2015) is two states away in Victoria.

Genre therefore seems to outrank culture in the discourse of truth in *The Straits*. As the series progresses, the clan and its predators become the sole focus, and the predators are within the clan. Harry deploys Sissi in scrutinising the family business in order to expose skullduggery on the part of employees. She is so effective that she also discovers Harry's own destructive secrets, including his affair with Natasha, and her sister-in-law, Lola's (Emily Lung), attempt to murder Harry. All is captured on the elaborate rig of surveillance cameras Sissi has installed in the house, and whereby she is often found gazing in horror at her laptop. This atmosphere of surveillance in the family home is layered externally by the gaze of the bikies, and the eyes of the Islander community on the Montebellos, and the ineffectual gaze of the bent police. It is, Blundell observes, suggestive of 'noir' but the 'landscape' of entrapment is not typical of the 'traditional nocturnal one of rain-slicked streets [...] rattling fire escapes' (2012, 27). 'This world', he says, 'is a daylit one, sensorially explosive' (27).

A kind of playful Orientalism emerges in *The Straits* towards the place of its tropical setting in Far North Queensland, described in the series website as a 'world' that is 'beautiful and dangerous' ('The Show' 2015; 'The Inspiration' 2015). If, as Edward Said argued, 'orientalism' is a style of thought premised on a distinction between 'the Orient' and 'the Occident', then, notionally at least, *The Straits* implies a comparable perspective – not between East and West, or Indigenous and non-Indigenous, but between Far North Queensland and its outside. Barring Noel's attempt to flee to South America, and Natasha's banishment to Melbourne, the world outside Cairns, the Islands and the shores of PNG might not exist. Wider Australia is wholly marginalised, and Queensland is figured as a hermetic space. When Sissi's Irish boyfriend, Joel (James Mackay), wants to run away from the family, she warns him that spies are everywhere and that he probably 'won't get out of the state'. The question of how this might measure some authenticity or 'truth' might also be filtered through the notion of the Orient that exists, as it were, despite or without correspondence with a 'real' Orient (Said 1978).

Among the clan's various illicit activities are legitimate ones, including a crocodile farm. The farm, and its nefarious uses, adds to the grotesquerie of gangster family drama in a tropical setting given the ecological status of crocodiles as top predators in the wild. The crocodile threat has been exploited in a number of Australian horror films (see Ryan 2010; Simpson 2010). While it is not horror, *The Straits* is at times horror-comedy and crocodiles figure in the ghoulish humour. As crocodiles retain mythic and totemic status in both Australian Indigenous and Papuan cultures, and quasi-mythic status in occidental cultures, these creatures have cross-cultural references. Catherine Simpson, in a postcolonial frame, suggests that large predators like crocodiles challenge 'the notion of human mastery', and that all animals contribute to the 'mystique and agency of a landscape that has not been tamed', and equally are potentially seen as 'victims of colonial enterprise' (2010, 45). The farming of crocodiles by the grotesque Montebellos treats this potential with energetic irony.

The series comes to rest in the final episode on Harry's perspectives on fatherhood and Harry's fears that he has turned his children into 'monsters' (Episode 10). The children, on the other hand, struggle for independence while retaining loyalty to the clan. Most poignant is Marou, the darkest-skinned man in the family, who is the most brutalised and makes the most sacrificial compromises of all in order to demonstrate his loyalty to the family, enduring torture and then executing his wife, Lola, for trying to kill Harry. Lola is a Lady Macbeth–type figure in the style of a contemporary gangster's moll, as Yaquinto defines them, more 'opportunist' than 'victim' (2004, 209), although Marou is an ambivalent gangster. Lola's politic intrusions in the family hierarchy on behalf of Marou's ascendancy are resisted by Harry, who regards her as 'trash'. Marou kills her in the nadir of his conflicted feelings towards family loyalty. Lola's fate, prefigured by an earlier encounter with a loose crocodile at the farm one night, leads to storage of her body at the crocodile farm by Marou, tearful and traumatised.

Marou's retreat to the family of origin is a pattern replicated in the stories of all the siblings, whose various efforts to establish independence fail. This is with the exception of Gary, who with the help of Eddie is a stoic stager and fixer of various escapades and is outposted on Zey Island throughout the series. But back in Cairns the family noir devolves, in the progressive absence of friends or community, from some version of paradise to dystopia. The white folks are either outright enemies or subordinate or dishonest allies of a coloured family of crooks, whose tense inner sanctum is wrought with filial insecurity, and lurches between love for and revulsion from the patriarch. Only the matriarch, Kitty, stands to level him, buoyed up by her ancestral connection to the islands.

'A Bit Tropical'

> Our land abounds with nature strips. (Paddy, Episode 1, *The Straits*)

The sense of tropical difference of *The Straits* is condensed in the pastiche micro-narrative of the credit sequence of the series. An electronic reggae theme, the music of David Bridie, accompanies the montage of images from the series of native flora and fauna and scenes of violence and crime. A coral reef, a pair of stingrays cruising beneath translucent waters, a rainforest canopy, a verandah, shell ornaments, colourful jellyfish, speedboats on channels, black hands passing drugs across a dug-out canoe, spearsmen in the scrub, a colonial church and Islander children, a religious icon decorated with shells, a colourful reptile, a knife-wielding man in a balaclava, a tree-lined highway with a dead kangaroo, a shipwreck, a body in a dumpster and a pod of crocodiles. As a single crocodile slinks into dark water, the face of the patriarch, Harry, comes into view, personifying the syncretism of the culture in the tropical place.

Aside from iconic animals, vegetation, islander peoples and tropical feasts, flamboyant weapons and methods of violence are adapted as signs of tropical difference. One bikie is dispatched in a swimming pool filled with marine stingers (the deadly jellyfish that pervades the waters of the region on migratory routes from south-east Asia) (Figure 7.2). Noel goes to jail for (mistakenly) avenging the hit on his father by firing on the bikies with a rocket launcher. Eccentricity and excess attach to Noel, who is given to characterising violent situations as 'a bit tropical'. When Eddie is speared through the face during a weapon run to PNG, Noel reports to his father that the assailants went 'totally tropical,' without mentioning his own bungled part in the escapade. Noel's hot-headedness earns a lecture from Harry about the need for cool: 'Our business is about minimising risk, Noel.'

Figure 7.2 The bikie goes into the swimming pool with the stingers as Noel (Aaron Fa'aoso, centre) and Harry Montebello (Brian Cox, right) look on in *The Straits* (2012). Image provided courtesy and with kind permission of *The Straits*, Matchbox Pictures, and Andrew Watson Photography.

Cool is not a climatic characteristic of the tropics of Far North Queensland and noir, traditionally, demands an urban setting. Cairns fills the role in the style of other cinematic (south-east Asian) tropical cities in which the natural converges with the urban environment (to adapt Chua 2008). Reprised from different angles in establishing views and transitions, always from the air, Cairns is a low- to medium-rise grid of buildings that pokes up amidst the surrounding green mountains and faces water. Much action takes place outside of Cairns in sites labelled with inter-titled place names that set up a playful mix of real and inauthentic sites of Montebello activity. 'Lockhart River, Far North Queensland' appears as a landing point for drugs from PNG; Lola is buried at 'Iron Range, Far North Queensland' (Episode 9). Both of these sites are authenticable, and refer to places in Aboriginal land on Cape York Peninsula, even if the vision shown is indeterminate except for the titles.

The offshore places in the islands and PNG are a mix of authenticable and false sites. 'Zey Island' is not one of the many islands of the Torres Strait and is figured on the website map 'of the region' as located near Marbuaig Island, the Torres Strait community acknowledged in the series credits. Neither are Lugaut or Dungal (that appear in Episode 9) part of the Torres Strait group of islands. (The notorious activities of the Montebellos are unlikely to honour the modern governance and conduct codes of the Torres Strait Regional Council, so perhaps some distancing was warranted.) Fly River exists in PNG; Waru is on the map, but is not an island. Inter-titles, as Jaikumar says, serve various purposes, sometimes suggesting the 'historicity or actuality of the representation'; or the 'relationship to the images is one of control' (2001, 59). Alternatively, inter-titles 'function to make the "otherness" of the place unthreatening', a trope of imperial film (59). In *The Straits*, these inter-titles serve to name the stamping ground of the Montebellos in Far North Queensland, and how the unknown and otherwise unmarked territory is identified with them.

Dubious dignity is afforded to the body of Lola, who is spared the abjection of disposal in feeding time at the crocodile park, unlike Harry's would-be assassin, Vlad (Richard Cawthorne). Vlad, for all his threat to Harry, falls victim to a gruesome death when he is frightened by a spider under the influence of Kitty's *puri puri* (magic) administered by Uncle George (Deba Pilot) to apprehend Harry's assassin. Marou pauses to say a prayer as he distributes Warren's mortal remains to the crocs.

The series ends with a question mark, as Sissi is seen abandoning her boyfriend, Joel, as he snorkels on the Reef. She powers away in the family launch, ignoring his cries, apparently returning to the fold after contemplating elopement with him. His fate and hers might have emerged in the touted second series that has not eventuated. The few messages linked to the still extant ABC Messageboard testify to appreciation of the series, and disappointment on its demise from a few viewers ('Discussion' 2014). It also records a viewer debate about 'a sea of missed opportunities' in the use of the region as setting for a genre crime drama ('Discussion' 2012). Some proclaim the 'bold, original, colourful' production and the 'risky, new, unchartered terrain'; another cynically bemoans it as 'just entertainment set in an interesting location' ('Discussion' 2012). There is little comment about the cultural perspectives, aside from one who perceives the treatment as fitting in showing Torres Strait Islanders as like everyone else, and not 'museum' spectacles ('Discussion' 2012).

The Straits does not comment explicitly on the politics of the region, on Torres Strait sovereignty, for instance. An allusion to the politics of West Papua is whittled into one of the comic-strip violence vignettes when Eddie hears a West Papuan band on the car radio, before the Raskol he is transporting shoots out the dashboard. While *The Straits* is no Robinsonade, it does feature a castaway, who emerges (in Episode 2) in the form of an earnest and optimistic Sri Lankan, Joseph (Chum Ehelepola). He is met on sea, washing along towards the mainland in a large esky. 'Is this a boat-people person?' asks Gary, as he stares, incredulous, towards the waving tub-mariner. It is one of the few moments in the series in which the island stands for the island of Australia, lampooning its excesses of border control. 'This island hates outsiders,' says Gary to Joseph, assisting him, blindfolded, out of the boat and up to the house on Zey Island, 'we're kind of racist that way.' The good-humoured refugee remains at the house, cooking and cleaning and denied use of the phone, and ably assisting in the various escapades. He eventually escapes on one of the flights from the island, disguised in a Quarantine officer's t-shirt, and is last seen walking euphorically through Cairns's tourist precinct and heading for a public telephone. Ironically, the item of greatest proximity to the Torres Strait on the 'Real Straits' tab on the series website is a news item about the disputed account of two Burmese fisherman found floating in an esky in the waters of the Torres Strait in 2009 ('Esky Ordeal' 2015).

The surveilling gaze of the state that Joseph evades is implied throughout both series, in the friendly participant observer, Helen, of *RAN*, and in the ineffectual police in *The Straits* who only arrest the Montebellos when they hand themselves in, as Noel does to settle a score with the DCs. The protagonists at the centre of each series, Helen in *RAN* and Harry in *The Straits*, are both posed as originating from beyond the narrative places and both have some anxieties about their connections to the families that draw them to the islands. While Helen is respectfully repatriated at the conclusion of *RAN*, Harry is not going anywhere, and there is no escape from Queensland for a Montebello. Of the various symbols of the tropics pasted into its melodrama, family and crocodiles are aligned. As to the threat posed by either, crocodiles are nearly as prevalent throughout Far North Queensland and its wider region, as the wearing of thongs as footwear. The threat of family, on the other hand, is not factored by prevalence but by functionality. It is as much a source of the mystique of the unknown in *The Straits* as the territories trammelled by the Montebellos. In the focus on family and community, it has much in common with *RAN*, which does without crocodiles, and presents a more persuasive portrait of family as a central institution of culture in the Torres Strait.

In diverging ways, family persists as an aspect of the drama in the films in the next chapter. Like *The Straits* and *RAN*, family is barely subordinate to the spectacle of the setting but in a wholly different space of inland western Queensland.

Chapter 8

BACK TO THE BACK: GENRE QUEENSLAND AND WESTERNS IN WINTON

Filmakers [sic] welcome. Winton is a film friendly town. (Close 2015)

Film Acres

The western Queensland town of Winton recently has acquired a résumé as a centre for film production. A website details the several productions made or partly made since 2004, and proclaims the 'film friendliness' of Winton and its district.[1] Its film-historical past is acknowledged in a reference to the production of *Bushranging in North Queensland* in 1904 (see Introduction). The annual 'Vision Splendid Outback Film Festival', held in the town's historic outdoor cinema, celebrates the growing attention of the film industry to the region. The 'vision splendid' alludes to Banjo Patterson's poem, 'Clancy of the Overflow', about a shearer in the outback. It bespeaks the attractions of heritage culture and landscape spectacle and the role of the region in settler history, in grazing and agriculture. Like all small towns in remote regions, Winton's economy is prone to fluctuations due to the effects of droughts or floods, and other fortunes.[2] For some years, Winton, along with a number of similar towns in western Queensland, has attracted tourism to its extraordinary archive of dinosaur fossil finds in the region. Its reception of the film industry represents another stage in diversification of its economy.

The production that stimulated this rebirth of Winton as a film town in 2004 was *The Proposition*. It is listed on the website in the gallery of the mounting number of domestic and international productions since, and it is one of the focal films of this chapter, along with the more recent production of *Mystery Road*, which will be followed up by *Goldstone* (Sen 2016).[3] These films exploit the stark landscapes that surround Winton, rather than the town itself, for the resemblance to the landscapes of the classic American Western. Among other (non-Western) titles is the outback thriller *Gone*

(Ledwidge 2006), and a heritage title, *Banjo and Matilda* (O'Neill, forthcoming), is currently in production about the writing of the folk song 'Waltzing Matilda', which is believed to have been first performed in Winton in the 1890s. The producer, Bill Leimbach, claims he was considering locations in Broken Hill, New South Wales, when he was contacted by the mayors of Winton, Longreach and Townsville to make the film in Queensland where it 'belongs' (Lewis 2013).

Press coverage of these various productions predominantly focusses on the economic benefits to Winton and its neighbouring hamlets, especially the nexus between film-making and the seasonal economics of tourism. 'Every small town wants to create a point of difference for itself, something to pitch to tourists to encourage them to stay a day or two, spend some money and hopefully create some local jobs' (Lewis 2013). Film-making is seen as supplementing the tourism economy at the quieter times of the year. '"[E]very time that Winton is shown as a location it's almost like an advertisement to wave the flag and tell the world about Winton as a tourist destination,"' according to John Elliott, Winton Shire Council's tourism and events manager (quoted in Moore 2015). Elliott highlights the 'momentum' gained from earlier productions, and the action of governments, state and local, to '"generate film making into an area"' (quoted in Moore 2015). One article suggests a mildly surreal sense of the boom in prospects in the news that a set built for *Goldstone* in the tiny community of Middleton, 170 kilometres west of Winton, with a population of three people, had brought employment to the town. This arrived, according to producer David Jowsey, '"with all the transportation, the accommodation, with the buying of resources – we are spending all the money out here basically [...] Locally we are probably employing some 50 people, many of those will be actors and cast in the film"' (quoted in Arthur 2015b).

Also pronounced in reportage is alignment of the region with the masculine semiotics of film Westerns. Of Middleton, Jowsey says: '"[I]t looks like a little old town in the mid-west of America really,"' a town that '"Clint Eastwood might ride into"', but '"it just happens to be in the middle of [...] outback Queensland"' (quoted in Arthur 2015b). The local publican of Middleton comments that he had always thought the place would suit a Western because of its resemblance to 'Monument Valley', with the '"flat top hills with the straight sides,"' which are '"pretty arid and it looks pretty harsh now"' (quoted in Arthur 2015b). He observes that, '"if John Wayne knew this country was here, he would come back and make one more movie, just for old time's sake"' (quoted in Arthur 2015b). This uncanny recollection of Wayne, long deceased, in the perceived boomtime of a community numbering three persons, gestures to the paradoxical conflation of nostalgia and prospect that is also immanent in Winton's publicity for its film-production assets.

Among the 'infrastructure' touted on film-friendly Winton's website are a selection of natural and engineered assets (they do not mention Internet access). Along with 'mechanical repairs', 'ample water supplies', 'Tyre store', 'waterholes', 'outback flora and fauna', 'road trains', the 'Diamantina Truck Museum', 'water bores' and 'windmills', is a unique cultural icon, the 'musical fence' (Close 2015). This playable instrument, iconic of the pastoral identity of the region, has not to date been featured in any fiction film, although it is occasionally featured in documentary television. Fences, moreover, are ubiquitous elements of pastoral landscapes in Australia (and elsewhere), and carry a sinister resonance in *The Proposition* and *Mystery Road*. Fences pose a distinct trope in these films when coupled with another of Winton's natural assets that might well be added to the infrastructure listed on the website, the spectacular horizon lines so prominently figured in *The Proposition* and *Mystery Road*.

If fences suggest the finiteness of property, horizon lines evoke a sense of infinite. In the Western genre, Melinda Szaloky argues, horizon lines visually trope diverging quests, for (national) myths of origin and eschatological quest, and sometimes, in postmodern adaptations, the illusoriness of either (2001). In the Western, horizons frame the frontier and 'mark the fringes of the impenetrable "beyond"' that 'obsess' the genre (Szaloky 2001, 64). In *The Proposition* and *Mystery Road*, the trope of horizon is adapted with the accompanying figure of the fence. These images play together in dialogue with the genre conventions of the Western and the landscape aesthetic of Australian cinema in films that contain some of the more potent portrayals of race relations in recent years.

Horizons of Genre

As outlined earlier (in the Introduction to this book), the approach to these films is premised in Jaikumar's account of 'the colonial place as unproblematic backdrop' in British imperial films of the post-war years. Jaikumar (2001, 2006) points to the break in this tendency in British films in which the imperial subject is disturbed or agitated by the colonial place, no longer a backdrop and cannot be ignored. Something comparable occurs in *The Proposition*, and more so in *Mystery Road*, where landscape is deployed to expose the blight of *terra nullius*; and to provoke attention to land, that substance that is somehow evaded in the landscape aesthetic of Australian cinema. If playful excess characterises the regional semiotics of *The Straits* (see previous chapter), then purposeful excess more describes the deployment of landscape in *The Proposition* and *Mystery Road*.

The effect is rendered as parody of the conventions of the Western, and of the landscape aesthetic of Australian cinema. It is in contrast with the sentimental nationalism of landscape in films like *The Irishman* or the exoticism of *Jedda* (see Introduction). By parody, however, Linda Hutcheon's account of postmodern parody is intended. The conventions of the Western are not ridiculed in these films, but attention is drawn through parody as 'critical distance' that signals the 'difference at the heart of similarity', to adapt Hutcheon (1988, 27). The effect in *The Proposition* is to deconstruct the landscape myth by confronting the 'splendour-image of the landscape' with the 'action-image of [colonial] violence' (Collins 2008, 65–66). In *Mystery Road*, the cowboy detective, Jay Swan (Aaron Pederson), explicitly questions the ownership of the land in the spectacle, seen stretching eerily to the horizon. Both films appropriate and subvert the sign of pastoral settlement, the fence, in insinuating the colonial legacy and racial divisions that have resulted. In *The Proposition* the gaze is led to fence lines and horizon lines that suggest the dimensions of settler and outlaw communities. In *Mystery Road*, views of fences accompany the hero's encounters with racism in pastoral spaces. Diurnal rhythms adumbrate the action and the spectacles of horizons. The conventions of Western and film noir are threaded together through Swan, the cowboy detective, and his relationships to women in the community. Although these films do not directly revise the masculine associations of the genres, the play with conventions highlights perspectives on colonialism and its ongoing impact through the lens of gender and race.

Australian adaptation of the Western is not new. Peter Limbrick argues that the Western has been appropriated in various national cinemas for decades because it represents 'a settler colonial mode of cinema' that is part of a cultural project of 'grounding white settler cultures within colonised landscapes' (2007, 69). This is not simply mimicry or appropriation of 'an exclusively American frontier mythology' but concerns the 'negotiation of the tensions and contradictions of building "home" in a disputed space, the demarcation of territory between European settlers and indigenous inhabitants' (70). But he emphasises the significance of the site in which the Western is retold. The 'white cottages and fenced paddocks' of the Australian 'cattle duffer' and 'bushranger' films of the early twentieth century signify 'the successful demarcation of space' in landscapes already colonised (Limbrick 2010, 102). Pre–World War II films, *Girl of the Bush* (Barrett 1921) and *The Squatter's Daughter* (Hall 1933), established the 'racialised nature of the outback, and set white settlers, Aboriginals, Chinese, and even Afghans in asymmetrical relations of gender, sexuality, labor, and property' (Limbrick 2010, 102). The post-war films made by Ealing Studios in Australia, *Bitter Springs* and *The Overlanders*, also adapted the Western but '[rewrote] white conquest as peaceful coexistence' (87).

Subjectivity, space and (white) masculinity are seamlessly aligned in Limbrick's account of the Western as settler cinema. In the classic (American) Western, the associations of land underpin the traditional centrality of male protagonists, and the marginality of women, according to Jane Tompkins. The classic Western emphasises the importance of manhood as an ideal, and pursuit of the ideal is a spiritualised quest that concerns death and transcendence that is marked in the landscape. To 'go west' is to die; death, she says, 'is everywhere' in the Western and the death is transfigurative and ritualised (1992, 17–24). The arid landscapes figure this transfigurative potential, where (white) men may dominate women, animals, and each other but nature is the 'one thing larger than man' and it is 'constantly portrayed as immense' through the figure of landscape (72).

The relationship between land and gender in the classic Western is regarded in a diverging account by Virginia Wright Wexman. For her, the myths of origin of the (American) nation results in a 'fundamental contradiction' between 'a wilderness that fosters a noble individualism and the advent of a desired civilisation that is [...] accompanied by a less-heroic regime of socialisation and domestication' (1993, 70). The myth of the frontier is used to focus on race and on the danger 'hostile Indians' pose to '"our women"' (101). But what is most at issue, she argues, is 'not the right to possess women but the right to possess land' (75). This idea of the Western envisages the bucolic landscape, where the setting is 'animated by the placid movements of horses, wagon trains, or cattle' and where the presence of domestic animals 'ties [...] the European intruders into the landscape in a bucolic portrait of people whose activities are harmoniously integrated with nature' (78). Accordingly, the genre's 'ideal of the family farm' is nostalgic for 'the dynastic model of marriage' which is understood not as 'individual emotional fulfilment but as an economic partnership, the object of which is to make use of land to build a patrimony for future generations' (81). It is often contaminated by the rivalries of brothers (82). Dynastic marriage is associated with 'separate spheres for men and women' and contrasting ways of being: men 'domineering' and 'unsentimental'; women 'loyal, self-effacing and submissive' (82). If romance is marginal, marriage, she says, is central to the Western (83).

The women in these feminist accounts of the classic Western are white women. While there is no suggestion that these specific ideas about gender and the Western are explicitly addressed, they can inform the connections raised between genre, gender and land and the effect of parody in *The Proposition* and *Mystery Road*.

The Gothic Backdrop in *The Proposition*

An account of the shoot appears in The Winton Herald: 'The Major having arranged his kinematograph camera, two pictures were taken. The first was a scene of fearful carnage, in which the passengers, including the ladies, were shot, and the mails rifled.' (From '1904 *Bushrangers in North Queensland*', n.d.)

It was just on 100 years after the making of the first bush-ranging film in Australia in Winton that *The Proposition* was made wholly on location in the same district. It was co-produced with international interests, written by the musician Nick Cave and directed by (the Queensland-born and Canadian-raised) John Hillcoat. Cave also composed the haunting musical score that accompanies the action. The filming of Cave's screenplay took place in late 2004 in locations around Winton in the withering, fly-ridden heat of summer.[4] Sets were constructed in nearby Bladensburg National Park and on private stations in the district, with the post-production set demolition apparently assisted by the combined forces of windstorms and termites. The punishing conditions befitted the tale of Captain Stanley (Ray Winstone), the grizzled British police officer assigned to the remote fictional town of Banyon, and his efforts to contain the vicious Irish bushranger Arthur Burns (Danny Huston) and his gang made up of his brothers Charlie (Guy Pearce) and Mikey (Richard Wilson) and offsiders Sam Stoat (Tom Budge) and Two-Bob (Tom E. Lewis), and Queenie (Leah Purcell).

The proposition of the title is made following the capture of two of the brothers. Stanley propositions Charlie to pursue and kill Arthur in exchange for his and Mikey's freedom, and he sets a deadline of fast-approaching Christmas. Charlie grimly agrees, but the decision is fraught with his residual family loyalty, tempered by awareness of Arthur's appalling violence and Charlie's mistrust of the police. Stanley proposes the bargain in a quest to 'civilise this place'. The place-to-be-civilised, the narrative place, is not Queensland but pre-Federation Australia, apparently minus state borders (although the 1870s setting post-dates the 1859 separation of Queensland from New South Wales[5]), an imperial terrain figured in Captain Stanley's words as this 'fresh hell'. The squalid little (fictional) town of Banyon is made to appear emblematic of the minute dent made by colonial 'civilisation'. The sustained and lingering images of western Queensland not only reference the landscapes of Westerns, but bespeak the abject colonial context of *terra nullius* that pervades Cave's screenplay, in his attempt to expose a history of black resistance to settler violence, a depiction he perceived as an 'absence' in earlier films.[6]

Yet history is elusive in Westerns.[7] Bushrangers replace cowboys in *The Proposition*, although bushrangers were little known in this region of Queensland.[8] Carol Hart criticised the incorporation of historical photographs in the credit sequences of *The Proposition*, seeing this as pastiche in its blending of fictionalised history and folklore (Hart 2005). Felicity Collins

(2008) regarded this approach as effective in articulating deeper and allegorical truths about the past. The figurative power of the landscape is critical to the allegory, and death pervades the landscapes of *The Proposition*, but in no transcendent way, like Tompkins's idealised template.

The Burns brothers embody the risk of brotherly rivalry as the threat of fratricide, and the dead are everywhere in *The Proposition*. Human and animal corpses appear in many scenes, imposing a sense of moribund futility on Captain Stanley's quest to civilise the place. The squalid mining community of Banyon grotesquely parodies the bucolic agrarian myth as the placid wagon trains of Wexman's description transmute to prison wagons, in which brutalised criminals and enslaved Aborigines are rolled into town. The economics of Banyon are subordinated to a struggle over the means of civility and justice, which thinly conceals the deep divisions of two acute racial conflicts that permeate the imaginary community and hence the view of colonial Australia: between Indigenous people and white settlers, and between English authorities and Irish bushrangers. The grotesque English bounty hunter, Lams (John Hurt), who is familiar with Darwin's *Origin of the Species*, makes vile jokes, describing the Irish as 'niggers inside out', drawing together the dual racial conflicts British colonialism introduced to the place.

Fence lines and horizon lines are hauntingly incorporated into the mise-en-scène staking out the mythic borders between the terrain of Stanley's governance and the 'fresh hell' beyond, the vast territory inhabited by bushrangers and Aboriginals. Horizon lines rim the arid territory in which Charlie searches for Arthur. Numerous vivid and largely still or postcard-like images of sunsets and horizon-trimmed landscapes suggest the liminality of the town and the wider territory of the villainous Arthur Burns. Landscape is made sentient and haunted by the evocative song lyrics that play over Charlie's journey towards Arthur. The abject ambience of convict Australia and *terra nullius* is iterated through the explicit images of violence. Jon Fortgang senses the influence of Sam Peckinpah in the 'visceral' violence, and David Stratton found some passages 'unwatchable' (Pomeranz and Stratton 2005). Stephen Gaunson associates this violence with the bush-ranging genre, observing that *The Proposition* revives the 'blood, gore and depravity' that led to the banning of bush-ranging films in the early twentieth century (2010, 92).

The element of strong violence also refigures a key trope of the American Western. While shoot-outs form the climax in most Westerns, Tompkins argues this goes to the performative competencies of the cowboy. In *The Proposition*, gun-slinging is less featured, as people are flogged, kicked, beaten, knifed and shot to death. The director, Hillcoat, reflected that 'nation building is founded on violence [...] we definitely wanted to look at [...] how it actually affects people' (quoted in Pomeranz 2005). In production, there was a certain continuity between themes and history, as *The Proposition* was subject to legal requirements arising from the Queensland government's Aboriginal Cultural Heritage Act 2003 (which was apparently aimed at the mining industry). Pearl Eatts, a cultural induction officer, advised the cast and crew on issues of cultural sensitivity and directed the production away from a site in which an historical massacre of Indigenous people is believed to have occurred (Bush TV 2004). Awareness of landscape and a sense of colonial place therefore converged in the film's production and mise-en-scène.

The civility Stanley desires to impose is embodied by his genteel wife, Martha (Emily Watson). Her visits to town are discouraged, and when she appears in the squalid township, her opulent garments and genteel bearing mark her as an outsider. Their homestead dwelling, with a colonial 'homesick garden' of roses, and surrounded by a bush picket fence, is an oasis of civility out of town. At home in their bedchamber or taking breakfast on the veranda, Captain and Mrs Stanley appear to live Wexman's agrarian myth, reminiscent of outback pioneers. But they are childless with no prospect of patrimony, and the 'homesick garden' is a travesty of Eden. Martha's infertility is emphasised through her affinity with the murdered Eliza Hopkins and her unborn baby. In a key scene, directly following the violent murders of Jacko (David Gulpilil) and the sergeant (Robert Morgan), Martha, recalls to Stanley a dream in which Eliza's unborn child grasps her finger. Stanley, too emotional to respond, secures the house again, an isolated and flimsy barricade surrounded by the stark fence. As Christmas approaches, Toby (Rodney Boschman), the Aboriginal servant in the Stanley house, heads back to country, removing his shoes before passing through the picket gate.

The bushrangers strike the house on Christmas Day. Arthur, accompanied by Sam Stoat, breaches the flimsy dwelling, and Martha is raped on the table amidst the festive fare, while Stanley, with Union Jack wrapped around his head, is beaten senseless in the adjoining room. It is a gruesome parody of Christmas in the bush and the Nativity, prefigured by the insubordinate staff of Stanley's jail subversively singing the 'Twelve Days of Christmas'. But Charlie comes through, arriving and firing on Arthur and Stoat. Fatally injured, Arthur departs through the homesick garden until he sits to die, facing away from fence and horizon. The quest of the proposition is completed, and Stanley is vindicated, but at a price, and there is no reflection on how this grisly conclusion transforms the quest for civility. If the fence figures the ineffectual defence against the forces of violence, horizon promises no dawn but lingers as a gloomy, gothic image of the violence of colonialism. With its period style and pastiche code, *The Proposition* parodies the Western and paints a disturbing picture of the past. But in its violent resolution, it does not transform the implications for Indigenes or settlers. This is in contrast to *Mystery Road*, where the cowboy is an agent of change.

The Detective in the Backdrop in *Mystery Road*

> Bitumen road to Brisbane, Townsville, Longreach, Mt Isa etc. (Close 2015)

The figure of the cowboy is often, as Sarina Pearson suggests, seen as 'paradigmatic of cinema's imperial legacy' through the 'genre's tendency to reaffirm the dominance of white masculinity at the expense of Indigenous people' (2013, 161). In historical colonial sites in Oceania, she argues, cowboys in early Westerns embodied a 'masterfully masculine corporeality' regarded as 'objects of affection, desire and empowerment, as well as contradiction and ambivalence' (161–62). She emphasises the 'attention to the cowboy's body and its gestural archive', and contends that recognition of Indigenous attitudes towards the cowboy 'paradoxically demands the recognition and remembrance of colonial cultures and practices' (161).

This commentary resonates with *Mystery Road*, which is readily recognised as an adaptation of the Western, and more subtly as a hybrid of Western and neo-noir, or, as coined, 'outback noir' (Blatchford 2013a; 2013b). The Western genre frame of *Mystery Road* has been received as either 'ironic' or as an adaptation of the 'iconography' of the Western (Harkins-Cross 2014), and Dolgopolov says it 'dances with genre' and Jay Swan is a 'superhero' (2013, 10). But while the treatment is pastiche, the scenario is not ironic or playful. Jay Swan, the cowboy detective, is a stirring portrait of a man of Aboriginal heritage who, as a senior detective, returns to his remote hometown to investigate the murder of a teenage girl, Julie Mason, a member of the local Indigenous community, whom he knows as a friend of his daughter. A 'Lone Ranger' type (12), Swan is unmistakably iconic with his Stetson (Akubra) and hip gunholster, and doubly armed with his police-issue (silver) automatic pistol and his late father's Winchester hunting rifle. But he rides no horse and is accompanied by no Tonto. His efforts to detect the culprits in the murder are conducted mostly alone because his senior officer denies him resources (telling him to 'ride bareback'), and effectively any priority to solving the case. His peers all appear to be implicated in the malevolent network responsible for the death, and apparently connected to a corrupt undercover police drug operation.

Also conspiring against his efforts of detection are the Indigenous community members who see him as a black tracker, commandeered to do the work of white authorities. An Aboriginal child, Marbuk (Michael Connors), asks: 'You a copper, bro? We kill coppers, bro.' He mimes shooting. This view is expressed in more explicitly racist terms by the white citizens Farmer Bailey (David Field) and Pete (Ryan Kwanten), his son, who eventually prove to be involved in the murder. *Mystery Road* might be an 'epic revision of the black tracker narrative' (Dolgopolov 2013, 13; and see Rutherford 2015, 313). But it seems a red herring because Swan is more than a tracker, he is a deliverer of justice, and a force for reconstruction of the dysfunctional community, and mindful of his own survival of dysfunction. Neither is the tracker story supported by Sen's comments, who speaks in interview of how Swan has more in common with a pen-pushing bureaucrat than the 'tracker' or 'trooper', someone who knows the system and tries to make a difference (Luskri 2013). Jay Swan has an 'agenda' to make a difference (Luskri 2013). Moreover, Sen's comments about the film suggest that the Western genre was suggested to him by the potential of the Winton landscapes as locations.

Landscape and remote towns are intertextual signs in Sen's cinema.[9] But *Mystery Road* was originally conceived as a metropolitan procedural about a detective working in his own community (Luskri 2013). In an interview, Sen explains that he sought to combine attention to Indigenous teenage girls, like those from his home community in Moree in New South Wales (Luskri 2013). He seems to have had a pastoral setting in mind – he mentions that he considered shooting the film in cotton-growing areas of Moree. Sen's concern that the resulting film might overly resemble his previous film, *Toomelah* (Sen 2011), which was set and filmed in Moree, combined with his encounter with the landscape in western Queensland, he says, culminated in the turn to the Western genre, and the setting for the production, although it is fictionalised as an unnamed town (that might or might not be in Queensland).[10]

The Winton locations, however, are iconic of Swan's quest. The arid landscapes represent the place that his family lived after moving from a mission. His father was a head stockman in the district, and Jay's first memory is on his father's horse on a station. These details of his past come to light in Swan's conversation with the paternalistic sergeant (Tony Barry) as they size up a horse across a paddock fence while the sergeant observes his grandchildren riding a pony. It seems innocent, bucolic. Yet, Jay, the cowboy detective, is subordinately figured in the pastoral landscape, still on his father's horse but riding 'bareback', like an Indian. Out of town, the road signs connote histories of genocide in the same landscape, 'Massacre Creek' where the murder victim's body is found; 'Slaughter Hill' where Jay's showdown occurs with the druglords, a 're-visioning of the Mexican stand-off' (Dolgopolov 2013). Thus the 'featureless' (13) landscape is brought to life by signs that connote the violent history which is otherwise invisible, even if its legacy persists in the present action. In this landscape, the cowboy detective's authority is treated with contempt as he confronts racism and the indifference of the police and the community towards the fate of the murdered girl.

In a bleak way, like Wexman's account of the dynastic Western, Swan's dysfunctional world could not function without women. Nor could its mystery be unravelled entirely without the blending of neo-noir and Western codes. The fatal trail of *Mystery Road* leads to a series of teenage girls, all connected in some way to the murder victim. These various femmes fatale or ingénues defy the traces of John Wayne in the look-a-like Western landscape. The circle of teenage girls who are the 'dramatic core' of the film (Dolgopolov 2013, 10), are also targets of the same racist and corrupt system, and the most disturbing witnesses to the racist dysfunction afoot in the town. One of them is Swan's own daughter, Crystal (Tricia Whitton). Harkins-Cross compares her to youth in earlier Sen films, like *Beneath Clouds* (2002), for the way 'it's nearly impossible for Crystal to break out of these destructive cycles' (2014). Various characters, Mary (Tasma Walton), his ex-wife, Johnno (Hugo Weaving), his grungy colleague, and a criminal, Wayne (Damien Walshe-Howling) taunt Swan about his commitment to his daughter.

Sexual and racial difference govern the space of authority in the town. The police world is a white man's world. Roads are iconic channels of masculine power in the landscape. It seems no coincidence that the film is named for one, Mystery Road. The highway is the space of sexual exploitation of the drug-addicted girls, and the arteries for the drug trade, which 'seems to be the town's only thriving industry' (Harkin-Cross 42). The mysterious death of Swan's deceased colleague, Bobby Rogers, occurred on the highway. The coroner (Bruce Spence) creeps out to the murder site in his spruce, vintage Holden vehicle. The drug lords drive around in a dated gold Holden Statesman, iconoclastically in contrast with the contemporary police four-wheel-drive that conveys Johnno, Swan's ambiguous peer, and the hunting muscle-truck that houses the sinister Pete Bailey's super-dogs. Youthful men drive contemporary cars, older men drive retro cars. It is not a strict guide to goodies and baddies but suggests the hierarchy of the highway in *Mystery Road*.

Swan pounds the earth in his detective practice and swivels around in his car. During his traversal of the fatal highway, back and forth to the crime scene, around town to his contacts and sitting out in surveillance, his car is his cover and becomes his shield when the shootout gets underway. Swan is seen intermittently at his desk, receiving updates on a landline from his one ally, the coronial pathologist, whose telephone calls convey the off-screen action of the post-mortem on the victim that helps piece together her fate. Meanwhile, the youth of the community, wired through texts and photographs on mobiles, surreptitiously or inadvertently slip clues to Swan.

Amidst the traffic of the case, the landscape figures vividly, its horizons illuminated by a diurnal rhythm that calibrates the narrative. Dolgopolov speaks of the 'endless horizons that are so prevalent in the film' (2013, 14); Harkins-Cross notes the cultural connotations of the 'ochre' coloured light that 'stains the dimming horizon' (2014). Key events occur at dawn and dusk when those horizons are most vivid: the discovery of the body occurs at dawn; Swan's possible reconciliation with his family occurs at deep sunset, or 'twilight' (Harkins-Cross 42). The shootout takes place at something like high noon. The pattern is internally parodied in the 'Dusk till Dawn' Hotel. Swan is directed there in his investigation by Jasmine (Angela Swan) because a missing girl used to meet a whitefella there. The receptionist (Zoe Carides) is helpful: she remembers the car.

By broad daylight the landscape is just as haunted and disturbing in the pastoral setting. Swan's two interviews with his key suspects, Mr Bailey and his son, Pete, are accompanied by vision of property fencing and a sense of the wasteland of patrimony. His tense interview with Mr Bailey takes place pointedly across a stockyard fence.[11] Bailey is evasive and says he has sheep to drench, but no animals are seen. 'Are you a real copper or one of them black trackers who turns on his own type?' Bailey asks the question and then spits on the ground. 'No disrespect intended.' Swan responds with a question. 'How much land you got here, Mr Bailey?' 'Far as you can see', replies Bailey. 'That's a lot of dirt', says Swan, and 'your children'll have a pretty good future, won't they? You're a lucky man.' In a subsequent scene, the child, the son, Pete, greets Swan equally disparagingly, as the tracking vision of fence line gives way to Swan's point of view on Pete on his shabby verandah. 'You that Abo copper?', he asks. Pete reveals that he's a 'roo shooter' and that he runs the 'meat freezer' in town. He says that 'we shoot uninvited fellas, specifically ones of the dark breed'. Pete reports that his father, Bailey, is out 'droving', but there is no sign of livestock, only the hunting dogs chained in the truck. It is not the death-strewn landscape of *The Proposition*; there is no sign of an active pastoral industry at all. The stockyards and fences that enter the frame are residual, even ghostly, markers of the history of the region, like the road signs that mark the massacres of the past. Even the wild dogs, the roaming metaphor of predation, are not visible, except for the scarring left on the bodies of the murder victims.

For all the tension of *Mystery Road*, there is tender optimism in the conclusion. Jay, seasoned by the rambling counsel of elderly Mr Murray (Jack Thompson), and by his own near demise in the shootout, seems destined for reconciliation with Crystal and his ex-wife, Mary. In the fading twilight of another vivid horizon, he meets with them on a roadside, not in a property. This ending recalls the road as a space of interval (Probyn-Rapsey 2006), and the conclusion of *Radiance* (see Chapter 3). It is hopeful and the future is essentially unknown. Sen speaks of the importance for the film and for the Indigenous youth who will view it to see Jay Swan 'comes home' to the 'family unit' (Luskri 2013). Obliquely, this speaks to Wexman's thesis on the dynastic Western. Swan's success as a cowboy and as a detective inverts the outcome of the plot of patrimony, and benefits the dispossessed members of the community. Crystal's future holds some dim promise signalled by the reunion with Swan at the vanishing point where the land in the fenced properties and the horizons of colonial history meet. But the day is entering dusk when this occurs in *Mystery Road*.

Land and region pervade *Mystery Road* and carry over into the experience of the director and star in their recollections of the production. Sen says the role of Swan was written for Aaron Pederson, and that their combined perspectives on the challenges of family 'dysfunction' in Indigenous communities was a strength of the production (Luskri 2013). Both Sen and Pederson have spoken of the bond they formed in the production, and how it was established and sealed in an extended reconnoitre in the landscape seeking locations (Blatchford 2013b; Luskri 2013). Aaron says: "'We went for a drive. [...] We checked our locations; pretty much lived out of each other's pockets for ten days. We became brothers in arms. We actually didn't talk about the script much [...] we got to the same place when it came to making this film. [...] We talked about a lot of personal stuff – we just made a connection'" (quoted in Blatchford 2013b). Sen recalls that it was important for Aaron as an actor 'to know the land that the character's going to walk on' (Luskri 2013).

In the basic plot that brings an Aboriginal man back to his home town, and in the concluding reunion with his estranged family, and in the revisioning of the landscape of violence, the trope of return is deep in *Mystery Road*. It is amplified in the context of the revisiting of outback settings in the Westerns in Winton. Pederson's skilful adaptation of the 'gestural archive' of the cowboy, and the strategic way this retro figure is inserted into the complex challenges of modern Indigenous communities compares positively with the outcomes of the bush-ranging plot of *The Proposition*. Distanced by period, *The Proposition* illustrates an obscure and haunting history. By comparison, the re-enactment of the cowboy in *Mystery Road* is more than merely a pastiche spectacle of subversion.

In a way, too, the masculinity of the Western genre is reclaimed in both of these films to moral purpose, in Charlie Burns's judgement on his vile brother, Arthur, that vindicates Stanley's methods, and in Jay Swan's triumph over the corrupt police and drug lords. Swan triumphs not only because he wins the shootout, but as a superior moral entity, a better man. The fate of the young woman murder victim is a grim scenario, but in her connection to Swan's daughter and the promise of Swan's reconciliation with Crystal, it becomes a story of the possibility of change. If the cowboy 'constitutes a complex site around which political critique, corporeal desire and modern spectacle coalesce' (Pearson 2013, 153), Jay Swan enables a sense of how this complexity is also figured in a space marked by the fenced history of colonialism and transfigured by the overarching image of horizon that frames the land as far as can be seen.

Queensland Unfenced

As for Winton, it is another case study in the transitional economies of regions, the profound illusion of place in cinema, and yet another instance of the passage of nature to culture in the wake of film production in Queensland. The issues raised in these films extend far beyond Queensland. The iconic landscapes of Winton have the power to convey meaning that resonates in regional, national and transnational imaginaries and to garner attention to these issues in specific localities or wider settings. The singing fence resounds far beyond the horizons around Winton.

CONCLUSION

ON LOCATION IN QUEENSLAND

The excitement generated by productions like *Mystery Road* exudes in publicity for its follow up film, *Goldstone*. 'We are seeing a whole new "Queensland-genre" film mixed with outback western grit and characters who survive in our tough yet spectacular outback terrain. *Goldstone* showcases the very best in Queensland storytelling, craftsmanship and, indeed, our unique cultural diversity and voice on screen,' says the CEO of Screen Queensland, Tracey Vieira (quoted in Press Release 2015). The praise is fully warranted for Ivan Sen, except that it is not for Sen, it is for Queensland. It is no slight to Winton or to Sen to observe, as the previous chapter shows, that the same film was nearly set in Moree. In fact, some of it was filmed in Moree, which, in any case, sits very close to the border between Queensland and New South Wales. *The Proposition* was made in Winton in preference to Bourke in New South Wales.

The competition for film spaces goes back much further than this to *Buddies* (see Introduction), for instance, which was made in Queensland in preference to South Australia, and South Australia won out for *Bitter Springs* over Queensland (Verhoeven 2006). There are stories, too, of the local film-makers who could not make their films in Queensland and had to go elsewhere (see Craven 2013). Ivan Sen, moreover, is a case study in how these distinctions of state-based identity can be arbitrary and fluid. He is not usually identified as a Queenslander, although his birthplace, the small community of Toomelah, is on the state border and he spent his early life 'about 60kms upstream in […] Queensland', and later lived in Tamworth and Inverell, in New South Wales (Mills 2015).[1] While he acknowledges the impact of the Winton landscape on the development of his script for *Mystery Road*, Queensland's contribution is mainly infrastructure, in the form of locations, and the local impetus of the townspeople and local authorities (see Chapter 8). Attribution of all the 'storytelling', 'craftsmanship' and 'cultural diversity' and 'voice' to Queensland suggests a consuming influence of infrastructure.

Vieira's excitement is more the exuberance of the state in cultivating identity as a brand. Queensland now appears in dozens of movies as the source of locations and place of production. Vieira's praise begs the question of what exactly Queensland represents in films made in its locations. It is a challenge to objectify Queensland so confidently, so diverse are its dimensions and when a place, like a state or region, gains presence in a film through the collaborative processes of interests that might or might not be fundamentally connected to it. Rachel Perkins memorably speaks of coming to Queensland for the 'atmosphere' when she made *Radiance* (see Chapter 3). The setting of 'North Queensland' is a general one in *Radiance* and the places of production skim away from the actual region (see Chapter 3) in a way that foils local knowledge, even the anachronism of the burning cane. But the ubiquitous sugar cane fields that stretch throughout large tracts of coastal Queensland are taken for granted as iconic of the north, even though it is a crop grown in multiple regions, and in other states. Sugar cane is not unique to Queensland.

Perhaps the historical strength of the sugar industry, and the relative size of it, broadcast in *The Cane Cutters* (see Introduction), coalesces with the visual imagining in a film like *Radiance*, or perhaps it is the contradiction of industry in the holiday tropics that clinches the iconography to Queensland rather than other places, or the lurking memory of the practices that exploited labour from the Pacific region. Whether prosperous or insidious, the associations of sugar cane as a localised spectacle signifies Queensland as an international competitor in a global industry. It is something of a mirror to the film industry, or the aspirations at least, of what it has lately become. The resonances of sugar cane in fiction film speak, too, to the equation of space with cultural products, and how it is not unique in the creative industries. Conversely, locations as commodity in Queensland suggest how the production of film is akin to a form of primary industry, and faces comparable challenges and cycles of prosperity. But film locations are elusive once a production is concluded. It is a challenge to retrace the precise locations of a film, and so the general locations become the reference points. This does not deny the colonial frame of a settler place and the relevance of land in every act of film production, even in the controlled and privatised world of a studio environment.

Retracing film locations moves the premise of this book as 'backtracking' through visions of Queensland, where 'backtracking' has connotations of moving back through changed territory. The changes are marked by the dramatic growth of capacity for film production, and the heightened consciousness of Indigenous rights and interests in the perspectives presented in the films, and owing, at least symbolically, to the influence of Native Title. Queensland emerges in *The Irishman* (in Chapter 1) as a symbolisation of Australia, anchored in its provenance as an AFC film, and in spite of its production affiliations with Queensland and South Australia. The place of its making and the regional signs of Queensland are visible but muted in the heritage discourse of the film.

The profile of Australia in the national cinema is one that derives national identity from localised spaces. The stereotyping lens of nationalist cinema is shown in *Jedda* and *The Irishman*, in Chapter 2, to literally dub a view of the place and the people that has specific resonances for the historical silence of Indigenous people in the conjunction of industrial and cultural forces.

Queensland in the abstract has gained greater prominence in the film industry in the years since these films, as the domestic industry has grown and become more transnationalised. The space of paradise in Queensland continues in iteration as largely associated with the coastal tropics and islands, especially in Far North Queensland (see Chapters 3, 4 and 7). Long championed in state-aligned practices, the myth continues in the 2015 government-sponsored *Paradise through Your Lens* tropical North Queensland marketing campaign that attracted international competitors for a large cash prize (Jones 2015). Tropical paradise still derives meaning from natural phenomena and notions of aesthetics influenced by the colonial imaginings of the South Seas. It seems more important than ever to highlight the counter-discourse that emerges in *Radiance* (Chapter 3) where paradise is only for some. It is reiterated in *The Tall Man* (Krawitz 2011), based on Chloe Hooper's book of the same title about the death in police custody of an Indigenous resident of Palm Island. Palm Island is the former place of detention for displaced Indigenous people that lies a short distance off Townsville in North Queensland. It is a unique community with a presence in regional literature and film (see Taylor 2009). The tagline of *The Tall Man*, 'life in Paradise, death in custody', knowingly alludes to the sinister side of the holiday tropics. As one reviewer observed, 'The contrast between the shots of violence and the cutaways to serene landscapes is heart-stopping.'[2]

Constructions of paradise are unstable in settler tales, too, as seen through the eyes of the characters in the films discussed in Chapter 4. The paradise desired as escape by the artist Bradley Morahan in *Age of Consent* is a place Cora longs to leave. The holiday paradise of *Uninhabited* is reflexive of the historical context of exploitation of islanders in the uncanny gaze of the vengeful, resident ghost, Coral. Nim's Island is a pastiche outpost where the Queenslanders are unwanted. The objectification of Queensland, the Torres Strait and Papua New Guinea, in the scenic melodrama of the Australian South Seas films, is parodied in the monstrousness of the Montebellos in *The Straits*, and their identification with crocodiles that grotesquely reference the serpentine threat in the paradisiacal myth of Eden.

There is some irony that the naturalism of the settings in *Age of Consent* and *Uninhabited* are now spaces of heritage, although not in a directly comparable way to the heritage worlds of *The Irishman*. The Great Barrier Reef is a World Heritage site, and its preservation involves the cultivation of the mystique of its unchanging presence. But the Reef has transformed from 'Australian bush to generic ideal', according to Celmara Pocock, through the influence of colour visual media, where, in tourist literature, 'vegetative framing of photographs has given way overwhelmingly to the palm' in contrast to the predominant vegetation of casuarinas and she-oak trees, and their aromas and distinctive sighing sounds recorded in historical documents (Pocock 2002, 374–76). The various sensory qualities that imparted a sense of place to Reef visitors in the early twentieth century, she says, have been superseded by the visual spectacle of the Reef (379). The visual aestheticisation of the Reef and its islands is visible in the institutional documentaries (discussed in the Introduction) that adapted Hollywood narrative to documenting the nation. Subsequently these spaces emerged in fiction film allied with a feminine spectacle, as suggested in Chapter 4. Paradise through a lens is subject to more influences than only a local environment.

Setting plays a more subordinate role in the masculine dramas of the coast in Chapters 5 and 6. The cave of *Sanctum* is not especially aestheticised, nor is it paradise in the spectacle of adventure gone wrong (Chapter 6). The aim to suggest a glamourous lifestyle in *The Coolangatta Gold* (Chapter 5) is wholly upstaged by the localised domestic troubles of the central family in dissonance with the ambitious aims of the production and the formative role of the film that was envisaged in the process of state-building. While it was not received warmly at the time, *The Coolangatta Gold* does not seem such a bad film today, and the family melodrama, the rivalry of the brothers and the parental tensions, seems a fairly convincing 'slice of life', if a little over-dramatised. There is no doubt that the passion for sport and outdoor leisure is an abiding aspect of life for many middle-class Queenslanders, especially those who live on the coast. *The Coolangatta Gold* belongs to another time and another model of filmmaking compared to *Peter Pan*. Indeed, many films have since been made in the space of the hub that now exists on the Gold Coast, and my adoption of *Peter Pan* as the marker of the coming of age of the film industry on the Gold Coast is a tad arbitrary, although not unjustified. It serves a purpose in bringing to light the iconography of Queensland, its beaches and crocodiles in a film meant to transcend Queensland. Neverland becomes Queensland in *Peter Pan*, in a way that predicts the identity of its creative industries today.

In the 1990s, in the run-up to this era of industry flourishing, ambivalence about this kind of production hub was felt to risk production of 'global films' in which digital effects 'create imaginary cities or worlds that are ubiquitous rather than geographically located', and thus downgrading of 'national cinema into an offshore service industry for global Hollywood' (Collins and Davis 2004, 28–30). Others saw the potential for outward-looking production and growth of production infrastructure, including in sites in Queensland (O'Regan and Venkatasawmy 1999). This perspective has been vindicated since, and the range of films produced, only a few of which are discussed in this book, is not evidence of globalised dystopia. But the film industry, like any industry, is subject to currency and commodity flows, and its strength cannot be guaranteed, no matter how excited the sponsoring rhetoric. The appeal of the capacity to render the fantasy of the coastal tropics and marine culture, or the horizon lines of the interior, or the depths of a cave, still depends on significant support from the state, and so the industry of state-sponsored paradise will persist.

But Jay Swan is not Peter Pan, and it does not diminish the strength of social statement in films like *The Proposition* and *Mystery Road* (Chapter 8), which reflect the continuing relevance of cinema as a public sphere. *Mystery Road*, like *The Straits*, *RAN*, and *Radiance*, in varied ways, exhibits the 'aftershock' of Mabo and demonstrates the potential for entertainment media to speak to political concerns. Neither does this overwrite the lengthy history in Queensland (and elsewhere) of goodwill-based involvement of residents and regional authorities in the making of films in regional locations (see Chapters 1, 3 and 8). Participants in the past, in a film like *The Irishman*, did not identify their participation in an industry, but experienced the activity of film-making as a glamourous novelty. The goodwill now has become more strategic in Winton, where the residents have embraced the ideology of film-friendliness (Chapter 8) in the interests of economic stability of the town and region, or so it seems. The 'vision splendid', that 'spectacular' quality of the land that is attracting film production to Winton, is not the substance of what location means in Queensland or in any place.

Places in film and television are always in some way grounded in a place and in time, and what this means to people who consume or produce it reflects their differences, regional, racial and gendered. In the television productions of *The Straits* and *RAN* (Chapter 7), there is generous acknowledgement of regional and Island communities that participated in the productions, and there is evidence of reciprocal appreciation, while some viewers saw the vision of Cairns in *The Straits* as cynically aligned with a touristic rhetoric (Chapter 7). If the show had been made in another place masquerading as Far North Queensland, this criticism might not be levelled, or might take another form. Location production with the involvement of the local population inevitably stimulates the dynamics of the place in more ways than are apparent in the textual semiotics. It matters that it is Queensland, a construct in time and place, because, in spite of the ineffable propensities of film and television to suggest that somewhere is anywhere, location is land, even in Neverland.

NOTES

Introduction: Regional Features

1. See http://screenqld.reel-scout.com/loc_results.aspx.
2. This film was made two years before the *Story of the Kelly Gang* (Charles Tait 1906), which is thought to be the oldest Ned Kelly film (and regarded by some as the world's first feature film) (Gaunson 2010, 89).
3. The allusion might refer to either *Mutiny on the Bounty* (Lloyd 1935) or *Mutiny on the Bounty* (Milestone 1962). The former was made after the Australian film by Charles Chauvel, *In the Wake of the Bounty* (1933).
4. *Jedda*, it must be noted, was made largely in Central Australia, not in Queensland. It has slim connection to the state through the film-maker, Charles Chauvel, who was a Queenslander, and some of his films were made there. However, *Jedda* is discussed in this chapter more for the perspective it provides on *The Irishman* and with respect to the national cinema more generally.

1. Period Features, Heritage Cinema: Region, Gender and Race in *The Irishman*

1. In the audio commentary, Crombie gives the mayor's name as 'Tiger Brennan', who, in fact, was mayor of Darwin, Northern Territory, in the same period. Thanks to Michael Brumby, local historian at Charters Towers Library, for the mayor's name in 1978.
2. *Beneath Hill 60* was produced in Townsville with support from the City Council and warm encouragement from locals and press. Its central production unit was located in suburban Townsville, and key warfront scenes were shot in suburban locations. *Beneath Hill 60* is in the style of a number of earlier military period dramas, the main prototype of which is *Gallipoli* (Weir 1981). Support for *Beneath Hill 60* also benefitted from the defence profile of Townsville and its identity as a garrison city since the 1960s.

2. Heritage Enigmatic: The Silence of the Dubbed in *Jedda* and *The Irishman*

1. Thomas cites, for instance, Orson Welles's extensive use of both post- and pro-syncing as a creative project, as Welles himself apparently supplied the dubbed voices in a number of his films (Thomas 2000, 186).

3. Tropical Gothic and the Music of the Cane Fields in *Radiance*

1 The setting of *Radiance* as 'North Queensland' is barely qualified within either the play or the screenplay, and might at times bamboozle a North Queenslander. One of Nona's speeches in the play that is not transposed to the film tells how she once ran away to 'Ayr' to go to a rodeo in 'Rocky' (Rockhampton) and left a note for her mother saying she was going to 'Cairns' (Nowra 1993, 13; 2000, 18). Ayr is around 700 kilometres north of Rockhampton. It suggests, at least, that she lived much further north than the locations of the film.
2 See the explanation for this shift given by Nowra (2000, xi).
3 The burning of the house is an act of arson suggested by Mae but instigated mostly by Cressy. In the play, Mae has a history of stealing and is on a good behaviour bond. This lends criminality to her desire to burn the house, and Nona comments that she has 'a criminal mind', but this aspect of Mae is not transposed to the film.

4. Island Girls Friday: Women, Adventure and the Tropics

1 *Robinsonade* is the literary term for a narrative modelled on Robinson Crusoe's solo survival on an island in the eighteenth-century novel *Robinson Crusoe* by Daniel Defoe (see Maher 1988; Bristow 1991).
2 The scene was between James Mason, as Bradley, and Clarissa Kaye as Meg. They later married after meeting during the making of *Age of Consent*.
3 See also David Stratton's comments regarding the treatment of the Queenslanders in *At the Movies*, broadcast 2 April 2008, ABC Television.'

5. The Sunshine Boys: Peter Pan and the Iron Man in the Coastal Cinema of Queensland

1 See www.movieworldstudios.com.au/.
2 A succession of state agencies has supported film production and infrastructure in Queensland since the 1980s, beginning with the Queensland Film Corporation (QFC), then its replacement, the Queensland Film Development Office in 1988, which became Film Queensland in 1993, and, later, the Pacific Film and Television Commission (PFTC), and now Screen Queensland (Goldsmith et al. 2010, 167).
3 More recently, Goldsmith, Ward and O'Regan reflect on the role of De Laurentiis in the film industry on the Gold Coast, describing him as a 'risk-taking speculator, a gambler whose currency was images and stories' (2014, 71). They also quote an obituary published following De Laurentiis's death in 2010, in which he is referred to as a '"pirate captain"' (quoted in Goldsmith, Ward and O'Regan 2014, 70), although not framed within the Peter Pan myth.
4 Terry Jackman's career is more distinguished than this connection suggests. Goldsmith, Ward and O'Regan note that he was 'former head of Australian exhibitor Hoyts and the broker of the distribution deals for *Crocodile Dundee*' (2014, 72).
5 See http://sls.com.au/coolangattagold/event-info.
6 Latter-day sources, such as the DVD and film databases, list Auzin as director and name writers and producers. The film credits acknowledge an 'idea' from Max Oldfield, and 'story' from Ted Robinson and Peter Schreck. Auzin, Schreck and John Weily

are named in a corporate opening title, 'presents', in association with 'Michael Edgley International and Hoyts' (Auzin 1984).
7   The telemovie *Mermaids* (Barry 2003), the feature film *Aquamarine* (Allen 2006) and the pre-teen television series, *H20: Just Add Water* (Shiff 2006), all featuring mermaids, were partly filmed there.
8   Tiger Lily, the Redskin princess, is another of Barrie's precocious child characters and also the most orientalised, and Barrie's Redskins are a relic of imperial times, portrayed as axe-wielding goons. Tiger Lily is described as: 'the most beautiful of Dusky Dianas and the belle of the Picaninnies, coquettish, cold and amorous by turns; there is not a brave who would not have the wayward thing to wife, but she staves off the altar with a hatchet' (Barrie 1996, 58).
9   *Peter Pan* (Herbert Brenon 1924), where Peter is played by Betty Bronson.
10 Regarding the monkeys, see: http://www.theguardian.com/world/2015/feb/18/animal-rights-groups-condemn-plan-to-import-monkeys-for-pirates-film. Johnny Depp was warmly received in Queensland and participated generously in publicity for the production, interacting with fans and visiting the children's hospital in Brisbane (in costume as Captain Sparrow). However, controversy arose over Depp's spouse, Amber Heard, who is alleged to have imported their pet dogs in breach of the Australian Quarantine Act. Headlines were made when the federal minister charged with administering the Act, Barnaby Joyce, threatened to have the dogs put down if they did not leave the country by an appointed deadline. See www.theguardian.com/film/2015/nov/16/amber-heard-fails-to-turn-up-to-court-appearance-over-johnny-depps-dogs.

6. A Pacific Parable: Cave and Coastal Masculinities in *Sanctum*

1   New Guinea was also the setting for Alister Grierson's first feature film, *Kokoda* (2006), a drama set in World War II and also made in locations in Queensland.
2   Imdb.com also mentions the Cave of the Swallows, Mexico.
3   Pike and Cooper note that this film was purchased by Joseph E. Levine, 'embellished with additional jungle footage' and rereleased in the United States as *Walk into Hell* (1998, 222).
4   Several sources claim this joke. See 'Why no matches in the FedEx box?' http://money.cnn.com/2003/01/27/news/companies/superbowl_fedex/index.htm (2003), where it is said to have been scripted for a FedEx advertisement; and 'What was in the box with the angel wings?' an 'FAQ' entry at www.imdb.com/title/tt0162222/faq#.2.1.1 that attributes it to Zemeckis.

7. Unknown Queensland in Torres Strait Television: *RAN* and *The Straits*

1   *RAN* also attracted praise, and an award from an international centre, for its realistic portrayal of nurses on television (see Milner and Brigden 2014, 112).
2   Nearly 7,000 Torres Strait Islanders reside on the islands, and more than twice that number now live on the Australian mainland. See: www.abc.net.au/ra/pacific/places/country/torres_strait_islands.htm#facts; see further information on the website of the Torres Strait Islander Regional Council: www.tsirc.qld.gov.au/.
3   In fact, 'top end' normally refers to the Northern Territory rather than North Queensland. *Underbelly* was the successful television series set in Melbourne, Victoria, and based on a notorious Melbourne family.

8. Back to the Back: Genre Queensland and Westerns in Winton

1. See www.wintonoutbackmoviecapital.info/index.php?p=1_1b.
2. More unexpected was the disastrous fire in the Waltzing Matilda historical centre in Winton, in which the iconic tourist centre and a significant collection of historical artefacts were lost (see Arthur 2015a).
3. *Goldstone* is still in post-production at the press time for this book.
4. Thanks to Ms Linda Elliott, who discussed the production of *The Proposition* with me in Winton in May 2008; and Ms Margaret Oxley who spoke with me in August 2010.
5. The 1870s setting might allude to the conflict between Kalkadoon people and settlers which occurred in north west Queensland in that period. See: https://www.qld.gov.au/atsi/cultural-awareness-heritage-arts/community-histories-mount-isa/
6. Carol Hart (2005) queries this perception, referring to a number of earlier films, including *The Tracker* (De Heer 2002) and *The Chant of Jimmy Blacksmith*, and the many documented sources on black–white conflicts now available to researchers.
7. See, for instance, Szaloky 2001; Wexman 1993; White 2011.
8. Bushrangers were apparently rare in Queensland and appear to have been associated with what is now known as central and southern Queensland rather than the district around Winton. See, for instance, Cyril Grabs, *Queensland Desperadoes: Wild Tales of Bushranging Days*, Sydney: Angus and Robertson, 1983; Robert Coupe, *Australia's Bushrangers*, French's Forest: New Holland, 1998.
9. Sen has revealed that the fictional events of the film had germinal connection to events in his life, namely the unsolved murder of his cousin. His commentary on *Mystery Road* also refers to his earlier science fiction film, created in Nevada, *Dreamland* (2009). Sen cites this film as formative in leading to both *Toomelah* (2011) and *Mystery Road* (Luskri 2013).
10. Winton was not the only location, as the police station and the 'Hong Kong Cuisine' restaurant were filmed in Ipswich (Gould 2014), and Moree briefly appears as the setting for some domestic action. Swooping 'topographical helicopter shots' (Dolgopolov 2013, 13) provide context for shifts between the town and the city in *Mystery Road* and disguise the movement between locations in Ipswich, Moree and Winton.
11. See Rutherford (2015, especially 315–17). Within this potent essay (which was published after this book was prepared for publication) on *Mystery Road* and Aaron Pederson's performance in it, Rutherford analyses with scouring detail the framing, dialogue and 'material density' (316) of the stockyard fencing in this scene.

Conclusion: On Location in Queensland

1. See Mills (2015) regarding Sen's life and connection to the country of his mother, a Gamilaroi woman.
2. See 'User Reviews': www.imdb.com/title/tt1864549/?ref_=fn_tt_tt_3.

FILMOGRAPHY

Adamson, Andrew, and Jenson, Vicki, dir. 2001. *Shrek*. USA: DreamWorks Animation, DreamWorks SKG, Pacific Data Images.
Allen, Elizabeth, dir. 2006. *Aquamarine*. USA/Australia: Twentieth Century Fox.
Andrikidis, Peter, Rachel Ward and Rowan Woods, dirs. 2012. *The Straits*. TV Series. Australia: Matchbox Pictures.
Auzin, Igor, dir. 1982. *We of the Never Never*. Australia: Adam Packer Film Productions and Film Corporation of Western Australia.
———. 1984. *The Coolangatta Gold*. Australia: Michael Edgley.
Barrett, Franklyn, dir. 1921. *A Girl of the Bush*. Australia: Barrett's Australian Productions.
Barry, Ian, dir. 2003. *Mermaids*. USA: Viacom Productions.
Batty, David, and Kelly, Francis Jupurrula, dirs. 1998. *Bush Mechanics*. TV Series. Australia: Film Australia.
Bennett, Bill, dir. 1986. *Backlash*. Australia: Mermaid Beach Productions.
———. 2010. *Uninhabited*. Australia: Screen Australia, SC Films.
Brenon, Herbert, dir. 1924. *Peter Pan*. USA: Famous Players/Lasky Corporation.
Bush TV 'Switch On', prod. 2004. *Managing Cultural Heritage on a Major Feature Film Shoot*. Queensland Government Department of Natural Resources and Mines.
Cameron, James, dir. 1997. *Titanic*. USA: Twentieth Century Fox/Paramount/Lightstorm Entertainment.
Caesar, David and Catriona McKenzie, dir. 2006. *RAN Remote Area Nurse*. TV Mini-series. Australia: SBS Independent/FFC Australia/ Chapman Pictures.
Chauvel, Charles, dir. 1933. *In the Wake of the Bounty*. Australia: Expeditionary Films.
———. 1949. *Sons of Matthew*. Australia: Greater Union Theatres/Universal International.
———. [1955] 2004. *Jedda*. Charles Chauvel Productions. Australia: ScreenSound Australia, National Screen and Sound Archive.
Crombie, Donald, dir. 1976. *Caddie*. Australia: Anthony Buckley Productions.
———.[1978] 2002. *The Irishman*. Australia: Forest Home Films/SAFC, Roadshow Entertainment.
De Heer, Rolf, dir. 2002. *The Tracker*. Australia: Vertigo Productions/Adelaide Festival for the Arts/South Australian Film Corporation.
———. 2006. *Ten Canoes*. Australia: Adelaide Film Festival/Fandango Australia.
'Featurette'. 2003. *Radiance* DVD. Universal Studios.
Foster, Marc, dir. 2004. *Finding Neverland*. USA: Miramax Films and FilmColony.
Funatoko, Sadao, and Toyama, Toru, dir. 1962–65. *The Samurai*. Japan: Senkosha Productions.
Geronimi, Clyde, Jackson, Wilfred and Luske, Hamilton, dirs. 1953. *Peter Pan*. USA: Walt Disney Productions.

Grierson, Alister, dir. 2006. *Kokoda*. Australia: AFFC/GFN Productions/Pacific Film and Television Commission.
———. 2011a. *Sanctum*. USA/Australia: Universal Pictures/Relativity Media/Great Wight Productions/Osford Films.
———. 2011b. *Sanctum: The Real Story*. Australia: Great Wight Productions/National Geographic Channels.
Hall, Ken G., dir. 1932. *On Our Selection*. Australia: Cinesound Productions.
———. 1933. *The Squatter's Daughter*. Australia: Cinesound Productions.
———. 1937. *Lovers and Luggers*. Australia: Cinesound Productions.
Hillcoat, John, dir. 2005. *The Proposition*. Australia/UK: Surefire Films.
Hogan, P.J., dir. 1994. *Muriel's Wedding*. Australia: CiBY 2000/Film Victoria/House and Moorhouse Films.
———. 2003. *Peter Pan*. Australia/USA/UK: Universal Pictures.
Honda, Ishiro, dir. 1954. *Gojira*. Japan: Toho Film (Eiga) Co. Ltd.
———, and Morse, Terry O., dir. 1956. *Godzilla, King of the Monsters!* USA and Japan: Toho Company and Jewel Enterprises Inc.
Honey, John, dir. 1980. *Manganinnie*. Australia: Tasmanian Film Corporation.
Hurley, Frank, dir. 1926a. *Hound of the Deep*. UK: Stoll Picture Productions.
———. 1926b. *Jungle Woman*. Australia/UK: Stoll Picture Productions.
Judge, Mike. 1993–2011. *Beavis and Butt-Head*. USA: Film Roman Productions, J.J. Sedelmaier Productions, Judgemental Films.
Krawitz, Tony, dir. 2011. *The Tall Man*. Australia: Blackfella Films.
Lander, Ned, dir. 1981. *Wrong Side of the Road*. Australia: Aboriginal Advancement League of South Australia/Aboriginal Arts Board/Australian Film Commission.
Larkin, John, dir. 1989. *Nullabor Dreaming*. Australia: Great Wight Productions/Osford Films.
Laughren, Pat. 1996. *Queensland's First Films: Surprising Survivals from Colonial Queensland*. Research and narration by Chris Long. Australia: Mungana Films. Released by National Film and Sound Archive.
Ledwidge, Ringan, dir. 2006. *Gone*. UK/Australia: Universal Pictures/Working Title Films/Australian Film Finance Corporation.
Levin Mark, and Flackett, Jennifer, dir. 2008. *Nim's Island*. USA: Walden Media.
Lloyd, Frank, dir. 1935. *Mutiny on the Bounty*. USA: Metro-Goldwyn-Mayer.
Longford, Raymond, dir. 1920. *On Our Selection*. Australia: E.J. Carroll.
Luhrmann, Baz, dir. 2008. *Australia*. Australia/USA/UK: Twentieth Century Fox Films and Bazmark Films.
Maher, Brendan, dir. 2013. *Return to Nim's Island*. Australia: Pictures in Paradise/Mazur/Kaplan Company/ Walden Media.
Mason, Richard, and Lee, Jack, dirs. 1964. *From the Tropics to the Snow*. Australia: Commonwealth Film Unit.
McElroy, Di and McElroy, Hal, creators. 2007–. *Sea Patrol*. Australia: Australian Film Finance Corporation/McElroy All Media.
McInnes, Hugh, dir. 1948. *The Cane Cutters*. Australian Department of Information/Australian National Film Board.
Milestone, Lewis. 1962. *Mutiny on the Bounty*. USA: Metro-Goldwyn-Mayer and Arcola Pictures.
Milson, John, dir. 1967/8. *Will the Great Barrier Reef Save Claude Clough?* Australian Commonwealth Film Unit.
Moffatt, Tracey, dir. 1993. *Bedevil*. Australia: Anthony Buckley Productions.

Nicholson, Arch, dir. 1986. *Buddies*. Australia: JD Productions/Queensland Film Corporation.
Noyce, Philip, dir. 1977. *Backroads*. Australia: Backroads Productions.
O'Neill, dir. Forthcoming. *Banjo and Matilda*. Australia: Lucky Country Pictures/Two Heads Media.
Parker, David, dir. 1993. *Hercules Returns*. Australia: Philm Productions.
Perkins, Rachel, dir. [1998] 2003. *Radiance*. Australia: Australian Film Commission and Eclipse Films. Universal Studios.
Powell, Michael, dir. 1966. *They're a Weird Mob*. Australia/UK: Williamson/Powell.
———. [1969] 2009. *Age of Consent*. USA: Columbia Pictures. Sony Pictures Home Entertainment.
Robinson, Lee, dir. 1954. *King of the Coral Sea*. Australia: Southern International.
———, and Pagliero, Marcel, dir. 1956. *Walk Into Paradise*. Australia: Southern International.
Ronning, Joachim, and Sandberg, Espen, dir. 2017. *Pirates of the Caribbean: Dead Men Tell No Tales*. USA: Walt Disney Pictures/Jerry Bruckheimer Films.
Safran, Henri, dir. 1976. *Storm Boy*. Australia: South Australian Film Corporation.
Schepisi, Fred, dir. 1978. *The Chant of Jimmie Blacksmith*. Australia: The Film House, and Victorian Film Corporation.
Schultz, Carl, dir. 1987. *Travelling North*. Australia: Australian Film Commission/Cineplex Odeon/Queensland Film Commission/View Pictures.
Sen, Ivan, dir. 2002. *Beneath Clouds*. Australia: Australian Film Finance Corporation and Autumn Films in association with Axiom Films.
———. 2009. *Dreamland*. Australia/USA: Bunya Productions.
———. 2011. *Toomelah*. Australia: Bunya Productions.
———. 2013. *Mystery Road*. Australia: Screen Australia, Mystery Road Films.
———. Forthcoming. *Goldstone*. Australia: Dark Matter.
Shiff, Jonathan M., dir. 2006. *H20: Just Add Water*. Australia: Film Finance and Jonathan M. Shiff Productions.
Sims, Jeremy, dir. 2010. *Beneath Hill 60*. Australia: Lucky Country Productions/The Silence Productions.
Smart, Ralph, dir. 1951. *Bitter Springs*. UK: Ealing Studios.
Spielberg, Steven, dir. 1991. *Hook*. USA: Amblin Entertainment/Tristar Pictures.
Tenant, Andy, dir. 2008. *Fool's Gold*. USA: Warner Bros. and De Line Pictures.
Thornton, Warwick, dir. 2003. *Rosalie's Journey*. Australia: Central Australian Aboriginal Media Association (CAAMA), Ronin Films.
———. 2009. *Samson and Delilah*. Australia: Central Australian Aboriginal Media Association (CAAMA) Productions, Scarlett Pictures.
Universal. 2003. 'Princess Tiger Lily'. Short. In *Peter Pan*. Dir. P.J. Hogan. Universal Pictures.
Various. 2008. *Underbelly*. Australia: Film Finance Corporation Australia; Film Victoria; Nine Network Australia.
Wargnier, Régis, dir. 1992. *Indochine*. France: Paradis Films/Bac Films.
Watt, Harry, dir. 1946. *The Overlanders*. UK/Australia: Ealing Studios.
Weir, Peter, dir. 1975. *Picnic at Hanging Rock*. Australia: Australian Film Commission/Picnic Productions.
———. 1977. *The Last Wave*. Australia: Ayer Productions and Australian Film Commission.
———. 1981. *Gallipoli*. Australia: Associated R & R Films.
Zemeckis, Robert, dir. 2000. *Cast Away*. USA: DreamWorks and Twentieth Century Fox.

WORKS CITED

'1904 Bushranging in North Queensland'. n.d. www.wintonoutbackmoviecapital.info/index.php?p=1_5. Accessed 2 October 2015.
'Animal Smuggling'. 2015. www.abc.net.au/tv/thestraits/#Stories:warfare. Accessed 30 September 2015.
Arthur, Chrissy. 2015a. 'Fire Rips through Waltzing Matilda Centre at Winton in Western Queensland'. www.abc.net.au/news/2015-06-18/fire-rips-through-waltzing-matilda-centre-at-winton/6554830. Accessed 2 October 2015.
———. 2015b. 'Movie Set Built in Outback Queensland Brings Employment to the Region'. www.abc.net.au/news/2015-05-04/middleton-movie-set-brings-employment-to-small-town/6441810. Accessed 2 October 2015.
Augé, Marc. 1995. *Non-places: Introduction to an Anthropology of Supermodernity*. Translated by John Howe. London and New York: Verso.
Bachelard, Gaston. 1994. *The Poetics of Space*. Translated by Maria Jolas. Boston, MA: Beacon.
Barrie, J. M. 1996. *Peter Pan*. Ware, Hertfordshire: Wordsworth Editions Limited.
Blatchford, Emily. 2013a. 'Road to Success'. *Inside Film* 156 (December): 14.
———. 2013b. 'The Long Road Home'. *Inside Film* 155 (Oct.): 25.
Blundell, Graeme. 2012. 'Straight Up'. *The Weekend Australian* January: 28–29. 26–27.
Bodey, Michael. 2011. 'Sanctum Scores a Century at the Box Office'. *The Australian* 'Film Arts', 5 October: 17.
———. 2015. 'Anniversary Screening for Jedda at Cannes'. *The Australian* 29 April: 15.
Bourne, Christopher. 2005. '*Age of Consent*'. *Senses of Cinema*. http://archive.sensesofcinema.com/contents/cteq/05/36/age_of_consent.html. Accessed 7 June 2009.
Bowles, Kate. 2008. 'Rural Cultural Research: Notes from a Small Country Town'. *Australian Humanities Review* 45: 83–96.
BP Australia. 1984. 'The Making of *The Coolangatta Gold*'. Short. In *The Coolangatta Gold*. Heliograph Pty Ltd. Magna Pacific, 2004.
Brennan, Claire E. 2013a. 'Crocodile Hunting'. *Queensland Historical Atlas* 21 August: 1–3.
———. 2013b. 'Australian Safari: Hunting Dangerous Game in Australia's Tropical North'. In *Lectures in Queensland History Series*. Edited by Annette Burns, 91–101. Townsville, Qld: Townsville City Council.
Bristow, Joseph. 1991. *Empire Boys: Adventures in a Man's World*. London: HarperCollins.
Brophy, Philip. 2001. 'Funny Accents: The Sound of Racism'. In *Cinesonic: Experiencing the Soundtrack*. Edited by Philip Brophy, 225–38. North Ryde: Australian Film, Television and Radio School.
Bulletin. 2014. ABC News 24. 3 October.

Carlsson, Susanne Chauvel. 1989. *Charles and Elsa Chauvel: Movie Pioneers*. St Lucia: University of Queensland Press.
Casey, Edward. 1998. *The Fate of Place: A Philosophical History*. Berkeley: University of California Press.
Casey, M., and Syron, L. 2005. 'The Challenges of Benevolence: The Role of Indigenous Actors'. *Journal of Australian Studies* 29, no. 85: 97–111.
Cashill, Bob. 2009. 'DVD Review: "The Films of Michael Powell (*A Matter of Life and Death* and *Age of Consent*)"'. http://popdose.com/dvd-review-the-films-of-michael-powell-a-matter-of-life-and-death. Accessed 7 June 2009.
'Characters'. 2015. www.abc.net.au/tv/thestraits/#Family. Accessed 30 September 2015.
Chauvel, Elsa. 1973. *My Life with Charles Chauvel*. Sydney: Shakespeare Head Press.
Chion, Michel. 1994. *Audio-vision: Sound on Screen*. Edited and translated by C. Gorbman. New York: Columbia University Press.
Chua, Beng Huat. 2008. 'Tropics, City and Cinema: Introduction to the Special Issue on Cinematic Representation of the Tropical Urban/City'. *Singapore Journal of Tropical Geography* 29: 1–7.
Clarke, Paul. 2005. 'Transcription. Oral History Program, Interviewer Ken Berryman and Gino Moliterno'. 8 August, Mavis Title No. 668089. Canberra: National Film and Sound Archive (NFSA).
Close, J. R. 2015. 'Filmakers Welcome'. www.wintonoutbackmoviecapital.info/index.php?p=1_13. Accessed 2 October 2015.
Collins, Felicity. 2002. 'Brazen Brides, Grotesque Daughters, Treacherous Mothers: Women's Funny Business in Australian Cinema from *Sweetie* to *Holy Smoke*'. *Senses of Cinema* 23: 1–10. www.sensesofcinema.com/contents/02/23/women_funny_oz.html. Accessed 10 November 2005.
———. 2008. 'Historical Fiction and the Allegorical Truth of Colonial Violence in *The Proposition*'. *Cultural Studies Review* 14, no. 1: 55–71.
———, and Davis, Therese. 2004. *Australian Cinema After Mabo*. Cambridge: Cambridge University Press.
Combs, Richard. 1969. '*Age of Consent*'. *Monthly Film Bulletin* 36 (December): 256.
Coyle, Rebecca. 2001. 'Speaking "Strine": Locating "Australia" in Film Voice and Speech'. In *Cinesonic: Experiencing the Soundtrack*. Edited by Philip Brophy, 203–24. North Ryde: Australian Film, Television and Radio School.
Craik, Jennifer. 1990. 'The Cultural Politics of the Queensland House'. *Continuum* 3, no. 1: 188–213.
Craven, Allison. 2010. 'Paradise Post-national: Landscape, Location and Senses of Place in Films Set in Queensland'. *Metro* 166: 108–13.
———. 2013. 'Fencelines and Horizon Lines: Queensland in the Imaginary Geographies of Cinema'. In *Selected Lectures on Queensland History from the Lectures in Queensland History Series 30 November 2009–27 February 2012*. Edited by Annette Burns, 61–73. Townsville, Qld: Townsville City Council, 2013.
———, and Mann, Chris. 2010. 'The Girl with the Bush Knife: Women, Adventure and the Tropics in *Age of Consent* and *Nim's Island*'. *Etropic: Electronic Journal of Studies in the Tropics* 9: 1–12. www.jcu.edu.au/etropic/ET9/CravenMann.html.
Crombie, Donald. 2002. 'Audio Commentary with Director Donald Crombie and Stars Michael Craig and Simon Burke'. In Special Features, *The Irishman*. Sydney: Forest Home Films/AFC, Roadshow Entertainment.
Cunningham, Stuart. 1987a. 'Charles Chauvel, the Last Decade'. *Continuum: The Australian Journal of Media and Culture* 1, no. 1: 26–46.

———. 1987b. 'To Go Back and Beyond'. *Continuum: The Australian Journal of Media and Culture* 2, no. 1. wwwmcc.murdoch.edu.au/ReadingRoom/2.1/Cunningham.html. Accessed 11 February 2012.

———. 1991. *Featuring Australia: The Cinema of Charles Chauvel*. North Sydney: Allen & Unwin.

Danks, Adrian and Verevis, Constantine. 2010. 'Australian International Pictures.' *Studies in Australasian Cinema* 4.3: 195–198. doi: 10.1386/sac.4.3.195_2.

De Certeau, Michel. 1984. *The Practice of Everyday Life*. Translated by Steve Rendall. Berkeley: University of California Press.

Dermody, Susan, and Jacka, Elizabeth. 1987. *The Screening of Australia: Anatomy of a Film Industry* (2 vols.), Vol. 1. Sydney: Currency Press.

———. 1988. *The Screening of Australia: Anatomy of a Film Industry* (2 vols.), Vol. 2. Sydney: Currency Press.

'Discussion: *The Straits*: A Sea of Missed Opportunities'. 2012. ABC TV Fiction Messageboard. www2b.abc.net.au/tmb/Client/Message.aspx?b=290&m=779. Accessed 30 September 2015.

'Discussion: Season 2 of *The Straits*'. 2014. ABC TV Fiction Messageboard. www2b.abc.net.au/tmb/Client/Message.aspx?b=290&m=1953. Accessed 30 September 2015.

Dolgopolov, Greg. 2013. 'Dances with Genre: *Mystery Road*'. *Metro Magazine* 177: 8–14.

'Drugs for Guns'. 2015. Real Life Stories. www.abc.net.au/tv/thestraits/#Stories:drugs. Accessed 30 September 2015.

Dyer, Richard. 2010. 'The White Man's Muscles'. In *The Masculinity Studies Reader*. Edited by Rachel Adams and David Savran, 262–73. Malden, MA and Oxford, UK: Blackwell.

Elliott, Bonnie. 'Period'. In *Directory of World Cinema: Australia and New Zealand*. Edited by Ben Goldsmith and Geoff Lealand, 147–50. Bristol, GBR: Intellect Ltd.

'Esky Ordeal'. 2015. www.abc.net.au/tv/thestraits/#Stories:esky. Accessed 30 September 2015.

Ferrier, Elizabeth. 1987. 'From Pleasure Domes to Bark Huts: Architectural Metaphors in Recent Australian Fiction'. *Australian Literary Studies* 13, no. 1: 40–53.

Flanagan, Martin. 1998. *The Call*. St Leonards: Allen & Unwin.

Fortgang, Jon. n.d. '*The Proposition* Review'. *Film 4*. www.channel4.com/film/reviews/film.jsp?id=1460&page=3. Accessed 17 March 2008.

Freadman, Anne. 1988. 'Untitled (on Genre)'. *Cultural Studies* 2, no. 1: 67–99.

Gaunson, Stephen. 2010. 'Bushranger'. In *Directory of World Cinema: Australia and New Zealand*. Edited by Ben Goldsmith and Geoff Lealand, 88–92. Bristol, GBR: Intellect Ltd.

Gibson, Ross. 1994. 'Formative Landscapes'. In *Australian Cinema*. Edited by Scott Murray, 45–60. St Leonards: Allen & Unwin.

Goldsmith, Ben. 2010. 'Outward-looking Australian Cinema'. *Studies in Australasian Cinema* 4, no. 3: 199–214.

——— and O'Regan, Tom. 2008. 'International Film Production: Interests and Motivations'. In *Cross Border Cultural Production: Economic Runaway or Globalization?* Edited by Janet Wasko and Mary Erickson, 13–44. Amherst, NY: Cambria.

———, Ward, Susan and O'Regan, Tom. 2010. *Local Hollywood: Global Film Production and the Gold Coast*. St Lucia: University of Queensland Press.

———. 2014. 'Dino De Laurentiis and Australia: Creating a Film Industry on the Gold Coast'. *Studies in Australasian Cinema* 8, no. 1: 70–75.

Gould, Joel. 2014. 'Murder Mystery Shot in Ipswich'. www.qt.com.au/news/murder-mystery-shot-in-ipswich/2149780/. Accessed 2 October 2015.

Hall, Ken G. 1977. *Directed by Ken G. Hall: Autobiography of an Australian Film Maker*. Melbourne: Lansdowne Press.

Harkins-Cross, Rebecca. 2014. 'Bloody Horizons: Ivan Sen's *Mystery Road*'. *The Lifted Brow* 20. http://theliftedbrow.com/post/72697679708/bloody-horizons-ivan-sens-mystery-road-by. Accessed 2 October 2015.

Hart, Carol. 2005. 'Portraits of Settler History in *The Proposition*', *Senses of Cinema*, www.sensesofcinema.com/contents/06/38/proposition.html. Accessed 13 February 2007.

Healy, Chris. 2008. *Forgetting Aborigines*. Sydney: University of New South Wales Press.

Herbert, Xavier. 2008. *Capricornia*. Pymble, NSW: HarperCollins. First published 1938.

Heung, Marina. 1997. 'The Family Romance of Orientalism: From *Madam Butterfly* to *Indochine*'. In *Visions of the East: Orientalism in Film*. Edited by Matthew Bernstein and Gaylyn Studlar, 158–83. New Brunswick, NJ: Rutgers University Press.

Holman, Tomlinson. 2002. *Sound for Film and Television*. 2nd edn. Boston, MA: Focal Press.

Hoorn, Jeanette. 2005. 'Comedy and Eros: Powell's Australian Films *They're a Weird Mob* and *Age of Consent*'. *Screen* 46, no. 1: 73–84.

Hutcheon, Linda. 1988. *Poetics of Postmodernism*. New York: Routledge.

'Interviews: Rachel Perkins – Director'. 2003. Special Features. In *Radiance*, dir. Perkins.

Jaikumar, Priya. 2001. '"Place" and the Modernist Redemption of Empire in Black Narcissus'. *Cinema Journal* 40, no. 2: 57–78.

———.2006. *Cinema at the End of Empire: A Politics of Transition in Britain and India*. Durham, NC: Duke University Press.

Jennings, Karen. 1993. *Sites of Difference: Cinematic Representation of Aboriginality and Gender*. South Melbourne: Australian Film Institute Research and Information Centre.

Jericho, Greg. 2005. 'War in the Tropics'. *Etropic: Electronic Journal of Studies in the Tropics* 4, 1–15. www.jcu.edu.au/etropic/ET4/Jericho.htm. Accessed 23 November 2011.

Jones, Kate. 2015. 'Media Statements'. http://statements.qld.gov.au/Statement/2015/4/16/filmmakers-capture-a-touch-of-tropical-north-queenslands-paradise. Accessed 10 October 2015.

Kelly, Veronica. 1998. *The Theatre of Louis Nowra*. Sydney: Currency Press.

Keon-Cohen, Bryan. 2013. *A Mabo Memoir: Islan Kustom to Native Title*. Malvern, Vic: Zemvic Press.

Khoo, Olivia. 2011a. 'Australian Cinema up in the Air: Post-national Identities and Peter Duncan's *Unfinished Sky*'. *Continuum* 25, no. 4: 547–58.

———. 2011b. 'Introduction: Regionalizing Asian Australian Identities'. *Continuum* 25, no. 4: 461–64.

———, Belinda Smaill and Audrey Yue. 2015. *Transnational Australian Cinema: Ethics in Asian Diasporas*. Lanham, MD: Lexington Books.

Kunoth-Monks, Rosalie. 1995. Transcript of interview by Robin Hughes, Australian Biography. www.australianbiography.gov.au/subjects/kunothmonks/intertext1.html. Accessed 30 June 2009.

Landman, Jane. 2006. *The Tread of a White Man's Foot: Australian Pacific Colonialism and the Cinema, 1925–62*. Canberra, ACT: Pandanus Books.

———. 2013. '*RAN: Remote Area Nurse*: SBS Protocols, Grassroots Collaboration and the Quality Mini-series'. *Studies in Australasian Cinema* 7, nos. 2–3: 201–13.

Langton, Marcia. 2003. 'Grounded and Gendered: Aboriginal Women in Australian Cinema'. In *Womenvision: Women and the Moving Image in Australia*. Edited by Lisa French, 43–56. Melbourne, Vic: Damned Publishing.

Lewis, Peter. 2013. 'Winton Scores another Movie Win'. www.abc.net.au/news/2013-04-12/winton-scores-another-movie-win/4626890. Accessed 2 October 2015.
Limbrick, Peter. 2007. 'The Australian Western, or a Settler Colonial Cinema Par Excellence'. *Cinema Journal* 46, no. 4 (Summer): 68.
———. 2010. *Making Settler Cinema: Film and Colonial Encounters in the United States, Australia and New Zealand.* New York: Palgrave MacMillan.
Luskri, Chris. 2013. 'In Conversation with Ivan Sen'. Melbourne International Film Festival. In *Mystery Road*, dir. Sen.
Maddox, Garry. 2005. 'Beyond the Age of Consent'. *Sydney Morning Herald.* 11 June. www.smh.com.au/news/Film/Beyond-the-age-of-consent/2005/06/10/. Accessed 7 June 2009.
Maher, Susan Naramore. 1988. 'Recasting Crusoe: Frederick Marryat, R.M. Ballantyne, and the Nineteenth Century Robinsonade'. *Children's Literature Association Quarterly* 13, no. 4: 169–75.
Maurice, Alice. 2002. 'Cinema at Its Source: Synchronizing Race and Sound in the Early Talkies'. *Camera Obscura* 49, no. 17.1: 31–71.
Miller, Benjamin. 2007. 'The Mirror of Whiteness: Blackface in Charles Chauvel's *Jedda*'. In *Spectres, Screens, Shadows and Mirrors: Journal of the Association for the Study of Australian Literature.* Edited by Tanya Dalzielland Paul Genoni, 140–56. www.nla.gov.au/openpublish/index.php/jasal/article/viewArticle/320. Accessed 30 June 2009.
Miller, Kylie. 2005. 'Distant Lives'. www.australiantelevision.net/remoteareanurse/articles/distantlives.html. Accessed 20 September 2015.
Mills, Jane. 2012. *Jedda.* Strawberry Hills, NSW: Currency Press/National Film and Sound Archive.
———. 2015. 'Bordering Activity in Ivan Sen's Film *Toomelah* (2011)'. *Screening the Past* 39. www.screeningthepast.com/2015/06/bordering-activity-in-ivan-sen%E2%80%99s-film-toomelah-2011/. Accessed 24 December 2015.
Milner, Lisa and Cathy Brigden. 2014. 'From Martyr to Robo-Nurse: the Portrayal of Australian Nurses on Screen'. *Studies in Australasian Cinema* 8, nos. 2–3: 110–22.
Molloy, Bruce. 1990a. *Before the Interval: Australian Mythology and Feature Films 1930–1960.* St Lucia: University of Queensland Press.
———. 1990b. 'Screensland: The Construction of Queensland in Feature Films'. In *Queensland Images in Film and Television.* Edited by Jonathan Dawson and Bruce Molloy. St Lucia: University of Queensland Press.
Molnar, Helen. 1997. 'Radio'. In *The Media in Australia: Industries, Texts, Audiences.* 2nd edn. Edited by Stuart Cunningham and Graeme Turner, 201–26. North Sydney: Allen & Unwin.
Moore, Blythe. 2015. 'Outback Queensland Town of Winton to Provide Backdrop for Historical American Mini-series'.www.abc.net.au/news/2015-03-20/winton-to-host-filmmakers-of-historical-american-mini-series/6335232. Accessed 2 October 2015.
Moran, Albert. 1985. '*From the Tropics to the Snow:* The Commonwealth Film Unit in the 1960s'. In *An Australian Film Reader.* Edited by Albert Moran and Tom O'Regan, 104–11. Sydney: Currency Press.
———. 1989. 'Constructing the Nation: Institutional Documentary Since 1945'. *The Australian Screen.* Edited by Albert Moran and Tom O'Regan, 148–71. Ringwood, Vic: Penguin Books.
———. 2001. *Queensland Screen: An Introduction.* Brisbane: Griffith University.
Morissey, Di. 1984. 'Good Morning Australia Segment'. Short. In *The Coolangatta Gold.* Heliograph Pty Ltd. Magna Pacific, 2004.

Murray, Rebecca. 2014a. 'Behind the Scenes of the Live Action Movie "Peter Pan": The Producers and Cinematographer Discuss "Peter Pan"'. About Entertainment. http://movies.about.com/cs/peterpan/a/petplf121303.htm. Accessed 3 July 2014.

———. 2014b. 'Director PJ Hogan Discovers Neverland with "Peter Pan"'. About Entertainment. http://movies.about.com/cs/peterpan/a/petpjs121303.htm. Accessed 3 July 2014.

———. 2014c. 'Jeremy Sumpter Soars in "Peter Pan": Interview with Jeremy Sumpter'. About Entertainment. http://movies.about.com/cs/peterpan/a/petpjs121303.htm. Accessed 3 July 2014.

Murray, Scott, ed. 1994. *Australian Cinema*. St Leonards: Allen & Unwin in Association with Australian Film Commission.

———. 2009. 'Michael Powell Down Under: Norman Lindsay's *Age of Consent*'. *Senses of Cinema* 51. http://sensesofcinema.com/2009/dvd/age-of-consent/. Accessed 23 July 2009.

Nelson, Victoria. 2001. *The Secret Life of Puppets*. Cambridge, MA and London: Harvard University Press.

Nowra, Louis. 1993. *Radiance*. Current Theatre Series. Sydney: Currency in Association with Belvoir Street Theatre, Sydney.

———. 2000. *Radiance: The Play and the Screenplay*. Sydney: Currency.

O'Brien, Patty. 2006. *The Pacific Muse: Exotic Femininity and the Colonial Pacific*. Seattle and London: University of Washington Press.

Oc Screen. 2004. 'Shooting Strait'. www.australiantelevision.net/remoteareanurse/articles/shootingstrait.html. Accessed 20 September 2015.

O'Conner, Elizabeth. 1960. *The Irishman: A Novel of Northern Australia*. Sydney: Angus and Robertson.

O'Hanlon, Seamus. 2002. *Together Apart: Boarding House, Hostel and Flat Life in Pre-war Melbourne*. Melbourne: Australian Scholarly Publishing.

O'Regan, Tom. 1989. 'Cinema Oz: The Ocker Films'. In *The Australian Screen*. Edited by Albert Moran and Tom O'Regan, 75–98. Ringwood, Vic: Penguin.

———. 1996. *Australian International Cinema*. London: Routledge.

———, and Potter, Anna. 2013. 'Globalisation from Within? The De-nationalising of Australian Film and Television Production'. *Media International Australia* 149 (November): 5–14.

———, and Venkatasawmy, Rama. 1999. 'A Tale of Two Cities'. In *Twin Peeks: Australian and New Zealand Feature Films*. Edited by Deb Verhoeven, 187–203. St Kilda, Vic: Damned Publishing.

Orr, Wendy. 2008. *Nim's Island*. Pictures by Kerry Millard. Crows Nest: Allen & Unwin. First published 1999.

Otto, Jeff. 2003. 'Interview: The Stars and Director of *Peter Pan*'. IGN Entertainment Inc. 23 December. 1996–2014. http://au.ign.com/articles/2003/12/23/interview-the-stars-and-director-of-peter-pan. Accessed 3 July 2014.

Pearson, Sarina. 2013. 'Cowboy Contradictions: Westerns in the Postcolonial Pacific'. *Studies in Australasian Cinema* 7, nos. 2 and 3, 153–64.

Penman, Ian. 2001. 'Garvey's Ghost>KLANG!<Heidegger's Geist'. In *Cinesonic: Experiencing the Soundtrack*. Edited by Philip Brophy, 105–23. North Ryde: Australian Film, Television and Radio School.

Pierce, Peter. 1998. 'The Adventure Novel and Imperial Romance'. In *The Encyclopaedia of the Novel* (2 vols.), Vol. 1 A–L. Edited by Paul Schellinger, 6–9. Chicago and London: Fitzroy Dearborn.

Pike, Andrew and Cooper, Ross. 1998. *Australian Film 1900–1977: A Guide to Feature Film Production*. Melbourne: Oxford University Press.
Plato. 2010. From *Republic: Book VII*. Translated by Robin Waterfield. In *The Norton Anthology of Theory and Criticism*. 2nd edn. Edited by Vincent B. Leitch, 60–64. New York and London: Norton.
Pocock, Celmara. 2002. 'Sense Matters: Aesthetic Values of the Great Barrier Reef'. *International Journal of Heritage Studies* 8, No. 4, 365–81.
Pomeranz, Margaret. 2005. '*The Proposition* Interviews'. *At the Movies: The Proposition*. 5 October. www.abc.net.au/atthemovies/txt/s147287.htm. Accessed 10 February 2012.
———, and Stratton, David. 2005. 'At the Movies: The Proposition'. 5 October. www.abc.net.au/atthemovies/txt/s1474241.htm. Accessed 17 March 2008.
Powell, Michael. 1992. *Million-Dollar Movie*. New York: Random House.
Press Release. 2015. 'Hong Kong Star Joins Sen's Thriller'. 5 June. http://if.com.au/2015/06/05/article/JCZAZQGAPK.html. Accessed 10 October 2015.
Probyn-Rapsey, Fiona. 2006. 'Bitumen Film in Postcolonial Australia'. *Journal of Australian Studies* 88: 97–109.
Rattigan, Neil. 1991. *Images of Australia: 100 Films of the New Australian Cinema*. Dallas, TX: Southern Methodist University Press.
Robinson, Victoria. 2008. *Everyday Masculinities and Extreme Sport*. Oxford and New York: Berg. [e-book]
Robson, Jocelyn, and Zalcock, Beverley. 1997. *Girls' Own Stories: Australian and New Zealand Women's Films*. London: Scarlet Press.
Rose, Jacqueline. 1994. *The Case of Peter Pan; or the Impossibility of Children's Fiction*. Rev. edn. London: MacMillan.
Rothwell, Nicholas. 2007a. *Another Country*. Melbourne: Black Inc.
———. 2007b. 'Thea Astley Lecture 2007, Byron Bay Festival'. *Etropic: Electronic Journal of Sstudies in the Tropics*, 6. www.jcu.edu.au/etropic. Accessed June 2009.
Routt, William D. 1989. 'The Fairest Child of the Motherland: Colonialism and Family in Australian Films of the 1920s and 1930s'. In *The Australian Screen*. Edited by Albert Moran and Tom O'Regan, 28–52. Ringwood, Vic: Penguin.
———. 2001. 'Demolishing a Wall (1)'. *Senses of Cinema*, May. 1–10. www.sensesofcinema.com/contents/01/14/demolishing_a_wall.html. Accessed 13 February 2007.
Rutherford, Anne. 2015. 'Walking the Edge: Performance, the Cinematic Body and the Cultural Mediator in Ivan Sen's *Mystery Road*'. *Studies in Australasian Cinema* 9, no. 3: 312–26.
Ryan, L. 2008a. 'Hugh Helps Local Flick'. *Townsville Bulletin*, December 20: 27.
———. 2008b. 'Investors Eye Bowen'. *Townsville Bulletin*, December 27: 11.
Ryan, Mark David. 2010. 'Australian Cinema's Dark Sun: The Boom in Australian Horror Film Production'. *Studies in Australasian Cinema* 4, no. 1: 23–41.
Said, Edward W. 1978. *Orientalism*. London: Routledge and Kegan Paul.
Schaffer, Kay. 1988. *Women and the Bush: Forces of Desire in the Australian Cultural Tradition*. Cambridge: Cambridge University Press.
Seidel, Michael. 1981. 'Crusoe in Exile'. *PMLA* 96, no. 3: 363–74.
Simpson, Catherine. 'Australian Eco-horror and Gaia's Revenge: Animals, Eco-nationalism and the "New Nature"'. *Studies in Australasian Cinema* 4, no. 1: 43–54.
———, Murawska, Renata and Lambert, Anthony. 2009. *Diasporas of Australian Cinema*. Bristol, UK: Intellect [e-text].
Stafford, Jeff. 2010. '*Age of Consent*'. Turner Classic Movies. www.tcm.com/tcmdb/title.jsp?stid=3772&category=Articles. Accessed 9 April 2010.

Stewart, Susan. 1984. *On Longing: Narratives of the Miniature, the Gigantic, the Souvenir, the Collection*. Baltimore, MD and London: Johns Hopkins University Press.

Szaloky, Melinda. 2001. 'A Tale Nobody Can Tell: The Return of a Repressed Western History in Jim Jarmusch's *Dead Man*'. In *Westerns: Films through History*. Edited by Janet Walker, 47–70. New York and London: Routledge.

Taylor, Cheryl. 2003. 'Gender and Race Relations in Elizabeth O'Conner's Northern Homesteads'. *Australian Literary Studies* 21, no. 1: 20–31.

———. 2009. 'This Fiction, It Don't Go Away: Narrative as Index to Palm Island's Past and Present'. *Queensland Review* 16, no. 1: 35–67.

'The Inspiration'. 2015. www.abc.net.au/tv/thestraits/#About:inspiration. Accessed 30 September 2015.

'The Show'. 2015. www.abc.net.au/tv/thestraits/#About:show. Accessed 30 September 2015.

'*The Straits*: Beautiful One Day, Deadly the Next'. 2015. www.abc.net.au/tv/thestraits/. Accessed 30 September 2015.

Thomas, Francois. 2000. 'Orson Welles' Turn from Live Recording to Post-synchronization: A Technical and Aesthetic Evolution'. In *Cinema and the Sound of Music*. Edited by Philip Brophy, 173–89. North Ryde: Australian Film, Television and Radio School.

Thomson, David. 2003. *The New Biographical Dictionary of Film*. 4th edn. London: Little, Brown.

Tompkins, Jane. 1992. *West of Everything: The Inner Life of Westerns*. New York and Oxford, UK: Oxford University Press.

Turner, Graeme. 1987. 'Breaking the Frame: The Representation of Aborigines in Australian Film'. In *Aboriginal Culture Today*. Edited by A. Rutherford, 135–45. Sydney: Dangaroo Press.

———. 1989. 'Art Directing History: The Period Film'. In *The Australian Screen*. Edited by Albert Moran and Tom O'Regan, 99–117. Ringwood, Vic: Penguin.

Verhoeven, Deb. 2006. *Sheep and the Australian Cinema*. Carlton, Vic: Melbourne University Press.

Voigts-Virchow, Eckart. 2007. 'Heritage and Literature on Screen: *Heimat* and Heritage'. In *The Cambridge Companion to Literature on Screen*. Edited by Deborah Cartmell and Imelda Whelehan, 123–37. Cambridge: Cambridge University Press.

Wexman, Virginia Wright. 1993. *Creating the Couple: Love, Marriage and Hollywood Performance*. Princeton, NJ: Princeton University Press.

White, John. *Westerns*. Abingdon, UK and New York: Routledge.

Whitley, David. 2008. *The Idea of Nature in Disney Animation*. London: Ashgate.

Whitlock, Gillian. 1994. 'The Child in the (Queensland) House: David Malouf and Regional Writing'. In *Provisional Maps: Critical Essays on David Malouf*. Edited by Amanda Nettlebeck, 71–84. Nedlands: The Centre for Studies in Australian Literature, University of Western Australia.

Yaquinto, Marilyn. 2004. 'Tough Love: Mamas, Molls and Mob Wives'. In *Action Chicks: New Images of Tough Women in Popular Culture*. Edited by Sherrie A. Inness, 207–29. Palgrave MacMillan.

INDEX

ABC (television network) 40, 99, 109–10
Aboriginal Arts Board 53
Aboriginal Cultural Heritage Act 2003 120
Aboriginals
  dubbing and 33–34, 39–41
  in *The Irishman* 26–27, 34–36
  in *Jedda* 7, 37–39
  Mabo Native Title Legislation 5–6, 8–9, 13, 45–47, 131
  in *Mystery Road* 121–22
  in *The Proposition* 119–20
  in *Radiance* 41, 47
AFC. *See* Australian Film Commission (AFC)
AFC genre
  overview 6
  The Irishman in 17, 21–23, 27, 128–29
  terra nullius and 59
Agelessness in *Peter Pan* 79
Age of Consent (1969)
  overview 57–58
  "bush woman" figure in 58–60
  "girl Friday" figure in 58, 60
  locating Queensland in 5
  naturalism in 60–63, 129
  paradise myths in 9–11, 129
  Revival and 57
  sex in 60–63
  Uninhabited compared 65
Agnes Water in film 45–46
Anderson, Andy 105
Aphrodite 11
Aquamarine (2006) 135
Atherton Tableland in literature 20
Auge, Marc 3
Australia (2008)
  overview 18–19

The Irishman compared 27–29
Jedda compared 28
Australian Film Commission (AFC). *See also* AFC genre
  The Irishman and 6, 17
Australian United Foods 73
Australia Zoo 65
Auzin, Igor 76, 134–35
Avondale Studios 39
Ayshford, Blake 104

Backlash (1986) 51
Backroads (1977) 51
"Backtracking" 7, 128–29
Bani, Jimi 99, 102, 104–05
Banjo and Matilda 113
Barrie, J.M. 12, 71, 77–81, 135
Barry, Tony 122
Bateman's Bay in literature 61
Bayes-Morton, Suzannah 104
Beavis and Butt-Head (1993 – television) 32
Bedevil (1993) 34–35
Belvoir Street Theatre 53
Beneath Clouds (2002) 51, 123
Beneath Hill 60 (2010) 18, 29, 133
Berryman, Ken 38
Bikie gangs in *The Straits* 105
Bitter Springs (1951) 7, 59, 116, 127
Bjelke-Petersen, Joh 71–72
Bladensburg National Park in film 118
Blake, Rachel 105
Blundell, Graeme 103–04, 106
Boschman, Rodney 120
Bowen in film 27–29
Brazil, release of *Sanctum* in 92
Breslin, Abigail 58, 65
Bridie, David 101, 107

Brisbane
  actors from 20, 27, 35
  in film 63
Bronson, Betty 135
Brophy, Philip 32
Brown, Jamie 104
Brown, Lou 26
Brumby, Michael 133
Buckley, Anthony 20
Buddies (1983) 9, 127
Budge, Tom 118
Bundaberg in film 45–46
Burdekin River in film 18
Burgoyne, Marcella 24
Burke, Simon 22, 35–36
Bush Mechanics (1998) 51
Bushrangers
  overview 136n. 7
  in *The Proposition* 118–19
Bushranging in North Queensland (1904) 3–4, 113
"Bush woman" figure
  overview 10, 57–58
  in *Age of Consent* 58–60
  in *RAN: Remote Area Nurse* 102–03
  in *Uninhabited* 65–67
Butler, Gerard 63

Caddie (1976) 20
Cain, Cramer 88, 105
Cairns in film and television
  The Cane Cutters 4
  RAN: Remote Area Nurse 102
  Sea Patrol 99
  The Straits 97, 100, 104–05, 109, 131
Cairns Post 105
Calypso 11
Cameron, James 88, 92
The Cane Cutters (1948) 4, 55, 128
Cannes Film Festival 7
Cape York Peninsula in television 109
Capricornia (Herbert – novel) 28
Cardwell in film 20
Carides, Zoe 124
Carlsson, Susanne Chauvel 38–39
Carroll, Luke 98
Casey, Edward 7
Casey, M. 27
Cast Away (2001) 87–88

Cave, Nick 118
Caves in *Sanctum* 87–90, 130
Caving in *Sanctum* 87–90
Central Queensland in film 45–46
Central Queensland University 53
Certeau, Michele de 3
The Chant of Jimmie Blacksmith (1978) 24
Chapman, Penny 99–104
Charters Towers in film 18–21, 25
Chauvel, Charles 5, 7, 37–40
Chauvel, Elsa 39
Childers in film 45–46
China, release of *Sanctum* in 92
Cinematic sense of place 2–3
Circe 11
"Clancy of the Overflow" (Patterson) 113
Clarke, Paul 37–40
Coleridge, Samuel Taylor 91
Collins, Felicity 5–6, 8, 47, 49–50, 118–19
Colonial setting of *The Proposition* 115
Columbia Pictures 61
Community participation in film production 131
Community perspectives in *RAN: Remote Area Nurse* 100–03
Competition for film location 127
Connors, Michael 121–22
The Coolangatta Gold (1984) 73–76
  overview 11–12, 71–72, 82–83
  family dynamics in 130
  masculinity in 71–72, 75
  Queenslander houses in 75
  Sanctum compared 86
Coolangatta Gold Iron Man Marathon 11–12
Coolangatta in film 76
Cooper, Ross 135
Coppola, Francis Ford 104
Cowboy figure in *Mystery Road* 121, 125
Cox, Brian 99
Coyle, Rebecca 40
Craig, Michael 18, 22–23, 35–36
Craik, Jennifer 21
Cratchley, Alison 88
Crocodiles
  in *Peter Pan* 78, 82–83, 130
  in *The Straits* 107–09, 129
Crombie, Donald 19–22, 26–27, 35–36, 39–40, 133

INDEX

Crooke, Ray 21
Croydon in film 19–20
Cunningham, Stuart 7, 33, 37–39

Darling Downs in film 3
Darwin, Charles 119
Darwin in film 28
Davis, Therese 5–6, 8, 47, 49–50
Decorous aesthetic in *The Irishman* 17–18, 34
Defoe, Daniel 134
de Laurentiis, Dino 72
Denham Studios 39
Depp, Johnny 83
Dermody, Susan 21, 23, 26
Dirani, Firass 104
Dolgopolov, Greg 121, 124
Double Take (1993) 32
Dreamland (2009) 136n. 8
Dubbing
  overview 31–34
  Aboriginals and 33–34, 39–41
  in B-cinema 31–32
  in *The Irishman* 31, 34–36, 39–41
  in *Jedda* 31, 34, 37–41
Dunk Island in film 9, 59, 61–62, 85
Dunphy, Kristen 104
"Dusky maiden" figure 10–11, 57–58, 66–67, 135
DVDs 33
Dyer, Richard 88–90
Dystopia in *Radiance* 49–51

Ealing Studios 116
Eatts, Pearl 120
Edgley, Michael 73, 76
Ehelepola, Chum 110
Enoch, Wesley 51
Eurocentrism, landscape aesthetic and 8
Expansion of film production in Queensland 1
Extreme sports in *Sanctum* 90–92

Fa'aoso, Aaron 99, 102–04
Family dynamics in *The Coolangatta Gold* 130
Far North Queensland in film and television
  Fool's Gold 63

Nim's Island 63
RAN: Remote Area Nurse 13, 99
Sea Patrol 99
The Straits 13, 97, 99, 105–06, 109
Father figures in *Peter Pan* 81–82
Feminine myths
  "Hollynesians" 10
  within paradise myths 10–11
  "sarong girls" 10
Fences
  overview 115–16
  in *Mystery Road* 116, 124–25
  in *The Proposition* 119–20
Field, David 122
Film friendliness 12, 72, 115, 131
Film Queensland 134
Finding Neverland (2004) 79
Flynn, Errol 79–80
Fool's Gold (2008) 63
Fortgang, Jon 119
Foster, Jodie 63–64
4GG (radio station) 73
"Freedom Ride" 51
Friels, Colin 73
From the Tropics to the Snow (1964) 4

"Gaia's revenge" 67
Gallipoli (1981) 133
Garvin, John 88
Gaunson, Stephen 119
Georgetown in film 20
"Girl Friday" figure
  in *Age of Consent* 58, 60
  in *Nim's Island* 58
  in *Uninhabited* 58
Girl of the Bush (1921) 116
"Global films" 130
The Godfather (1972) 104
Godzilla: King of the Monsters! (1956) 32
Gojira (1954) 32
The Gold and the Glory (1984) 73
Gold Coast City Council 73
Gold Coast in film and television
  overview 4, 11–12
  The Coolangatta Gold 71–76
  Nim's Island 63
  Peter Pan 71–72, 130
  Sanctum 85–86, 92
Goldenberg, Michael 77

Goldsmith, Ben 72
Goldstone (forthcoming) 13, 113–14, 127
Gone (2006) 113
Good Morning Australia (television) 73
Grant, Roberta 24, 36
Gray, Carsen 78
Great Barrier Reef in film
  overview 12
  Age of Consent 58–61
  islands 4–5
  Uninhabited 65
  as World Heritage Site 129–30
Grierson, Alister 135
Gruffudd, Ioan 88
Gulpilil, David 40–41, 120
Gyngell, Kym 105

H20: Just Add Water (2006 – television) 135
Haddon, A.C. 3, 97
Hakewill, Geraldine 58
Hall, Ken 58–59
Hanks, Tom 87
Harkins-Cross, Rebecca 123–24
HarperCollins 28
Hart, Carol 116, 118–19, 136n. 7
Harvey, Margaret 98
Heidelberg School 7
Herbert, Xavier 28
Hercules Returns (1993) 32
Heritage film, *The Irishman* as 19, 22–24, 27, 34
Hervey Bay in film 45–46
Hillcoat, John 118–20
Hinchinbrook Island in film 57, 63–65
Hogan, P.J. 76–82
"Hollynesians," 10
Homer 11
Hook (1991) 78–79, 81–82
Hooper, Chloe 129
Hoorn, Jeanette 60–63
Horizons
  overview 113–15
  in *Mystery Road* 116, 125–26
  in *The Proposition* 119
Hound of the Deep (1926) 85–86
Hueng, Marina 48
Hughendon in film 3–4

Hurd-Wood, Rachel 77
Huston, Danny 118
Hutcheon, Linda 116

Indigenous people. *See* Aboriginals
Indochine (1992) 48–49
Ingham in film 4
Innisfail in film 4
Ipswich in film 136n. 9
The Irishman (1978)
  Aboriginals in 26–27, 34–36
  AFC and 6, 17
  in AFC genre 17–19, 21–23, 27, 128–29
  Australia compared 27–29
  community participation in 131
  decorous aesthetic in 17–18, 34
  dubbing in 31, 34–36, 39–41, 129
  as heritage film 19, 22–24, 27, 34
  Jedda compared 7, 26, 29
  landscape aesthetic in 6–7
  locating Queensland in 19–22, 128–29
  masculinity in 22–24
  mise-en-scène in 17–18, 26, 34
  Mystery Road compared 115–16
  The Proposition compared 115–16
  Queenslander houses in 21, 24–27
  region in 6
  Revival and 6, 17, 34
  women in 24–27
The Irishman: A Novel of Northern Australia (O'Conner – novel) 18
Irwin, Bindi 65
Irwin, Steve 65
Isaacs, Jason 77
Islands of Great Barrier Reef in film 4–5

Jacka, Elizabeth 21, 23, 26
Jackman, Terry 72–73
Jaikumar, Priya 13–14, 115
James, Henry 65
Japan, release of *Sanctum* in 92
Jedda (1955)
  Aboriginals in 7, 37–39
  Australia compared 28
  dubbing in 31, 34, 37–41, 129
  The Irishman compared 7, 26, 29
  landscape aesthetic in 7

locationism in 7
Mystery Road compared 115–16
The Proposition compared 115–16
Jennings, Karen 37
Jowsey, David 114
Jungle Woman (1926) 85–86

Kapernick, Greg 99
Katter, Bob, Jr. 20–21
Kellogg's 73
Kelly, Veronica 47–49, 51
Kennedy, Gerard 22–23
Kennedy Valley 20
Kenny, Grant 73–76
Kidman, Nicole 28
King of the Coral Sea (1954) 86
Kinka Beach in literature 53
Kokoda (2006) 135
Kunoth, Ngarla 31
Kunoth, Rosalie 31
Kunoth-Monks, Rosalie 39
Kwanten, Ryan 122–23

Lamington National Park in film 9
Landman, Jane 12–13, 85–86, 89, 97–98, 100–03
Landscape aesthetic
 overview 6–8, 13
 cultural themes and 8
 Eurocentrism and 8
 in *The Irishman* 6–7
 in *Jedda* 7
 in *Mystery Road* 122, 124–25, 131
 in *The Proposition* 119–20
Langton, Marcia 45
The Last Wave (1977) 24
Leimbach, Bill 114
Levine, Joseph E. 135
Lewis, Tom E. 118
Limbrick, Peter 13, 116
Limelight Department 3–4
Lindsay, Norman 60–61
Locating Queensland in film and television
 overview 3–6
 Age of Consent 5
 The Irishman 19–22, 128–29
 Peter Pan 78
 Radiance 128

RAN: Remote Area Nurse 99, 101–02
The Straits 99
Locationism 7, 37
Locations Gallery 2
Long, Michael 51
"Long Walk" 51
Lovers and Luggers (1937) 85–86
Lung, Emily 106
Lurhmann, Baz 28

Mabo Native Title Legislation 5–6, 8–9, 13, 45–47, 131
Madam Butterfly (Puccini – opera) 47–48
Mailman, Deborah 9, 46
Male body in *Sanctum* 90
Manganinnie (1980) 24, 34–35
Mann, Chris 57
Martin, Mary 78
Masculinity
 overview 11–12
 in *The Coolangatta Gold* 71–72, 75
 fences in 116, 122, 124–25
 in *The Irishman* 22–24
 in *Mystery Road* 123, 125–26
 in *Peter Pan* 78–79
 in *Sanctum* 86–88
 as Western 121–22, 125–26
Mason, James 59, 61
Masthead Island in film 65
Matchbox Pictures 99
Maternity in *Radiance* 47
Max Film Studios 45–46
Maza, Rachel 9, 46
McClintock, Anne 86, 89
McMahon, Tina 24, 27, 34–36
McMann, Doug 37
McNamara, Barbara 19
McWilliam, Joss 73
Mermaids (television) 135
Michael Edgley International 73, 134–35
Middleton in film 114
Miller, Benjamin 37
Mills, Jane 7
Mirren, Helen 58–62
mise-en-scène
 overview 2
 in *The Irishman* 17–18, 26, 34
 in *Nim's Island* 57–58

mise-en-scène – *continued*
  in *The Proposition* 119–20
  in *Sanctum* 86
Mission Beach in television 99
Miss Saigon (play) 48
Mitchell, Billy 103
Mixed races in *The Straits* 104
Moliterno, Gino 37–38
Molloy, Bruce 8–9
Moran, Albert 4
Moree in film 122, 127
Morgan, Robert 120
Morris, Judy 27, 35
Morris, Meaghan 60
Morrissey, Di 73, 76
Morton-Thomas, Trisha 9, 46
Mount Gambier in film 85
Muriel's Wedding (1994) 76–77
Murray, Scott 21
Mutiny on the Bounty (1935) 5
Myers, Mike 32
Mystery Road (2013) 121–26
  overview 13–14, 113, 115, 127
  Aboriginals in 121–22
  colonial setting in 115
  cowboy figure in 121, 125
  fences in 116, 122, 124–25
  horizons in 116, 125–26
  The Irishman compared 115–16
  Jedda compared 115–16
  landscape aesthetic in 122, 124–25, 131
  masculinity in 123, 125–26
  The Proposition compared 122, 124–25
  sense of place in 3
  The Straits compared 115
  terra nullius and 115
  as Western 115–17, 121–22, 125–26
  women in 116–17, 123
Myths of home in *Radiance* 46–47

Narracoorte Caves in film 85
National Film and Sound Archive 39
Naturalism
  in *Age of Consent* 60–63, 129
  in *Uninhabited* 65, 129
Ned Kelly films 133
Neill, Bill 105
Neill, Ray Doa 105

Nelson, Victoria 87
Nevin, Robyn 24, 75
New South Wales in film 76
New Wave. *See* Revival
Nim's Island (2008)
  overview 10–11, 57–58
  "girl Friday" figure in 58
  mise-en-scène in 57–58
  paradise myths in 63–65, 129
  Robinson Crusoe motif in 63–64
  Uninhabited compared 65
Nim's Island: The Return of the Pirates (2013) 65
Nora Island in film 9–10
North Queensland in film
  overview 3
  Age of Consent 57, 59–62
  Nim's Island 57
  Radiance 45–46, 128, 134
  Sanctum 86, 92
  Uninhabited 57
Nostalgia in *Peter Pan* 77–79
Nowra, Louis 45, 47, 49, 51, 53–54, 57
Nullabor Dreaming (1989) 88
Nullabor Plain cave rescue 88
Numinbah Valley in film 9

Oberea (Tahitian Queen) 10
Objectification of Queensland in film 127–29
O'Brien, Patty 10–12, 57
"Ocker" comedies 17, 23
O'Conner, Elizabeth 18–20, 22–26, 35–36
Odyssey (Homer – epic) 11
O'Hanlon, Seamus 46
Oldfield, Max 134–35
On Our Selection (1919) 9, 60
Orientalism in *The Straits* 106
Origin of the Species (Darwin – book) 119
Orr, Wendy 63–64
The Overlanders (1946) 7, 9, 59, 116
Owen, Rena 99

Pacific Film and Television Commission 134
Palm Island in literature 129
Panckhurst, Helen 103

INDEX

Pannikin Plains cave rescue 88
Papua New Guinea in film and television
   overview 12–13, 129
   Kokoda 135
   Sanctum 12–13, 85–86, 89
   "South Seas films" 85–86
   The Straits 97, 100, 109
Papua-New Guinea Post 105
Paradise myths
   overview 8–11
   in *Age of Consent* 9–11, 129
   "dusky maiden" figure 10–11, 66–67, 135
   dystopian nature of 9–10
   feminine myths within 10–11
   "girl Friday" figure in 58, 60, 66–67
   in *Nim's Island* 63–65, 129
   Queensland and 129
   in *Radiance* 9–10, 129
   Robinson Crusoe motif (*See* Robinson Crusoe motif)
   in *Uninhabited* 65–67, 129
   women in 57–58
"Paradise Through Your Lens" (marketing campaign) 129
Parkinson, Alice 88
Parsons, Nick 104
Passi, Charles 98
Pate, Michael 61
Patterson, Banjo 113
Pearce, Guy 118
Pearson, Sarina 121
Peckinpah, Sam 119
Pederson, Aaron 116, 125–125
Penman, Ian 31, 40
Period genre. *See* AFC genre
Perkins, Charlie 51
Perkins, Rachel 45, 47, 49, 128
Peter and Wendy (Barrie – novel) 71, 77
Peter Pan (1924) 135
Peter Pan (1953) 78
Peter Pan (2003)
   overview 12, 71–72
   agelessness in 79
   crocodiles in 78, 82–83, 130
   father figures in 81–82
   gender in 78–79
   locating Queensland in 78

nostalgia in 77–79
Pike, Andrew 135
The Pirates of the Caribeean: Dead Men Tell No Tales (forthcoming) 83, 135
Plato 87–88
Pocock, Celmara 130
Port Douglas in film 63
Porter, Susie 97
Powell, Michael 58–62
Probyn-Rapsey, Fiona 51
The Proposition (2005) 13–14, 18, 29, 118–21
   overview 113, 115
   Aboriginals in 119–20
   bushrangers in 118–19
   colonial setting of 115
   fences in 119–20
   genre of 115–17
   horizon lines in 119
   The Irishman compared 115–16
   Jedda compared 115–16
   landscape aesthetic in 119–20
   mise-en-scène in 119–20
   Mystery Road compared 122, 124–25
   The Straits compared 115
   terra nullius and 115, 118–19
   violence in 119–21
   as Western 115–17, 122, 125–26
   women in 116–17
Puccini, Giacomo 47–49
Purcell, Leah 118

Queenslander houses
   in *The Coolangatta Gold* 75
   in *The Irishman* 21, 24–27
   in *Radiance* 49–51, 54–55
Queensland Film Corporation 73, 134
Queensland Film Development Office 134
Queensland Theatre Company 51

Radiance (1998)
   overview 45–46, 54–55
   Aboriginals in 41, 47
   aftershock of Mabo in 131
   arson in 134
   dystopia in 49–51
   locating Queensland in 128
   Madam Butterfly parody in 47–50

Radiance (1998) – continued
  maternity in 47
  myths of home in 46–47
  paradise myths in 9–10, 129
  Queenslander houses in 49–51, 54–55
  sense of place in 3
  sugar cane plantations in 45–46, 51–53, 128
  terra nullius and 50–51
  tidal mudflats in 53–54
Radiance (Nowra – play) 45
RAN: Remote Area Nurse (2006 – television) 100–03
  overview 13, 97–100
  "bush woman" figure in 102–03
  community participation in 131
  community perspectives in 100–03
  locating Queensland in 99, 101–02
  The Straits compared 103, 105, 110
  Torres Strait Islanders in 98, 100–01
Rattigan, Neil 25
Redgrave, Lyn 77
Region
  in *The Irishman* 6
  sense of place 2
Revival
  Age of Consent and 57
  Crombie and 36
  The Irishman and 6, 17, 34
  "Ocker" comedies and 17, 23
Reynall, Paul. *See* Clarke, Paul
Reynell, Paul. *See* Clarke, Paul
Robinson, Ted 134–35
Robinson, Victoria 90–91
Robinsonade. *See* Robinson Crusoe motif
Robinson Crusoe motif
  overview 58, 134
  in *Nim's Island* 63–64
  in *Uninhabited* 65–66
Rosedale in film 45–46
Rothwell, Nicholas 8–10
Rousseau, Jean-Jacques 63–64
Routt, William 3, 25, 58, 60
Roxburgh, Richard 86
Russia, release of *Sanctum* in 92

Sacdpraseuth, Sri 105
Said, Edward 106
Salvation Army 3–4

Samson and Delilah (2009) 41
The Samurai (television) 32
Sanctum (2011)
  overview 12–13, 92–93
  actors in 105
  caves in 87–90, 130
  caving in 87–90
  The Coolangatta Gold compared 86
  extreme sports in 90–92
  foreign markets, release in 92
  male body in 90
  masculinity in 86–88
  mise-en-scène in 86
  scenic melodrama in 86–87
"Sarong girls" 10
Saunders, Justine 53
SBS Independent 99
Schaffer, Kay 25, 58
Schreck, Peter 73, 76, 134–35
Screen Australia 2, 11, 28
Screen Queensland 2, 4, 11, 127, 134
Sculthorpe, Peter 62
Sea Patrol (2007 – television) 99
Sea World in film 76–77
Sen, Ivan 113, 122, 125–125, 127, 136n. 8
Sense of place
  overview 2–3
  in *Mystery Road* 3
  in *Radiance* 3
Settler themes 129
Sex in *Age of Consent* 60–63
Shrek (2001) 32
Simpson, Catherine 67, 106
Skiles, Wes 88
Smulders, Josephine 75
Sons of Matthew (1949) 9
The Sopranos (1999 – television) 104
South Australia in film 86, 127
South Australian Film Corporation (SAFC) 20–22
Southeast Queensland in film 9
South Korea, release of *Sanctum* in 92
"South Seas films" 12–13, 85–86, 97–100, 129
Spielberg, Steven 81–82
The Squatter's Daughter (1933) 58, 116
Stafford, Jeff 59–60
Standard Committee on Spoken English 40

Starling, Paul 75
Stevenson, R.L. 77
Storm Boy (1976) 24
Story of the Kelly Gang (1906) 133
The Straits (2012 – television)
  overview 13, 97–100
  Asians in 104–05
  bikie gangs in 105
  community participation in 131
  crocodiles in 107–09, 129
  cultural themes in 103–07
  locating Queensland in 99
  mixed races in 104
  Mystery Road compared 115
  Orientalism in 106
  The Proposition compared 115
  RAN: Remote Area Nurse compared 103, 105, 110
  Torres Strait Islanders in 99, 104–05, 110
  tropical themes in 107–11
Stratton, David 21, 119, 134
Sugar cane plantations in *Radiance* 45–46, 51–53, 128
Sumpter, Jeremy 77–80
Sunshine Coast in film 3
Surfer's Paradise in film 75–76
Swan, Angela 124
Syncretistic nature of Queensland 14
Syron, L. 27

The Tall Man (2011) 129
Tarzan films 90
Tate, Nick 73
Taylor, Cheryl 18, 20, 23–25, 36
Taylor, Rod 62
Taylor, Valerie 62
Television, film compared 99
Ten Canoes (2006) 40–41
Terra nullius
  overview 5, 8–9
  AFC genre and 59
  Mystery Road and 115
  The Proposition and 115, 118–19
  Radiance and 50–51
  Uninhabited and 57
They're a Weird Mob (1966) 61
Thomas, Francois 32, 133
Thompson, Jack 124

Thomson, David 59
Thursday Island film 102
Tidal mudflats in *Radiance* 53–54
Titanic (1997) 28
Titley, Thomas "Tiger" 20–21
Tompkins, Jane 117, 119
Toomelah (2011) 123, 136n. 8
Torres Kreole 101
Torres Strait Islanders
  overview 3, 5
  population of 135
  in *RAN: Remote Area Nurse* 98, 100–01
  in *The Straits* 99, 104–05, 110
Torres Strait Islands in film and television
  overview 12–13, 129
  RAN: Remote Area Nurse 97–98
  The Straits 97–98, 109
Townsville in film 20, 29, 133
Transnational cinema, Queensland cinema contrasted 1
Treasure Island (Stevenson – novel) 77
Tropical North Queensland in film 129
Turner, Graeme 17–18, 20–21, 23–24, 34

Underbelly (2008 – television) 104
Uninhabited (2010)
  overview 10–11, 57–58
  actors in 105
  Age of Consent compared 65
  "bush woman" figure in 65–67
  "girl Friday" figure 58, 66–67
  naturalism in 65, 129
  Nim's Island compared 65
  paradise myths in 65–67, 129
  Robinson Crusoe motif in 65–66
  terra nullius and 57

Vancouver (Canada) in film 72
Venus 11
Vieira, Tracey 127–28, 131
Village Roadshow Studios 11–12, 63, 72, 76–77
Violence in *The Proposition* 119–21
Vision Splendid Outback Film Festival 113
Voigts-Virchow, Eckart 19, 27

Wakefield, Rhys 86
In the Wake of the Bounty (1933) 5
Walk into Hell (1956) 135

Walk into Paradise (1956) 86
Walshe-Howling, Damien 123
Walt Disney Studios 78, 82–83
Walters, Brandon 28
Walton, Tasma 123
"Waltzing Matilda" (song) 113, 136
Warner Brothers Movieworld
   Studios 72
Watson, Emily 120
Weaving, Hugo 123
Weily, John 134–35
Welles, Orson 133
We of the Never Never (1982) 34–35, 76
Western Queensland in film 13
Westerns
   overview 13–14
   Mystery Road as 115–17, 121–22, 125–26
   The Proposition as 115–17, 122, 125–26
Wexman, Virginia Wright 117, 119–20, 123, 125
White, Robyn 100
Whitlock, Gillian 20, 45, 50
Whitton, Tricia 123
Wight, Andrew 85, 88
Williams, Olivia 77
Will the Great Barrier Reef Cure Claude Clough? (1968) 4–5
Wilmington (USA) in film 72
Wilson, Richard 118

Winstone, Ray 118
Winton in film 113–15
   overview 3–4, 29
   community participation 131
   economic benefits of 114
   Goldstone 127
   infrastructure in 115
   Mystery Road 125–26, 136n. 9
   The Proposition 127
Women
   "bush woman" figure (*See* "Bush woman" figure)
   "dusky maiden" figure 10–11, 57–58, 66–67, 135
   "girl Friday" figure 58, 60
   in *The Irishman* 24–27
   in *Mystery Road* 116–17, 123
   in paradise myths 57–58
   in *The Proposition* 116–17
World Heritage Sites 129–30
The Wrong Side of the Road (1981) 51
Wyllie, Dan 88

Yanthalawuy, Mawayul 34–35
Yaquinto, Marilyn 104, 107
Yorke Island in television 97

Zalar, Tasia 10, 105
Zemeckis, Robert 135

www.ingramcontent.com/pod-product-compliance
Lightning Source LLC
Chambersburg PA
CBHW021832300426
44114CB00009BA/407